renewed hearts, changed lives

FOCUS ON THE FAMILY®

renewing
the heart™

renewed hearts, changed lives

stories of faith
from everyday
women

by Betsy Holt

Commentary by Lisa Harper

TYNDALE

Tyndale House Publishers, Wheaton, Illinois

RENEWED HEARTS, CHANGED LIVES

Copyright © 1999 by Focus on the Family
All rights reserved. International copyright secured.

Library of Congress Cataloging-in-Publication Data
Renewed hearts, changed lives: stories of faith from everyday
women / by Betsy Holt, with commentary by Lisa Harper.
    p.   cm.
   ISBN 1-56179-679-4
    1. Christian women—United States—Biography. 2.
Christian biography—United States. 3. Renewing the Heart
Conference. I. Holt, Betsy. II. Harper, Lisa. III. Focus on the
Family (Organization)
BR1713.R45   1999
270'.082'092273—dc21
[B]   98-55068
                               CIP

A Focus on the Family book published by Tyndale House
Publishers, Wheaton, Illinois.

Scripture quotations are from the HOLY BIBLE, NEW
INTERNATIONAL VERSION ®. Copyright © 1973, 1978,
1984 by the International Bible Society. Used by permission
of Zondervan Publishing House. All rights reserved.

The song "Small Sacrifice," in Story 4, pp. 136–37, is reprinted
by permission of Donna Shearron. Copyright © 1994.

Some names and certain details in women's stories in this
book have been changed to protect the privacy of the individuals involved.

Editor: Michele A. Kendall
Cover Design: Candi Park D'Agnese
Cover Photo: Steve Smith/FPG International

Printed in the United States of America

99 00 01 02 03 04 05/10 9 8 7 6 5 4 3 2

To my wonderful and patient husband, Sky—Your constant love and support made writing this book possible. I love you.

And to all the women who contributed their stories—Your testimonies of God's grace, power, and love have affected me more than you'll ever know.

Betsy

To Patti, my mother, and to Judy and Kim, my best friends—You have been and continue to be a wonderful extension of God's grace and mercy. Your prayers and wisdom help illuminate the steps He's ordered for me; your laughter and encouragement are the music to which my heart dances.

Lisa

Contents

How It All Began

I can hardly believe all that's taken place in the year and a half since I first spoke with Dr. Dobson about the possibility of hosting a women's conference. We were talking after a small Focus on the Family women's event, and he asked me if I had a dream, if there was something creative I'd like to pursue. I told him about the vision I had for Focus on the Family to sponsor a large national women's conference similar to Promise Keepers. I told Dr. Dobson that I thought women of all ages longed to be spiritually encouraged and rejuvenated, and that we could help accomplish this by offering sound biblical teaching, engaging praise and worship, and a clear presentation of the gospel in a conference setting. Dr. Dobson smiled and asked me to send him a proposal so we could discuss it further. I was excited because he seemed open to the idea, and I set out to put together what I hoped would be a stellar proposal.

One of the first tasks in writing the proposal was to decide on a name for the conference and a theme verse. I was praying about several ideas when the Lord reminded me of a dear friend's story. We met at a small women's retreat where she shared about how she had been sexually abused by her stepfather when she was a little girl. She married young—mostly to escape from him—and had children of her own. The abuse from her childhood was a secret she had shared only with her husband, and she kept it locked in the distant past. But after a lifetime of silence, she finally shared her story of abuse with some Christian friends. And God began to heal her. Next, she shared the awful truth with her adult daughter, her only daughter, who confessed that my friend's stepfather had sexually abused her, too. Shortly thereafter, the stepfather was hospitalized with advanced Alzheimer's disease, and my friend and her daughter became his primary caretakers. She told me how difficult it was to care for, and extend grace to, the man who had not only scarred her but her daughter as well.

During the time they were caring for him, he had two moments of lucidity. During one of those moments, when her daughter was also in the room, he grabbed my friend's hand, looked toward heaven, and exclaimed, "Oh Father, forgive me for what I've done to these girls." He died a few days later. My friend said that on the day he died, she drove home from the hospital in a state of shock. She was overwhelmed with the conflicting feelings of joy and freedom and guilt.

Later that day, while catching up on the mundane chore of sorting laundry, she read the verse for the day from a small flip calendar. The verse was from the Song of Songs 2:11–12a: "See! The winter is past; the rains are over and gone. Flowers appear on the earth; the season of singing has come." She told me that she sank onto the floor of her laundry room, clutching the calendar to her bosom. And she said the peace of God filled the room as it filled her heart. She felt as if God had wrapped His arms around her in that room and whispered to her that the winter of her life was over and that spring was here. God has continued to bring about miraculous healing in both her and her daughter's lives.

As I remembered my friend, I thought, *Her story represents hundreds of thousands of women across America. Not that we've all been sexually abused by our stepfathers; but we've all been broken and disappointed by our own personal tragedies.* I believe that most women need spiritual renewal, need to be reminded that they are loved by God and that He orders their steps, even when circumstances seem otherwise. We all need to be reminded that Jesus represents springtime, even in the harshest of winters. So the verse for our proposed conference became Song of Songs 2:11–12a, and I put "Renewing the Heart" across the top of the proposal.

That was the fun, inspirational part. Then I had to assemble the logistical and financial requirements. I tried to get realistic numbers, but much of it was guesswork because very few ministries had ever attempted a national women's conference. And I didn't want to tell anyone what I was doing because I wasn't sure it would come to fruition. I felt a little sheepish telling people that I was trying to put my dream for a national women's conference into a concise, spiral-bound proposal. Rodlyn Davis—a good friend who also worked at Focus—became my confidante, and we spent several afternoons eating chocolate yogurt and trying to make the proposal sound relatively professional. When it was finished, I gave it to Dr. Dobson and then headed up to the mountains to go snowboarding, figuring if he didn't like it, maybe my bruises would take my mind off the disappointment.

I was thrilled when he responded positively several days later. But the thrill was tempered when he told me that I would have to make a formal presentation to the executive cabinet of Focus on the Family, which is composed of all the vice presidents. He said I needed to sell my idea to them before it could become a reality. Making presentations to the executive cabinet can be intimidating. They're wonderful, godly leaders, but when they're all sitting around a big conference table watching me squirm, it can feel like an inquisition!

Needless to say, my preparation time was intense. By now, I'd told the women on my team about the proposal, and they jumped in to help. I convinced these women that I needed them to put together a skit to "liven up" the executive cabinet before I gave the formal proposal. I told them that I really needed their help, that we were a team, and so on. I was sure they'd figure out that I was teasing, but then they started practicing their skit during lunch. They made giant signs with the letters "H," "E," "A," "R," "T," and they created a little cheer to go with each letter. I finally had to confess that I had been teasing about the skit when I found out they were planning on buying matching outfits to make it look professional! They weren't very amused—I was almost lynched by my teammates before I had a chance to appear before the Inquisition. They threatened to humiliate me and prance into the executive cabinet meeting with their signs and sing their cheers anyway!

The night before the big presentation, I stayed late at work and went through a "dress rehearsal" of the proposal with Eugenia, our resident computer expert. She had put the entire proposal in Power Point, a computer program, and had come up with an impressive multimedia presentation. All I had to do was watch the screen and narrate—at least in theory. We met back at the office early the next morning and nervously waited to be called before the executive cabinet. I was wearing my favorite suit and smiled confidently when we finally walked into the boardroom. I knew that as long as I stayed calm and focused on narrating the screen, everything would be okay. Then tragedy struck: The room was too bright for the Power Point presentation to show up on the screen; the latter remained completely white except for a few faint wisps of color.

I briefly considered screaming and racing from the room in tears, but by the grace of God, I regained some composure and went on to give the presentation from memory. The more I talked, the more excited I became, and before I knew it, I had finished the presentation and the vice presidents were asking questions. I didn't have the answers to all of their questions, but they were largely supportive. By the time it was over, they had voted to let me create and direct Focus on the Family's first national women's conference. The only catch was that they wanted to hold it before October, so we had only about six months to pull it off.

Boy, was I in over my head! We had a team of three and just a few short months to pull together a conference for thousands of women. We made up a registration system, designed a brochure, stuffed envelopes, worked late into the night, and prayed. A friend of mine had shared 1 Chronicles 4:10, in which Jabez asks God to bless him and to enlarge his territory. I started asking God to bless our team with wisdom and to enlarge our hearts and minds if He wanted to enlarge our territory. I also started claiming a verse in Isaiah 49 that says He will turn the mountains into roads. I knew we were facing some very big mountains, and I knew that only God could enable us to climb them; only He could keep our feet from slipping.

One day Dr. Dobson called me into the broadcasting studio to record a short radio "tag" (the announcement at the end of a broadcast program) for the conference. It was my first time in the studio and I was nervous, but he was gracious and coached me along. While we were waiting between takes, he asked me if I really thought thousands of women would register for Renewing the Heart. I told him that I knew they would because I really believed God was going to "enlarge our territory," as long as we purposed to give Him the honor and glory. Dr. Dobson smiled indulgently and said that he'd be surprised if more than 2,000 women showed up. I think most people doubted it was really going to happen.

A few weeks later, Dr. Dobson had to go back into the studio and record another announcement asking women to stop sending in registrations because we were sold out and already had several thousand women on a waiting list. God really had turned mountains into roads for us. As I look back on the months leading up to that first conference, I am amazed at God's mercy and provision—not just that thousands of women registered, but that God blessed us with the energy to work harder than we'd ever worked before, with the organization to somehow manage the overwhelming volume of details, and with the ability to avoid making any devastating mistakes even though there were many times when we had no idea what we were doing.

All the months of labor and prayer finally paid off when the weekend of September 20, 1997, arrived. Our conference team went to Nashville a few days early to handle the logistical details. We were so busy taking care of last-minute problems that we were shocked to wake up on Friday and realize that the conference was less than 24 hours away. I was both thrilled and terrified when busloads of women started arriving at our hotel from all over the country. Some of them had designed their very own "Renewing the Heart" T-shirts. Most of the hotels and restaurants in downtown Nashville were filled with women coming to the conference—19,600 women came from 48 states and Canada.

We spent the night before the conference praying over each of the speakers, the musicians, and the program. Then we headed over to the arena to pray. It was incredible to consider that within just a few hours, all of those seats would be occupied by women hoping for renewal. I was overwhelmed, watching hundreds of people walking through section after section, stopping at individual seats, praying earnestly for whoever would occupy them during the conference.

As people finished praying and headed back to the hotel, I started talking with Dan Brunelle, who was running the production portion of the conference. Dan is an experienced professional, always cool as a cucumber, so I wasn't the least bit worried about the lights, stage, sound, crew, or catering. At least not until he told me that our state-of-the-art sound system still wasn't working properly! It was almost midnight, there were women literally camping outside the arena entrance in order to get the best seats, the doors were opening at 6:45 A.M., and the sound system wasn't working. Then I found out we had forgotten to have a piano delivered for one of our musical guests. Where in the world were we going to get a piano at midnight? Suddenly, one of the huge video projectors started acting up. Then my stomach started acting up.

I returned to my hotel room at about 2 A.M. The next three and a half hours were really difficult. The Bible tells us that we don't fight against flesh and blood, but against powers and principalities, and there was certainly a battle going on in my hotel room. I spent most of the time on my knees beside the bed. I've never felt so much spiritual oppression in my whole life. It became obvious that the enemy—who wants to rob, kill, and destroy—was not going to stand idly by while we proclaimed the saving, miraculous gospel of Jesus Christ to thousands of women.

When the alarm went off at 5 A.M., I hadn't slept at all. I stood up, walked into the bathroom, and got violently ill. I couldn't believe it—the dark circles under my eyes were bad enough, but now I couldn't move without throwing up. Bill Knott, one of my coworkers at Focus, picked me up downstairs, took one look at me, and started laughing. He teased me all the way to the arena about my weak stomach and about how the makeup artist was really going to have her work cut out for her. And did she ever! I had to race to the rest room every few minutes while she painstakingly tried to make me look like a hostess instead of a hospital patient!

People were rushing to and fro backstage, and suddenly someone yelled, "They just opened the doors!" Everybody was so excited that the day we had dreamed about and worked toward and hoped for and prayed for was finally here. Every few minutes, someone would stop by my dressing room to update me on what was happening. Meanwhile, a friend whose husband is a doctor was picking up antinausea medicine for me.

Kim Hill led the praise and worship team onto the stage at 7:45 A.M. I stood alone at a backstage entrance and looked out at a coliseum filled with thousands of women. Then they began to sing "Holy, Holy, Holy." I'd never heard that many women's voices singing to the Lord before, and it was absolutely beautiful. Within a few minutes, I had the blessed opportunity to greet all of those women and welcome them to the first Renewing the Heart conference. Then I had the privilege of introducing our special, surprise guest, Dr. James Dobson. They clapped so hard that he couldn't talk for several minutes. The applause swelled into a thundering standing ovation; it was like a bear hug from 20,000 women! Dr. Dobson was visibly moved, and it was precious to see him honored in such an affectionate way for his faithful ministry.

The day went almost exactly as we had hoped and planned. It wasn't perfect, but there were no major emergencies or mishaps. God protected us. And it was wonderful to watch women's faces as they sang praise songs and listened to the speakers. Some of them clearly changed throughout the day— it was as if they let go of the burdens they had dragged in with them. It was as if they remembered to hope again.

Anne Graham Lotz (Dr. Billy Graham's youngest daughter) was the closing speaker, and after her message on heaven, she gave women the opportunity to come forward and commit their lives to Jesus Christ. You could have heard a pin drop as the first few women got up out of their seats and started walking toward the stage to pray with Anne. Then, as more women began walking toward the stage, the rest of the audience started applauding. The applause got louder and louder, but it wasn't rowdy or raucous. It was one of the sweetest times of rejoicing I've ever had the opportunity to participate in. Most women had tears streaming down their faces. I said to myself, *This must be how the angels in heaven rejoice when one who was lost is found.*

The days following the conference were filled with a whirlwind of media interviews, a special Focus on the Family broadcast, and hundreds of phone calls and letters. I was exhausted and exhilarated. While on the plane flying back to Colorado the day after the conference, I was thumbing through a *Reader's Digest,* and I came upon a story I won't soon forget. It was so pertinent, I both smiled and cried when I read it. The story was about an eight-year-old boy named Cory, who was the worst player on his Little League baseball team. The moment came when his team was in the league championship and the game rested on his frail shoulders. It was the bottom of the ninth inning, there were two outs, two runners on base, and his team was behind by two runs. The other little fellows in his dugout grumbled loudly when the coach announced that it was Cory's turn to bat. He trudged up to the batter's box and awaited his fate. But then grace stepped into the box with him. Cory closed his eyes and swung with all his might, and the ball sailed over the outfielder's head for the game-winning home run! When the celebration was over and the crowd had dispersed, he and his mom drove home. For some time he sat silently beside her; then he looked over at her and said, "Mom, I'm trying to stop grinning, but I just can't."

I knew exactly how Cory felt. I had been out of my league. I didn't possess all the necessary skills to make my dream for a national women's conference a reality. Our staff was far too small and inexperienced. I should have struck out and lost the game. But then grace stepped in. God kept our feet from slipping. He gave us wisdom where we had none. He multiplied our efforts and covered our mistakes. His mercies are new every morning; great is His faithfulness.

One of my favorite scriptures is Jeremiah 29:12–14a: " 'Then you will call upon me and come and pray to me, and I will listen to you. You will seek me and find me when you seek me with all your heart. I will be *found* by you,' declares the LORD" (italics added). I am constantly amazed that the God who spoke the universe into existence, who put stripes on zebras and breathed life into Adam, allows Himself to be found by us. He allows us to have an intimate relationship with Him through His Son, Jesus Christ. God allowed Himself to be found by many women at the five Renewing the Heart conferences held during 1997 and 1998. The following chapters communicate that in living color. These are true stories from women who sent letters to Focus on the Family after attending the conferences. Our hope and prayer is that you will be reminded of how wide and long and high and deep is God's love for you as you read this book. May He alone be praised.

Lisa Harper
Nashville, Tennessee

STORY ONE

Healed by Forgiveness

Get rid of all bitterness, rage and anger . . .
along with every form of malice.
Be kind and compassionate to one another, forgiving
each other, just as in Christ God forgave you.
—EPHESIANS 4:31–32

"*M*ARIA, I DIDN'T APPRECIATE YOUR COMMENT TO THE PASTOR today," Doug Jamesson said bitterly, turning to his wife in the car. Lowering his voice so their two boys in the backseat wouldn't hear him, he added crossly, "What did you mean by saying that you liked his sermon?"

Maria looked irritably at her husband and folded her arms, saying nothing. It was a Sunday morning, and they had just left church, where, in her opinion, Pastor Winters had preached a great sermon on integrity. As she often did when she enjoyed a message, Maria had thanked their pastor for his sermon as they had walked out the door.

Now, in the car, Doug's face was flushed. "I know you were making some kind of dig at me!" he persisted. "What exactly were you getting at?"

Maria squared her shoulders and tossed her short, dark-brown hair. "Oh, please, Doug," she said hotly. "The sermon was good. I gave our pastor a compliment. Why are you so paranoid?" Her comment to the pastor on his integrity sermon had been sincere, but now she tried to guess why Doug was so upset. *He must be feeling guilty about something,* she deduced, frowning at her husband.

"Maria, you know you always put too much stock into what Pastor Winters says," Doug retorted, ignoring her comment that he was being paranoid. He was uncharacteristically showing his emotion today—his knuckles were white against the steering wheel, and he glared out the window, his mouth set grimly. He clicked on the turn signal. "You don't even know why you believe the things you do. Keep your focus on God, and quit hanging on every word the pastor says."

Maria bristled, and she narrowed her brown eyes. It was one of Doug's standard arguments. "Well, at least I'm trying to live a good Christian life," she shot back. "If you loved God as much as you love bowling and karate and the TV, you'd be a wonderful Christian!"

Doug scowled at her and sped the car around a corner, saying nothing.

Their marriage had been in a shabby state for eight years—almost since the beginning. When they weren't fighting, she and Doug were leading separate lives. He went out bowling and taught karate five nights a week, and she filled her time taking care of David and Trevor, who were five and three years old. Maria rolled her eyes as she reflected on their marriage. *As seldom as he's around, I'd be better off without him,* she thought, vexed. *I already do everything by myself.*

Back and forth they argued, until they got home. Maria wasn't ready to give up the fight and immediately sent Trevor and David out to play in the backyard. She stalked into the living room, where Doug had lowered his tall frame onto his recliner. Maria sat tensely on the edge of the couch and cleared her throat.

"Doug, let's get to the bottom line," she said brusquely. "Are you happy?"

Doug folded his arms across his Sunday dress shirt. "No, I'm not."

Fighting feelings of rejection, Maria stood up quickly and took a few steps into the center of the room. She had expected Doug's answer, but it was still painful to hear. *I'm not going to let him see he's hurt me,* she thought determinedly. Whirling around to face him, she said rashly, "Well, maybe you should leave, then!"

Seated in his recliner, Doug gave no response.

*T*WO AND A HALF WEEKS LATER, MARIA FOUND HERSELF standing by the kitchen counter, holding a plastic mixing bowl and sobbing.

Doug was gone.

He had left four days before, telling her, "I think we should separate for a while, until I can get my head on straight, because I'm not . . . I'm not sure if I love you anymore."

As she recalled his words, Maria dropped the bowl and crumpled to the floor. *I didn't think he had really stopped loving me,* she thought miserably, staring at the blue and white tiles. *I didn't think he would actually leave.* The colors in the floor blurred together as a more harrowing notion came to her: *Maybe I was right when I suspected Doug was seeing another woman.* Maria shuddered, and burying her face in her hands, she wept.

For the past few months, she'd wondered if Doug were cheating on her. He had become distant, and he'd been taking motorcycle rides every night for many weeks—possibly to see another woman. Despite her hunch, though, Maria hadn't ventured to ask Doug for the truth. Knowing would be more painful than just suspecting, she'd often thought. But now, sitting alone with her suspicions on the kitchen floor, Maria didn't believe it was easier to be in the dark. Her stomach sank. Now she didn't even know where she stood with Doug or if she were competing with another woman for his affections. If she was, who knew when or if he would ever come back to her?

Even though Doug had never been around much before, now the house seemed huge and empty without him there— and Maria felt acutely lonely. Pulling her knees up to her chest, she rocked back and forth. *He hasn't even called to check up on me and the boys,* she cried to herself. *He doesn't care if we're dead or alive.*

She had been sitting on the floor for several minutes when a voice cut through her weeping. *Maria, I'm just as hurt that you haven't checked in with Me, either,* the Lord said. *When was the last time you prayed to Me or read My Word rather than watched TV? Why haven't you drawn closer to Me, especially during this hard time?*

It wasn't an audible voice, but Maria could feel the Lord speaking clearly to her heart. She frowned. "But that's different," Maria objected. "Lord, aren't You paying attention to what Doug has done to me? He's abandoned me. He doesn't even care about me!" Her words became lost in the swell of emotion, and Maria turned a helpless, tearstained face up toward God.

I don't see how you've handled your relationship with Me much differently than Doug has handled his relationship with you, the Lord persisted.

"But . . . ," Maria protested lamely, then stopped. She couldn't ignore the Lord's words anymore.

I know it hurts, God continued, *but you must let go of this and turn to Me. First learn to love Me wholeheartedly—and that will be the best chance you can give your marriage.*

Maria listened. That had struck a chord. She wiped her eyes.

"You're right, Lord. I'm so sorry," she whispered sadly. She leaned her head against the cupboard. "After all You've done for me, I still haven't spent the time with You that I should," she admitted. "So how can I expect Doug to care about me when I haven't loved him fully, either?"

For the first time since becoming a Christian 10 years before, Maria felt God's peace, and it eased her burden. "Okay, Lord," she said into the stillness. "I'll work on my relationship with You first—and You take care of Doug."

Fired up by her talk with God, Maria followed through as best she could. She read the Bible more consistently and got more involved in her church by joining the choir, attending Wednesday night prayer meetings, helping out in Sunday school, and counseling with her pastor.

Maria also began to pray with David and Trevor every night before they went to bed. She herself prayed constantly—in the shower, on the road, and at work in the advertising agency—asking God to bring Doug back to her. Now that she and Doug were separated, Maria could see that she'd pushed him away by endlessly preaching at him and trying to make him pay for his mistakes. It was a bitter realization, but there was nothing Maria could do now to fix the marriage. She couldn't try to control Doug anymore. Only God could mend things between them.

The day after Maria's breakdown in the kitchen, Doug finally contacted her, asking to see the boys. In the months after the separation, he continued to see David and Trevor twice a week—on Wednesday nights when Maria went to church, and on Saturdays. After a year of legal separation, both agreed to let the separation turn into a divorce, which was standard in the state of New Hampshire. Although Doug got an attorney, Maria never did. She and Doug had already written out an agreement several months before, detailing division of property and how much child support Doug would pay. Maria felt the agreement they'd typed up was sufficient. She secretly continued to hope that they would get back together, even if only for the boys' sake. Knowing that only a miracle from God would make reconciliation possible, however, Maria kept her thoughts and prayers to herself.

But several months after the divorce, Maria learned that there had been another woman in the picture—and that Doug had been seeing her months before his and Maria's separation. Maria's hunch had been right.

She found out one Saturday when Doug came to get David and Trevor. Doug approached Maria, who was folding laundry in the boys' room.

"Maria, I want to talk to you," he said, running his hands through his dark-brown hair. Doug was blunt. "I'm going to introduce the boys to someone today."

Maria shuddered slightly, and the blood drained from her face. *So he's found somebody,* she thought in despair. *He's going to get married now.* It was a depressing thought. For a moment she said nothing and continued folding the clothes.

Then, trying to sound nonchalant, she asked, "What's her name?"

"It's Jessie," Doug told her, shifting uncomfortably. "I wanted you to know before the boys came home and told you. That's all."

Maria walked abruptly to David's dresser and shoved some clothes in. Her eyes burned. *Keep calm,* she told herself. *Don't let him see you get upset about this.* Then, overwhelmed by another memory, she whirled around and glared across the room at Doug. "Remember when I asked you about some woman who answered the phone at your apartment a few months ago?" she asked accusingly.

Doug nodded.

She planted her hands on her hips. "Was that her?"

"Yes," he said.

Maria lifted her chin. "How long have you been seeing her?" she asked curtly. *If he's going to hurt me,* she thought with a vengeance, *the least I can do is make him feel guilty.*

"A long time," Doug said uneasily.

"How long?"

Doug hesitated, then said, "Actually, since a few months before you and I separated."

The truth almost knocked the wind out of her. "Oh," she whispered, blinking back what felt like a waterfall of tears that threatened to run down her face. "Well, I figured you were involved with somebody," she said quickly, trying to salvage her pride.

After Doug left with the boys, Maria wept bitterly into David's small sweatshirt. *He lied to me,* she thought bleakly, *and deep down I knew, but I chose not to see it. I didn't want to believe that he could really be with another woman.* She lifted her tearstained face to God. *This is ridiculous, Lord. Now that I can't have Doug, I want him even more.* But with Jessie in the picture, Maria felt that all her hopes for reconciliation were gone.

Doug's relationship with Jessie continued off and on for four years. He never married her, but a year after the divorce was final, he and Jessie had a son, Jimmy.

Jimmy's birth deeply hurt Maria, but she refused to let it break her. Instead, she focused on spending time with God, praying constantly, and staying busy. Still working full-time, she went to college and got her degree in marketing, started dating casually, and began to put her failed marriage in perspective.

One Bible verse that kept her from becoming bitter and judgmental was Romans 3:22–24: "This righteousness from God comes through faith in Jesus Christ to all who believe.

There is no difference, for all have sinned and fall short of the glory of God, and are justified freely by his grace through the redemption that came by Christ Jesus."

When Maria read it, she felt as if the Lord were speaking directly to her. Doug may have committed adultery, but she was guilty of other sins, such as wanting revenge, remaining bitter, and refusing to forgive. Because of this, she was just as sinful and just as responsible for the divorce.

This realization kept Maria from talking negatively about Doug, especially to the kids. Determined that David and Trevor learn something from their parents' situation, Maria spoke honestly with them about it, trying to give them a godly point of view. They needed to know not only that what their father had done was wrong, but also that he wasn't worse than the rest of them, because everyone is susceptible to temptation. Telling David and Trevor this kept Maria from bashing Doug or using the boys as pawns.

Doug never influenced his sons against their mother, either. In fact, when David and Trevor were with him, he upheld all of Maria's rules. If the boys weren't allowed to do something at their mother's house, Doug wouldn't excuse the same behavior at his apartment. This helped soften Maria's attitude toward her ex-husband. She knew that many divorced men and women did all they could to sway the children in their own favor. But Doug was different—always kind and generous, always supportive.

Both Doug's attitude and Maria's newfound understanding that they were equal in God's eyes enabled her to maintain a friendship with her ex-husband. Surprisingly, when he came over to spend time with the boys, they got along better than they ever had. Maria had learned a lot in the three years they'd been apart and was now more confident; she'd gotten her college degree, been promoted to manager of her advertising agency, and often had flowers on the kitchen table from one of her dates.

Doug was attracted to Maria's newfound independence

and enjoyed spending time with her. Now he and Maria laughed and talked, voicing feelings and opinions that they had never expressed when they were married. Doug was also generous, unselfishly helping Maria out when she and the boys needed extra money or repairs done on the house. They still quarreled, but even when they did fight, Maria couldn't stay angry for long. When Doug showed up at the door and she took one look at his gentle face, her anger melted away.

What am I going to do? she often wondered. *I can't let go of my feelings for him.*

ONE DAY A YEAR LATER, SHE SAT ACROSS FROM A MINISTER during a counseling session and poured out her heart. Maria's situation with Doug remained unchanged, and her love for him had only intensified. She grabbed a tissue and dabbed at her eyes.

"Doug and I have been apart for four years. I want to get back together with him, but I don't see how it'll happen," she confided to the pastor. "He's still seeing Jessie off and on." Jessie was always moving back and forth from New Hampshire to California, where her parents lived.

The pastor, whom Maria had driven an hour and a half from her home in New Hampshire to see, studied her. "Do you think Doug would come down to meet with us sometime?" he asked.

Maria shook her head. "I don't think he would, but I'll call him just to be sure," she said. She walked over to the phone and dialed the number, then sighed as the answering machine came on. "No one's home," she said despondently to the pastor. "Oh well, Doug wouldn't have agreed to marriage counseling anyway."

Before she could hang up the phone, however, she heard something.

"Maria?" a voice asked on the other end of the line.

"Doug? I thought you weren't home!" she said excitedly.

"I'm meeting with the pastor at Eastview Community Church right now. He wants to know if you'll come talk with us next week."

"Yeah, I heard you saying that on the machine," Doug said. "Sure, I'll come."

Maria blinked, amazed. A few years ago, Doug would never have wanted to discuss his relationship problems with a pastor. "Really? That's great!" she said exuberantly.

As she hung up the phone, she thought hopefully, *Maybe there's a chance for my marriage after all. Maybe my boys will finally have their mom and dad back in the same house again.*

Doug and Maria met with the pastor a few times and began to work more intentionally on their relationship. One night, a few weeks after they'd begun joint counseling sessions, Doug called and asked her if they could go for a motorcycle ride. He wanted to talk. Maria agreed and got her mother to watch David and Trevor.

When Doug showed up at the door, Maria could tell he had something serious to say. His jaw was clenched, and he kept running his hands through his hair. "Are you ready?" he asked quickly.

"Sure," Maria said, nodding. "Just let me grab my coat." She put on her coat, hopped on the motorcycle behind Doug, and threw her arms around his waist, holding on tightly. After about 10 minutes, they arrived at a neighborhood park, and Doug led Maria to a bench under a tree. He turned to her and gently took her hand.

"Maria, I still love you so much," he said quietly. His blue eyes were soft in the light of the park's lamppost. "And I feel terrible about all the things I've done to hurt you. I'm willing to continue marriage counseling with you. I'll even go in front of your church and admit my mistakes." He swallowed and took a deep breath. "Maria, you're a part of me—you're under my skin, and I just can't let go of you. I want for us to be together, and I'll do anything to make it happen."

Maria stared at Doug, unsure how to respond. This was the

moment she'd been praying for, but now that it was actually happening, she was scared. *Is he still going to feel like this next month?* Maria thought warily. *Is this really the right thing for us to do?*

"Well, what about Jessie?" she asked hesitantly.

"Jessie's not in the picture anymore," Doug said to Maria. "Things were never very good with us, and when she moved again to California, we broke the relationship off." He leaned forward. "Again, I'm so sorry for everything that I've done."

Maria sighed. *He feels really bad,* she thought. *He's serious about this. But is it best for us to be together again? It's been so long, and our marriage was so rocky before.*

Doug continued. "I can't take it back, though. There's nothing I can do except go forward and prove to you that I love you," he said hoarsely.

Maria looked intently at her ex-husband. "I don't want you to go in front of my church. You've already shown me that you're sorry." She paused, thoughtful. "Let's just take things slow," she told him. "We have a lot to work through, and I want to make sure this is what God desires for us."

"Okay," Doug said, nodding at her.

Over the next year, Doug worked hard to demonstrate his love for Maria. He gave her flowers—something he'd rarely done in the past—and discussed many things with her. During their separation and divorce, Doug had been afraid that Maria wouldn't completely forgive him for his adultery, that she might hold it over his head and never give him a chance to repent and move on. This fear had kept him going back to Jessie even though he had wanted to reconcile the marriage just as much as Maria did. And though Maria wanted to remarry, she sometimes fought feelings of dread that the same cycle of fighting and adultery would resurface if they got back together.

Talking with the minister helped Doug work through his issues, but prayer was the key that enabled Maria to overcome her fears and doubts. Each time she and Doug fought, each time she remembered the adultery, God would remind her, *You're not perfect either, Maria, but I still love you.*

Maria sought the advice of other pastors as well. They counseled her to lay down ground rules with Doug. For instance, since Maria's spirituality had always been a point of contention in the past, she needed to let Doug know that her relationship with God had only deepened since the divorce—and that remarriage wouldn't change her Christian beliefs and practices.

Rebuilding wasn't easy, though. Throughout that year, Maria often questioned why they were even trying to reconcile—there was just so much baggage in their relationship. She knew that because of Jimmy, Jessie would always be in the picture—and Maria wasn't sure she could handle that.

Doug hadn't thought to get rid of all his pictures of Jessie, and when Maria saw them still in his wallet, she almost went through the roof. There was a photo of Maria, David, and Trevor in front, but behind the family photo were several old pictures of Doug and Jessie.

"Are you sure you really want to be with me, Doug?" Maria said, her eyes smarting. "The pictures in your wallet seem to indicate that you'd rather have Jessie. Why are these photos still in here?"

Doug closed his eyes. "I'm sorry, Maria," he said sincerely. "They don't mean anything to me; I just didn't think to take them out. I don't usually flip through my wallet."

Maria stood with her arms folded, waiting.

"I'll tear them up right now," Doug promised. True to his word, he walked over to the kitchen trash can and ripped up the pictures.

Maria shook her head, wondering if she could endure Jessie being a part of her life forever. *Am I strong enough for this?* she wondered. *Lord, if this is what You want, make me the wife You want me to be. Help me to deal with all this in the way You want.*

That became her constant prayer as Maria sought the Lord's guidance in the months ahead. Finally, almost a year after they'd begun marriage counseling and working on their relationship, Doug proposed one spring afternoon. Maria was preparing dinner while Doug watched her from the kitchen table.

"Maria?" he said quietly.

Maria put down the pot she was holding and turned around. "Yes?"

"When would you like to get married?" Doug asked, fumbling with a small box.

"What? Doug, are you proposing to me?" Maria asked, taken aback. She wasn't expecting this today.

Doug looked at her tenderly as he walked toward her. "Yes." He pulled out her old diamond ring and slipped it on her finger. "I want to marry you again. When do you want to get married?" he repeated.

"I don't know," Maria said shakily. She stared at the sparkling diamond. She couldn't believe Doug was actually proposing. It had been five long years since they'd first separated.

"How about June 12th?" he asked seriously.

Maria blinked, unable to form words. Despite all her prayers for wisdom and guidance, she still felt a little nervous about this. *Lord,* she prayed silently, *I've wanted this to happen for so long. And I think that You want this, too, because You've brought Doug and me this far. Now please give me peace about this, that I'll be able to be the wife You want me to be, and that Doug and I will be able to have a strong, healthy marriage.* Right now, all she could think about were the difficult times they'd been through.

Doug put his arms around her. "I promise that things will be better the second time around."

Maria buried her face in Doug's chest and erupted into tears. In her mind, she'd always remained married to Doug throughout their separation and divorce, hoping for reconciliation—and now the Lord was making that hope a reality.

Maria still felt nervous, but she knew that this was what God wanted for her and Doug. The Lord would bring her peace, in His time. She smiled timidly. "June 12th sounds great," she said.

Later that day, after Doug had left, Maria received a package in the mail from her sister, Anna. *I wonder what this could be,* she thought, puzzled. *It's not anyone's birthday.* When Maria opened the package, she gasped.

It was a book: *Marrying Your Spouse for the Second Time.*

Anna, who lived in another state, didn't know Doug would propose that day, or even that Maria and Doug were talking of remarriage at all. Maria had told Anna only that they were working on their relationship.

Holding the book, Maria let out a sigh of relief and sank onto the couch. This was the confirmation that she'd needed. "Thank You, Lord," she whispered.

OVER THE NEXT FEW WEEKS, MARIA AND DOUG BEGAN TO plan the details of their second wedding. They picked the flowers, asked a friend to cater the reception and bake the cake, and sent out simple invitations to just 25 of their family members and closest friends. After much debate, Maria and Doug decided that the invitations would read like this:

> David and Trevor invite you to the wedding of their mom and dad, Maria and Doug Jamesson, on June 12, 1988, at 4:00 in the afternoon at the Jamesson home. Reception following.

Maria and Doug wanted their sons to be a big part of the ceremony. As good as their reconciliation was for the family, they still knew that their remarriage would cause ripples at home with the boys, now 10 and eight years old. David and Trevor's parents had been separated and divorced for most of their younger years, and they would face an adjustment period, having two parents in the same home again.

June 12th quickly crept up, and Maria and Doug were remarried at home in their backyard. It was a small, quiet ceremony. They had each chosen a close friend to serve as the matron of honor and best man, but there was a twist to the wedding—David carried the ring, and Trevor walked Maria down the aisle.

Maria had struggled with doubts and fears up until the

ceremony, but now she was radiantly happy, overwhelmed with emotion and gratitude to God. She couldn't believe all that had happened. She and Doug had been apart for five years, but now they felt closer than ever. Over the last year, Doug had shown her through his words and actions that he loved her and was completely remorseful about his mistakes, and Maria trusted that they would both honor their marriage vows.

Doug's attitude had truly changed. During their first marriage, he had been about as responsive as a brick wall when discussing their marital problems, but now he was willing to talk through everything with Maria. Though her confidence in Doug had been restored, the pain and jealousy Maria felt about his affair with Jessie didn't go away. In fact, it intensified after they remarried.

Maria had known that because of Doug's young son Jimmy, Jessie would still have to be a part of their life—but she didn't realize how difficult that would be for her. This made their first year of remarriage rocky at best. Maria couldn't put the adultery behind her—especially when she and Doug received pictures of Jimmy in the mail or when Jessie called to talk about the boy. Jessie didn't call often, but in Maria's mind, even once a year was one time too many.

"This marriage was a mistake!" she screamed at Doug one day when she opened a note from Jessie with a photo of Jimmy enclosed. "I'm leaving—I can't take this. I don't know what made me think I could!"

Rather than escape from the house or emotionally check out as he had done during their first marriage, Doug now simply let his wife yell and scream. He understood that she needed to express her feelings.

With barely a glance in Doug's direction, Maria raved on. "How would you feel if I were the one who had a baby with someone else?" she yelled. "How would you handle it?" Then, exhausted, she fell onto the bed, weeping hysterically.

Doug sat on the edge of the bed and laid his hand lightly on Maria's back. "Maria," he said gently, "I'm so sorry."

They remained that way for a long time, until Maria's sobs slowly quieted.

As the years passed, Maria gradually worked out most of her anger toward her husband—and Doug patiently let her do it. Soon he began going to church with her again, something he hadn't done since they had separated. Maria could see that he had matured. Doug loved Jimmy and wanted to see his son, but he never allowed his time with Jimmy to jeopardize his relationship with Maria and their boys. If Jessie wouldn't let him bring Maria when he had a rare chance to visit his son— Jimmy and Jessie lived in California now—Doug wouldn't go.

Although Jessie had gotten married and lived far away, Maria still made every effort to avoid any contact with her. If she called and Maria answered, Maria would simply hand the phone over to Doug, saying, "It's for you."

Just hearing Jessie's name, let alone her voice, made Maria burn with fury and bitterness. She was unable to let go of the perception that Jessie had wooed Doug away from her. It was easier to see Doug as the naive one who'd been tempted into an adulterous relationship by a manipulative seductress rather than remember that he'd been a willing participant in the affair.

One year, though, when Jimmy was about nine, Jessie brought him along from California to New Hampshire. She wanted to visit a girlfriend nearby and figured it would be a good time for Jimmy to see his dad as well. Doug picked up Jimmy and took him out for pizza, while Maria stayed home, not wanting to risk seeing Jessie. Although she'd released her bitterness toward Doug, she still couldn't stand the other woman. They'd only met briefly once before—and once was enough for Maria. She breathed a sigh of relief when Jessie and Jimmy left a few days later.

The next evening, Maria sat in the passenger seat of the family car as Doug drove to Trevor's basketball game. As she stared out the window, she thought ungraciously, *Boy, am I glad that woman is gone. She has caused me so much grief.*

"Maria," Doug said, breaking into her thoughts, "you know, I think Jessie got saved." He glanced at his wife.

Maria whipped around to look at Doug. "What?" she gasped, appalled. "Why do you say that?"

"Well, she was asking me questions about our church and talking about God," Doug told her calmly. "She doesn't seem like the same person."

Maria clapped her hand over her mouth and started to cry. "This is not fair!" she sobbed. "I don't want to spend eternity with *her!*"

"Maria . . . ," Doug began weakly. He braked at a stoplight and stared dumbly at her.

Trembling, she couldn't talk. In the back of her mind, Maria had always secretly hoped that Jessie was going to burn in hell because she didn't know the Lord. *Jessie can't be saved*, Maria thought desperately. *She's caused me so much hurt and pain. God wouldn't save her soul just like that . . . would He?*

Maria threw her head back against the seat. "This is awful!" she declared vehemently, her cheeks wet with tears.

She would have preferred to ignore Doug's news about Jessie and continue hating her, but over the next 12 months, she was bombarded with sermons and people who pointed her to forgiveness. Her pastor, for example, did a series on forgiveness and often would say, "If you want to experience the fullness of God, you have to forgive everyone who has ever hurt you." Maria would sit in church and think, *Yes, I should really try to forgive Jessie.*

But her intentions were always short-lived. When the service was over and she got home, Maria would change her mind. *What was I thinking?* she'd tell herself. *That's a really stupid idea. Jessie doesn't deserve forgiveness.* In her mind, Maria knew that she shouldn't be holding a grudge against Jessie, regardless of what she'd done—but in her heart, she felt Jessie was too wicked to forgive.

And as far as her being a Christian, maybe Doug believed Jessie had been saved, but Maria was doubtful. *How could God just forget the terrible sins Jessie has committed against me and my family?* she wondered.

Then the Lord brought Joy into Maria's life.

A FEW MONTHS LATER, MARIA LOOKED UP FROM HER DESK and saw an attractive woman about her age with frosted blonde hair walk into the advertising agency for an interview. *This must be Joy,* Maria thought, then sifted through her files for the woman's résumé and application. She had gotten Joy's résumé a few months before but didn't expect her to be hired—Joy didn't have a college degree, and James, the boss, never hired anyone for a marketing position who didn't have a four-year degree. Nevertheless, Maria smiled up at the stranger as she approached the desk.

"Hi, I'm Joy," the woman said, smiling brightly and holding out her elegantly manicured hand. She shook Maria's hand, then looked down at the nameplate on her desk. "Now, Maria, I wrote on the application that I have a felony charge against me for a DWI, but I served my time," Joy said, straightening her red blazer. She paused, then added, "I was in jail for five months."

Maria raised her eyebrows, aghast. "Oh, okay," she faltered, shrinking a little from Joy. *Jail? Oh my goodness!* she thought behind her plastered-on smile. *Well, honey, you can forget it. You're not going to get this job.*

Ignoring Maria's shocked reaction, Joy continued. "I told you that because I feel the Lord wants me to be truthful about my past," she said frankly.

Maria dropped her pen and leaned in closer. "You know the Lord?" she asked excitedly. *This changes everything!* she thought, amazed.

"Oh, yes!" Joy said, nodding. "Do you?"

"Absolutely," Maria responded emphatically. Out of the corner of her eye, she saw that James was ready for his appointment. Maria smiled at Joy and said sincerely, "Let me know how the interview goes, okay?"

Joy went into her interview, and to Maria's surprise, James was very impressed with her. That day, right after she left, he sent Joy a letter offering her the job even though he still had several other interviews scheduled. When James informed Maria of his uncharacteristically rapid decision, she realized that God had brought Joy into her life for some important reason.

Joy packed up and moved from Texas to New Hampshire, and Maria found a best friend. They had a spiritual connection in their love of Jesus. At the office, they prayed together on Fridays during lunch, and they eagerly told each other their life stories, detailing how they came to know God.

When Maria heard Joy's testimony, her big brown eyes grew even larger. Joy had changed dramatically since she'd become a Christian while in jail seven years before. She had been an alcoholic, a drug abuser, and sexually promiscuous most of her life. Even worse from Maria's perspective, Joy had cheated on her husband with her boss—for years.

Maria was speechless after Joy finished talking. To someone who had grown up a "good girl," as Maria had, Joy's former life sounded atrocious. Maria stared at her in amazement. *I can't believe that someone who once lived like that could now be my close friend,* she thought. "You know, Joy," Maria said honestly, "had I known you before you were saved, I would have crossed the street if I had seen you coming so I wouldn't have had to talk to you."

"Well then, I'm glad you know me now," Joy told her simply.

Through Joy, God was working on Maria's judgmental heart, causing her to see that even a substance abuser and *adulteress* could change and experience the fullness of God's love. In fact, Joy was so strong in her faith that she unknowingly challenged Maria to become more diligent about praying.

A few months after they met, Maria began writing down her prayers each day. It was through this prayer journal that God began to perform a miracle of forgiveness in Maria's life. Early one Monday morning, she sat at the kitchen table, writing her thoughts to the Lord. As she was journaling, Maria realized that Joy had done all the things Jessie had done—and more. Maybe Jessie was truly a Christian as well.

Maria stared at the spiral-bound journal, then in shame penned these words: "I call myself a child of God because I'm saved, and yet my heart is not glad that Jessie has been saved as well." Maria stopped and gazed at the wooden table. She could sense God was telling her to do something crazy.

Maria, I want you to write Jessie a note, telling her that you've forgiven her, the Lord said to her clearly.

Knitting her brow, she scribbled defiantly, "That's ridiculous, Lord. That's the dumbest idea You've ever had. What would Jessie say?" Maria clamped her mouth into a stubborn line. "Sorry, God," she wrote. "There's no way I'm going to write that note."

She continued to argue silently with God, but His instruction remained powerfully present in her mind. Finally, she set down her pen and surrendered. *Oh, Lord,* she prayed remorsefully, *I'm such a wicked person, and You forgave me for all the hurt I caused You. Help me to forgive Jessie. Help me to write this letter.* Maria realized that if Jessie really were a Christian, she would now be able to understand why Maria was forgiving her. Before, she probably would have laughed and mocked Maria for being a "Bible thumper." The timing certainly was right.

Okay, I'll write to her, Maria said ruefully to God. *But I still can't believe You're making me do this.* She knew it was the honorable thing to do, but that didn't make it easier. Maria walked to the bureau in the kitchen and pulled out a note card. Taking a deep breath, she wrote a brief paragraph:

> Jessie,
> Doug tells me you've gotten saved and now you're a Christian. Maybe, then, it won't sound so strange for me to tell you that I forgive you for everything that happened. I feel the Lord wants me to write this to you so that you know I'm not angry at you anymore.
>
> Maria

Maria still felt bitter toward Jessie, and she was still hurt, but she needed to write the words *I'm not angry at you anymore* out of obedience to God. She could only hope and pray that the feelings would follow now that she'd chosen to forgive Jessie. Maria wrote Jessie's name and address on the envelope and put the letter into her purse to drop off in the office mail. She wasn't going to tell Doug about this just yet, but she still needed support. So when Maria arrived at the advertising agency, she anxiously approached Joy.

"You've got to pray with me right now," she said, taking Joy's arm and leading her into the break room. "You're not going to believe what I did this morning."

Joy listened as Maria told her about the note. When Maria was done talking, Joy said, "You did what God wanted you to do. You're doing this for Him, not Jessie." She smiled comfortingly at her friend. "Don't worry about how Jessie might react. The Lord will take care of it."

Maria released her grip on Joy's arm. "You're right," she said more calmly. "I'm putting it in the mail now."

She left the break room, took the note from her purse, and placed it in the mail bin. Within five minutes, the mail was picked up and Maria's note to Jessie was gone. When Maria looked at the empty mail bin, peace swept through her. She had done what God had asked.

Joy was right—the Lord would take care of it.

*O*NE AFTERNOON A WEEK LATER, MARIA AND DOUG WERE cleaning up the kitchen when the phone rang.

Maria picked up the receiver and said, "Hello?"

"Maria?" a woman said hesitantly.

The voice on the other end was distinct, and Maria immediately recognized it as Jessie's. Her heart beating rapidly, Maria perched on the edge of a wooden chair, ready for anything. *Oh, Lord, please help me to stay calm. Make my heart willing to show Your love to her,* she prayed quickly. Then she saw Doug looking at her quizzically. *It's Jessie,* she mouthed to him, ignoring the shocked look that came over his face. Turning her attention back to the phone, Maria took a deep breath, then said, "Yes?"

"Hi. It's Jessie. I . . . I just wanted to thank you so much for the note," Jessie said awkwardly. "You know, I'd asked everybody else in my life to forgive me for the things I'd done to them, but I never could get up the courage to ask for your forgiveness. I was so moved that you would write to me."

Maria shifted nervously and began tapping her foot on the kitchen tile. "Well, the Lord told me to write that and send it to you," she said uneasily, then stole a glance at Doug. He was leaning toward her, trying to figure out where the conversation was leading.

"The Lord did? That's great!" Jessie responded, her voice becoming more relaxed. "I showed the note to some of the women in my church," she confided. "But you know what's really funny, Maria? You'd already made an impact on me for Christ a long time ago. Remember that one night I called you at home?"

Maria rubbed her forehead until her olive-toned skin turned red. She remembered that terrible night, but the only thing she recalled from the conversation was that she'd yelled at Jessie for almost two hours. Years ago, when Jessie and Doug were together, she had awakened Maria one night, hysterical after fighting with Doug, to ask for Maria's opinion on something he had said. Jessie had justified her phone call, saying that she knew Maria wouldn't lie to her.

Now Maria stared at the wall, confused. "What did I possibly say to you that was positive or helpful?" she said dubiously. "I thought we were only screaming at each other."

"You kept preaching to me, telling me that I needed to get saved, that I needed to become born again," Jessie told her, her voice intense.

I did? Maria puzzled, fingering the phone cord. *I sure don't remember that, but maybe God communicated those words through me without my realizing it.*

"I thought you were loony," Jessie continued bluntly. "A real holy roller. But last year, when I accepted Christ into my heart, I remembered what you'd said to me that night. Even though I didn't appreciate it at the time, you put the first nugget of God's truth in my heart, and now I'm so thankful."

Maria spoke with Jessie for 45 minutes, and for the first time ever, they had a completely cordial conversation. Jessie told Maria about how her family had all committed their lives to Christ—even 11-year-old Jimmy had—and Maria realized that this woman was no halfhearted Christian. She was totally excited about what God was doing in her and her family's lives, and she told everyone she met about Christ. Jessie was completely sold out to the Lord.

When Maria hung up the phone, David looked questioningly at his mother. "Who were you talking to?" he asked. The teenager had walked into the kitchen to raid the refrigerator and caught the last five minutes of their talk.

Doug, who had been sitting at the kitchen table the whole time, listening to the conversation in awe, answered proudly for Maria. "She was talking to Jessie," he said, grinning.

David stared at his mother and started laughing. "Yeah, Ma," he said, snickering. "Very funny, but I'm not that gullible."

Maria smiled wryly. "Well, God has a way of changing people—and Jessie and I are no exceptions," she said. Then she told Doug and David about the letter she'd sent to Jessie and about their conversation.

Still surprised that she and Jessie had actually managed a civil conversation, Maria contentedly put her feet up on the chair across from her. *I actually talked to Jessie and my heart didn't pound or stop beating,* she realized. Maria felt as though a huge burden had been lifted from her shoulders.

In the week since she'd written Jessie the letter, Maria had also begun praying for her, asking God to work in Jessie's marriage, to bless Jimmy, and to strengthen Jessie's faith. Maria was amazed that God had enabled her to do that—and now she'd also chatted with the other woman. It was incredible to her.

Maria didn't yet know it, but God's miracle hadn't ended there. Although she had forgiven Jessie in the letter, talked to her, and even had begun praying for her, Maria still had a long way to go before she'd be completely healed from the pain.

One evening a few months later, she and Doug sat watching TV on the couch in their closed-in porch. Maria yawned and stretched her arms above her head. It had been a long, tiring day. She had just pulled the afghan around her, enjoying the peacefulness of the evening, when the phone rang.

"Doug, would you get that?" she asked. "You're sitting closer to the phone anyway."

"Maybe two feet," Doug said, teasing her. He got up from the couch and retrieved the phone, which was sitting on a desk across the room.

Maria redirected her attention toward the TV, every once in a while catching snippets of Doug's conversation.

"Oh, you moved to North Carolina? . . . Well, I don't know if we can make it," he said into the receiver.

Maria's ears perked up. *He must be talking to Jessie about visiting Jimmy,* she realized. *She probably wants Doug to come out for Jimmy's twelfth birthday.*

Doug shook his head. "I have vacation scheduled that I have to take in June, but I don't think we could drive all the way to Greensboro."

Maria sat up on the couch. *Greensboro!* The city's name rang a bell in her head. *That's where the Renewing the Heart women's conference is going to be held in June! Maybe if we visit Jimmy, I can go,* she thought excitedly. She had heard about the conference a few weeks before but didn't think she'd be able to attend because it was so far away. This was her chance.

"Doug!" she said, waving her hands to get her husband's attention. "Doug, we can go! Jimmy's birthday is on the 9th, the Renewing the Heart conference is on the 13th, and you're supposed to take vacation that week anyway." She continued enthusiastically as she walked over to Doug. "And Jessie can go to Renewing the Heart with me!" The words bubbled out before Maria thought about what she was saying.

Doug gaped at her for a few seconds, then turned his attention back to Jessie on the phone. "Uh, Maria just said something about going to a conference and that you could go with her," he said tentatively.

As Maria listened, the hair stood up on her arms. *What did I just say?* she thought, panicked. *Did I really invite her to come to Renewing the Heart with me?*

Doug turned to his wife, and holding his hand over the mouthpiece of the phone, he said, "Jessie wants to know if you're talking about the ladies' conference in Greensboro."

Maria couldn't take her offer back now. "Yes, that's it," she said slowly, then sank into a nearby chair, the afghan still pulled around her. *Oh my goodness, what am I doing?* she fretted. *This is terrible.*

Doug motioned to his wife, who was now staring numbly at the floor. "Jessie says some of the women at her church are going," he told her. "Have you sent in your reservation or do you want her to do it?"

"No. I'll do it myself," Maria said gloomily. *I can't believe this is happening,* she thought. She had asked the Lord to help her forgive and love Jessie, and now He was sending them to the Renewing the Heart conference together! What kind of answer was that? Maria stood up and, folding her arms, walked back to the couch. "I should be more careful what I ask God for," she mumbled to herself. "He really does grant our requests."

*D*OUG AND MARIA SAT AT THE DINING ROOM TABLE IN THE home of Jessie and her husband, Steve, in Greensboro. It was a few months after Maria and Jessie had agreed to go to the Renewing the Heart conference together. Maria and Doug had just driven in from New Hampshire, and after their long trip, Maria felt frumpy—not the way she wanted to feel, or appear, when being in the same room with Jessie for the first time in almost 10 years. Jessie and Steve's three other children had gone to bed a few minutes after they'd arrived, and now the adults were alone.

Lord, please help me, Maria prayed. *I feel as if I'm going to throw up.* She eyed the other woman seated directly across from her. Jessie looked fresh and lovely in her beige outfit. All of a sudden, Maria—normally a confident woman—felt insecure, painfully aware of all the things she disliked about her own appearance. She sat fiddling with her teacup, unusually reserved.

Since Steve and Doug were quiet as well, Jessie carried the conversation. She handed a photo album to Doug and began to reminisce.

"Do you remember my brother and his kids?" she asked him eagerly, tossing her long, dark hair. "Look at how they've grown! Isn't it amazing?"

Maria squirmed uncomfortably in her seat, while Steve folded his arms.

Doug scooted his chair forward and looked at the pictures. "Boy, they really have gotten bigger," he commented.

Jessie talked easily, flipping pages and pointing to photos. "Oh, and look at Jimmy. He was only a toddler then."

She and Doug talked about her relatives, David and Trevor, and other friends. The memory-sharing seemed to go on for hours, and it hurt Maria deeply. *I wasn't a part of Doug's life then,* she thought, trying valiantly to hold back her tears. *He and Jessie have a history that I'll never be able to share. What am I doing here? This is only making me feel worse.*

Finally, she and Doug excused themselves and went back to their hotel. When they were alone in their room, Doug looked at her with concern. "Are you okay?" he asked.

"No, I'm really not," Maria said, sniffling. "Doug, this is harder than I thought. I don't know if I can deal with this."

She grabbed a pillow from the bed, cradling it tightly. The tears escaped from her eyes, and Maria finally released the painful feelings that she had kept pent up all evening. Holding a tissue to her face, she sobbed, barely able to get the words out. "But . . . but I just have to keep telling myself that since this is ha . . . ha . . . happening, I must be able to handle it because God won't give me anything more than I can handle." Maria looked at Doug through red, puffy eyes. "Right?" she asked.

Doug reached over and gently wiped the tears from her face. "Right," he said softly.

They got ready for bed and were soon asleep. Maria woke up a few hours later. She looked at the digital clock on the nightstand: 3:00 A.M. She sighed and, closing her eyes, tried to fall asleep. It proved to be useless. The emotional upheaval she'd experienced late that night had come back to her full force, and now completely distraught, she couldn't stop shaking.

Maria rubbed her puffy eyes, grabbed her Bible from the nightstand, and stumbled into the bathroom to read. She sat on the toilet lid for some time, trying to read psalms in the bright fluorescent light, but tears kept blurring her vision. *Help me, Lord,* she prayed desperately. *I'm such a mess. I need You to give me strength to get through the next few days, because it's for Your honor and glory, not mine.*

Finally, after a few hours of sitting, reading, and praying, Maria realized she might as well get up—it was already 6:00 A.M. Throwing on a sweatshirt and a pair of jeans and tucking her Bible and journal under her arm, she decided to venture into the lobby. Maybe a cup of coffee would perk her up physically and calm her emotionally.

After getting herself some coffee, Maria sat down at a tiny table in a corner of the lobby. Blinking back her tears, she wrote: "Lord, I thought that when I wrote that note, I had forgiven Jessie. I don't hate her anymore—but I don't want to be her friend, either. Why do I have to go to the conference with her? Lord, I need Your wisdom and comfort this morning, now more than ever." Putting down her pen, Maria closed her journal and then dabbed at her eyes with a tissue.

Suddenly, she realized that someone was standing by her table. She looked up in surprise.

"Hi, I'm Janet," a blonde woman said softly. "I was just having breakfast with my husband, and I noticed you sitting over here. Are you going to the ladies' conference tomorrow?"

Maria saw that Janet had a sweet, compassionate face. Letting down her guard, Maria told her tiredly, "I'm Maria, and yes, I'm going to the conference."

Janet leaned closer to Maria and put her hand on her shoulder. "Honey, do you need prayer?" she asked. Her southern accent was strong.

Maria nodded, then told Janet about the events of the night before. "Please pray that my going to the conference will be a testimony to others," she said. "And pray that God will strengthen me."

So Janet sat next to Maria and prayed for her, Doug, and Jessie. When she was done, Maria felt much stronger and more peaceful. *Thank You, Lord, for sending this woman to comfort me,* she prayed silently. *You'll take care of me at the conference tomorrow. I know You will.* Maria hugged Janet, then watched as the woman got up from the table to rejoin her husband.

She never saw Janet again.

Maria and Doug spent the day seeing the sights of Greensboro, and that evening, they took Jimmy out to dinner and shopping so he could pick out his birthday present. Usually, they sent him money, since they didn't know what he wanted or needed, but now that they were there, Doug wanted to do something more personal for his son. Jimmy picked out a fishing pole—he and Doug were going fishing while Maria and Jessie were at the conference the next day. Maria, who hadn't spent time with the boy for almost 10 years, was amazed at how kind, sweet, and thoughtful Jimmy was. He kept trying to make Maria feel included, showing her the fishing pole and thanking her profusely for buying it for him. It was a difficult evening for Maria, but Jimmy's attitude helped remind her that the boy hadn't done anything wrong. It wasn't his fault that Jessie and Doug had made a mistake.

Maria and Doug dropped Jimmy off at home later that

night and went back to their hotel. Maria needed a good night's sleep because she had to be up early the next morning. Exhausted, she flopped onto the hotel bed and closed her eyes.

"Tomorrow's going to be a long day," she told Doug ruefully.

*E*ARLY THE NEXT MORNING, SATURDAY, MARIA FOUND HERSELF sitting in the back of a church van next to Jessie, along with six other ladies from Jessie's church. The women chatted excitedly during the drive to the conference.

Maria nervously played with her wispy brown hair and tried to smile at Jessie. "It's a beautiful morning, isn't it?" she said, keeping the conversation safe. *Maybe if we stick to superficial topics, I can get through the day in one piece,* she thought.

Jessie turned to Maria and touched her shoulder with a gentle hand. "I can't believe we're here together!" she said happily. "This must be so hard for you, though. The Lord really worked a miracle in our lives, don't you think?"

Maria nodded silently. *So much for safe conversation,* she thought. *Lord, why are You doing this to me? It's not fair that You're making me talk to her like this!*

"Maria, you know I'm excited about God, and I want to serve Him, but my family is so hard to reach," Jessie suddenly confided. "I'm trying to get my parents to come to church with me, and my dad's almost there, but my mom's stubborn." She sighed. "And then there's Steve. He's not as spiritual as he could be," she said honestly.

Maria tried to tune out Jessie and concentrate on the scenery outside the van window. *I don't want to give her marriage advice,* she thought resolutely. *Why should I help her? This is ridiculous!*

But Jessie didn't seem to notice Maria's reticence. Gathering momentum, she talked on, gesturing with her hands. "I want to see Steve spend more time reading God's Word. I want him to be the spiritual leader of the family. I want him to pray with me more often. I want—"

"Jessie, you can't preach at him," Maria interrupted at last. No matter how hard it was for her to converse with Jessie, she had to address this issue. *This is so weird,* she realized uncomfortably. *Jessie and I are so much alike. She's doing to Steve exactly what I did to Doug—preaching at him and trying to control him.* Maria crossed her legs and reluctantly leaned in toward Jessie.

"You have to let the Lord work in Steve's heart," she said earnestly. "Praying is the only thing we can do that will change our husbands. Other than that, we need to love them and let God deal with them. That's what I did with Doug." The words were flowing from her mouth now, and Maria felt almost as if it were God doing the talking. *Lord,* she thought, shaking her head, *You're making me tell her these things, aren't You?*

Jessie, meanwhile, was nodding emphatically at what Maria had told her. "Oh, you're right, Maria," she said. "My goodness, I hope my telling you these things doesn't embarrass you. I hope I'm not saying too much." She searched Maria's eyes for her reaction.

Shrugging her shoulders, Maria just smiled weakly.

Shortly afterward, the van pulled into the arena parking lot, and the women filed into the auditorium and found their seats among the thousands of other women. Maria was, of course, seated next to Jessie. *Please don't make me talk with her very much, Lord,* she pleaded silently. *It's too painful.*

While they were waiting for the praise music and speaking to begin, Jessie told the six other women the story behind her relationship with Maria. They hung on her words in awe.

"Wow!" exclaimed Susie when Jessie was done. She shook her thick, red hair. "God is so good. You two have really encouraged me."

Jill, the woman seated on the other side of Maria, embraced her. "Yes," she agreed. "It's such a blessing to see you here!" Her deep blue eyes were kind, and Maria was comforted by her.

As the praise music began, Maria looked around at the thousands of women who filled the arena. *Lord, You are awesome,* she thought as she sang to God. *It's going to be wonderful to*

sing praises to You in heaven. This must be a taste of what it's like.
She realized that when she turned her attention from the
painful situation and concentrated on the Lord, her burden
with Jessie was eased. *Just keep your focus on God,* she told herself, *and you'll be okay.*

Maria noticed that the Lord was prodding Jessie's heart
that day as well. When Kay Coles James spoke about making
mistakes, Jessie leaned forward and listened intently, her hands
clasped tightly in her lap.

"Ladies," Kay's powerful voice boomed throughout the
quiet auditorium, "there are consequences for sin. You know
that. But God can turn your scars into beauty marks."

Sniff . . . sniff . . . sniff . . .

Maria stole a glance at Jessie, and her eyes widened in surprise. Jessie's tanned face was streaked with tears, and she
could hardly control her sobs. Hunched over in her seat, she
covered her mouth and nose with her hands as she tried to con-
tain her emotions.

Comfort her, God silently urged Maria.

Maria again looked at Jessie, then quickly turned her back,
biting her lip. *No way, Lord,* Maria told Him adamantly. *This is
asking too much. I'm not going to hug and comfort her. Shouldn't she
feel a little of my pain?*

But God's quiet voice persisted: *Comfort her, Maria.*

Maria sighed in surrender. Then, leaning over, she quickly
patted Jessie's knee. "God loves you, Jessie," she said dispassionately. *There, Lord,* Maria informed God. *That's all I'm willing
to do.*

Jessie feebly looked up, trying to smile her thanks to Maria.

When intermission began, Maria and her group found a
rest room. As they finished freshening up and walked out,
Maria started to head back to her seat, but Jessie stopped her.

"Can we go talk on the balcony?" she asked, pointing to an
area nearby where tables and chairs had been set up.

"Okay," Maria agreed. As she followed Jessie through the
crowd to a table in the corner, Maria thought wryly, *I wonder*

*what all these people would think if they knew whom I was walking
with?* Sitting across from Jessie, Maria noticed that the woman's
eyes were red.

"You know, Maria," Jessie began, fiddling with her conference program, "I didn't mean to fall in love with your husband.
It just happened." She swallowed, then continued, her voice
quavering. "I was lonely. I needed somebody to talk to."

As Maria looked at Jessie, pain began to well up in her
throat. "But you had no right to go after someone else's husband," she told her curtly.

"I know. I realize that now," Jessie said. "I knew it then, too,
but before I could catch my breath, I was in love with him."

Maria bristled. *She's talking about my husband! Does she have
any idea how much that hurts me?* Ignoring the pain in Jessie's
eyes, Maria said harshly, "You had no right to love him."

Jessie put down her program and looked at the other
woman. "Maria, I feel terrible about the things that I've done,"
she said, her voice catching in her throat. "But I can't do anything except to say I'm sorry." She leaned across the table and
gazed with pleading eyes at Maria. "I'm so sorry," she repeated.

Jessie's words continued to bore into Maria's psyche
throughout the rest of the day and evening. Maria left the conference feeling refreshed and encouraged, but also challenged.
Though she knew she'd truly forgiven Jessie, her heart was still
churning with anxiety and frustration. She realized she must be
holding something back.

That night after the conference, Maria and Doug went once
more to Jessie's house. While they were there, Jessie's mom
called. After chatting for a few minutes, Jessie waved Doug into
the kitchen. "My mom wants to talk with you," she said, hand-
ing him the phone.

Maria sat on the couch in the living room and heard Doug
discussing David and Trevor with Jessie's mother—how big
they were at 19 and 17 years old; where they were going to
school; and what their hobbies and interests were. *Those are my
children,* Maria thought angrily, crossing her arms. *And Jessie*

and her mother have both robbed me by sharing in their lives! She felt dizzy and nauseated. When Doug hung up the phone several minutes later, Maria leaped up from the couch.

"Doug, we need to leave—now!" she said decisively, brushing past a surprised Jessie as she grabbed her purse and headed for the door.

When she and Doug were both in the car and on their way back to the hotel, Maria tried to explain her feelings. With her voice shaking, she said, "Hearing you talk with her mother just reminded me of all the years that I had to share my family—the people I love most—with Jessie. It made me feel robbed."

Doug parked the car in front of the hotel and listened, smoothing Maria's hair from her face, trying his best to calm and comfort her. But nothing he did helped. Indignant, Maria looked defiantly up toward God. "What more do You want from me?" she yelled, clenching her fists. "I can't do any more. I've given Jessie all I can give! What more do You want?"

Deep down, Maria knew what the Lord wanted—He wanted her to *completely* let go of her anger and show His love to Jessie. Though Maria had forgiven Jessie, God wanted something more—He wanted Maria to take another step in the healing process.

$\mathcal{T}$HE NEXT MORNING, SUNDAY, MARIA AND DOUG WENT TO church with Jessie and Steve. As Maria stood between Jessie and Doug, singing praise songs to the Lord, her heart began to soften. She could feel God's presence filling her with peace and joy. *I love you, Maria,* the Lord reminded her. *I will work everything out for your good.*

Maria began to cry softly. Suddenly, Doug reached over and took her hand, squeezing it tightly. Maria looked up and saw a single tear roll down her usually reserved husband's cheek. Love, hope, joy, tenderness, and serenity rushed through her heart. She gazed at the wooden cross behind the pulpit and listened to the music, holding hands with Doug for the duration of the worship time. *Everything's going to be okay,* she realized.

After the service, Maria spotted Susie and Jill, two of the women who had attended the conference with her. Smiling, she walked over to them. "I just wanted to say good-bye," she told them. "Doug and I are leaving for New Hampshire this afternoon."

"Well, it was wonderful to meet you!" Susie said joyfully. Jill nodded her head in agreement.

"I enjoyed my time with you both so much," Maria said, her eyes shining. Susie and Jill were wonderful Christian women who loved God with all their hearts. Maria hugged them and said good-bye again. She wiped her eyes as she watched them leave the sanctuary. When Maria turned around, however, she froze. She was standing face-to-face with Jessie.

Embrace her, God told Maria. *Show her My love.*

Maria couldn't ignore the Lord's prodding anymore. *Okay, Lord,* she told Him, *I will.* Her heart pounding, Maria took a step toward Jessie and tentatively held out her arms, feeling as though her movements were in slow motion. As Jessie stepped into her embrace, Maria stiffly placed her hands on Jessie's back and hugged her as if she were made of glass.

For a few moments they embraced cautiously, then Jessie began to weep. Her small frame shaking, she clung to Maria, holding her tightly. "Thank you," she choked out. "Thank you for forgiving me."

Maria closed her eyes, feeling her spirits soar. All her bitterness was gone. Months ago, she had written the words "I forgive you" to the other woman, but now God had enabled Maria to finally *show* her forgiveness to Jessie, and by doing so, both women were enveloped in a blanket of joy and peace, making the healing process complete.

Maria Jamesson lives with her husband, Doug, and their sons, David and Trevor, in New Hampshire, where she recently started her own

sales and marketing business from home. Enthusiastic about the miracle of forgiveness that God has enacted in her life, Maria gave her testimony in church shortly after returning from the Renewing the Heart conference. Although Maria admits she and Jessie will probably never be friends, they have seen and talked to each other since the conference. Maria gives all the credit to God for reconciling her marriage with Doug and enabling her to forgive and accept Jessie. She believes that the Lord has truly healed her.

Heart to Heart

───────────────────────────────

C. S. Lewis, in his essay "On Forgiveness," said, "There is no use in talking as if forgiveness were easy. We all know the old joke, 'You've given up smoking once; I've given it up a dozen times.' In the same way I could say of a certain man, 'Have I forgiven him for what he did that day? I've forgiven him more times than I can count.' For we find that the work of forgiveness has to be done over and over again" (in Lewis, *The Weight of Glory and Other Addresses*, ed. Walter Hooper [New York: Macmillan, 1980]). The hardest thing for me about forgiveness is that it doesn't demand reciprocity. God calls me to forgive those who have wronged me because of the grace He has extended to me, not because I decide they deserve to be forgiven. Colossians 3:13 tells us that we are to forgive as the Lord has forgiven us; therefore, a readiness to forgive others is an indication of the state of our own hearts. A person who understands the constant, overwhelming grace needed to cover his or her own mistakes is much more likely to forgive others of their shortcomings.

While Maria's story demonstrates the fruit and peace that forgiveness brings, she—along with C. S. Lewis— also reminds us that true forgiveness isn't easy and sometimes is a long, painful journey. But if we yield to Jesus Christ and His precepts, we will be more like Him as a result of the process.

Walking by Faith ~

Lisa

Guided by an Unseen Hand

*Trust in the Lord with all your heart and
lean not on your own understanding; in
all your ways acknowledge him, and he will
make your paths straight.*
—PROVERBS 3:5–6

"KINDRA, COME IN! WE NEED TO TALK. I HAVE SOME GREAT news for you." Norman leaned back in his leather, swivel chair and waved her into his office. "Sit down," he said, peering at her through gold-rimmed spectacles.

Kindra Savage smiled at her boss and sank into one of the blue chairs facing his desk. She'd had several talks with Norman about her future since returning to work from maternity leave a few months before. "Okay, Norman. What's going on?" she asked.

"All your hard work has finally paid off!" Norman's mustache twitched with excitement. "You're going to be promoted to executive director of personnel. You really deserve this, Kindra. After everything you've done for this company—" He broke off suddenly. "What's wrong?"

Kindra was gazing through the glass walls of the office to the sprawling woods and rolling hills beyond. After working five and a half years for a large financial services institution here in San Antonio, Texas, she'd known that the promotion was highly likely, but the presence of her infant son, Eric, made her response less predictable than her boss had expected.

Tucking her short, straight brown hair behind her ears, she swallowed nervously. "Norman," she said slowly and deliberately, "please don't allow your bosses to promote me yet. You know that Bob and I have been praying about how to care for our son. My mom said she'd watch Eric for only a couple more months, and I don't know what I'm going to do after that. I might end up staying home with him."

Norman's eyes widened slightly. Then, with a loud laugh, he slapped the polished wood desktop. "There's no way you'd give up this promotion. You love your job, and a lot of people have spent several years mentoring and supporting you. I know you wouldn't let them down."

"I need some time," Kindra said, sighing. "I really don't know what I'm going to do."

"Well, when you figure things out, let me know," Norman

said as he picked up a pen and began signing some forms on his desk.

Realizing the meeting was over, Kindra stood up. "I will," she assured him. *If I ever do decide,* she thought dismally as she walked out the door and back to her office.

WORK HAD ALWAYS BEEN AN IMPORTANT PART OF KINDRA'S life. As a high school and college student, Kindra had worked as a cashier for a major grocery-store chain. After graduating from Oklahoma Christian University with a degree in social work, she had had several internships, but she soon became disillusioned with the cynicism she encountered in the field. The pay for social workers was low, and since Kindra had several student loans she needed to pay off, she decided to go back to her old job as a cashier, at which she had made good money.

One day about a year after Kindra had returned to the grocery business, her boss, Gary, approached her.

"Kindra, the other supervisors and I have been watching how you interact with the customers," he said, "and we're very impressed. As a matter of fact, we'd like you to be more involved in our training program."

"But I don't know anything about training," she said.

"Just teach the other employees what you already practice. You're a natural. Would you be willing to give it a try?" Gary asked.

"Sure," Kindra answered. How could she say no?

To her surprise, the program she put together was a huge success—and she loved the work. The chain of grocery stores saw an enormous lift in employee morale, and those who went through the course improved their customer-service skills dramatically. As a result, Kindra was promoted from cashier to equal employment opportunity coordinator, where she handled discrimination complaints and recruited staff for the company. It was the first time in the grocery chain's history that an operations person had been promoted to a corporate position.

Kindra's success was astonishing, especially to her. Her fear that people would find out she wasn't as competent as they thought drove her to put in countless hours of overtime and devote endless amounts of energy to her job. Soon her career began to take over her life—her identity was defined by who she was as an employee, and how she felt about herself as a person was determined by the success of her day. She had little time for hobbies or outside interests, let alone a social life.

Kindra had never dated much in the past, so when Bob, whom she met in the training department of the supermarket chain, began to show interest in her, she was stunned. At first she thought of Bob only as a friend—romance didn't fit into her 70-hour workweek. But he was persistent and patient, and soon Kindra was drawn in by his easygoing, fun personality. They began talking on the phone every day at work. And when Bob could get Kindra away from the office, he took her out to dinner.

Still, her career often got in the way, and Bob didn't like it. One night after they'd been dating for a few months, they went out to eat. It had been a particularly long day at work for Kindra. At the restaurant, she leaned against the cushioned booth across from Bob and sighed. "Bob, I don't know how I'm going to get everything done," she said. She had been given responsibility for overseeing the company's corporate move from Corpus Christi to San Antonio, which meant she not only needed to convince key employees to stay with the company, but she also had to hire staff for all the vacated positions, as well as organize the details of the move itself. "I'm in way over my head." Kindra rubbed her temples tiredly.

Bob put his menu on the table and looked at her intently. "You can do it," he said, "but you need balance in your life, Kindra. You're going to burn out."

"I know, I know," she said quickly, waving her hands as if to dismiss his concerns.

· "No, I really mean it. You're a workaholic."

Kindra nodded her head, trying to listen, but her mind was somewhere else. Suddenly, she clapped her hand over her mouth. "Oh no! Bob," she said as she slowly lowered her hand, "I've got to make a phone call to Steve at work. I completely forgot to talk to him about that invoice!" She sprang up from the table. "I'll be right back."

Kindra found the restaurant's pay phone and dialed Steve's number at work. A few minutes later, she hurried back to Bob, who was still waiting at the table. "This is a major crisis situation," she said. Throwing her coat on, she leaned over and kissed Bob on the cheek. "I'm sorry, but I have to go back to the office."

Bob looked at her incredulously. "Kindra, it's 7:30 in the evening. You're going to end up in the hospital if you keep this up!"

"You don't understand. I have to do this. The magnitude and visibility of this project is a huge responsibility," she said breathlessly. "Steve's in a crisis situation right now, and I've got to go back and help him fix the problem."

Bob shook his head. "This is ridiculous," he said in frustration. "You haven't even eaten yet. The 'crisis' can wait until tomorrow. But I know you won't listen to me, so go ahead. I'll see you later."

Though Kindra's crazy work schedule remained an issue throughout their dating relationship, Bob patiently put up with playing second fiddle to her job responsibilities. About a year later, Kindra accepted his proposal of marriage.

After she and Bob were married, Kindra continued working at the grocery-store chain for several more years before leaving to get her graduate degree in counseling. Within a few months of graduating, she got a job in the human resources department of a large, prominent financial services company. There, she was swiftly promoted, much to the chagrin of her coworkers, many of whom had worked for years hoping to reach the levels she now attained so quickly and easily.

With each promotion—the final one leading to corporate personnel manager—Kindra felt increasing pressure to excel at her position so that no one, particularly her bosses, would suspect that she couldn't handle the responsibility. So when she became pregnant with Eric, she didn't alter her schedule at all. It wasn't that Kindra didn't want a child. She loved kids. In addition, having miscarried the year before, Kindra deeply wanted to become pregnant again. So when she found out she was pregnant for the second time, she was ecstatic.

Kindra never planned on staying home with her baby, however. Being a stay-at-home mom was out of the question at this stage in her life—there was too much she still wanted to accomplish. So she and Bob decided the solution was simply to find someone who would take good care of their son for them. When Kindra's mother graciously offered to watch Eric for six months, Kindra found it easy to delay making a decision about day care. For a few months, she enjoyed the best of both worlds.

When Norman told her she was in line for a promotion, Kindra's situation suddenly became more complicated. Her bosses needed to know soon whether or not she would take the position. Also, the deadline Kindra's mother had given was fast approaching. Kindra could no longer put off making a decision.

For two months, she spent anxious days looking into child-care options and sleepless nights praying. She and Bob quickly ruled out the possibility of putting Eric in a day-care center. They wanted Eric to have one-on-one attention, and the centers in their area all seemed to be overcrowded and staffed with inexperienced, young workers. They decided to hire a nanny instead and contacted a referral service. The agency charged a $250 fee to set up three interviews for them, but only one of the nannies showed up for her appointment; Kindra wasn't impressed with her. The owner of the agency assured Kindra that the service would send her a good, dependable nanny as soon as one became available. So Kindra waited and prayed that God would find the right person, whether it was through the agency or someone else. But in spite of the agency's efforts and many well-meaning offers from friends and coworkers to find child care for them, nothing turned up.

To complicate matters further, Kindra began to question whether she really could leave her baby under a stranger's supervision all day. The sacrifices she was making by being away from her son became painfully clear to her one day when she received a call at work from her mother.

"You're not going to believe this," her mother said. "Eric just sat up." Kindra slumped in her chair as she realized, *I have a son, and I haven't given him a thought all day.* She sighed and, closing her eyes, said into the receiver, "Push him over, Mom."

"What?"

"Push him over. I'm not there to see it, and I don't want to just hear about it." Kindra hung up the phone, her eyes stinging and her throat tight because she had missed this important "first" in her son's life.

Bob was equally torn and offered to work at home and care for Eric so they wouldn't have to leave him with strangers. He had always wanted to start his own consulting business, and this would give him the opportunity to do it. Kindra quickly dismissed the idea, however, as she envisioned her easygoing husband forgetting the work part of the day and spending his time on the golf course with their infant son strapped to the back of a golf cart.

Lord, what do You want me to do? Kindra prayed. *Is the promotion opportunity Your way of telling me to stay at work? The new job would allow me to witness to more people. But then You've blessed Bob and me with a beautiful baby boy, and it's hard for me to accept that You would want us to leave him with strangers all day. Father, tell me what I should do, please!*

A week before Kindra had to give her bosses her decision on the promotion, she still didn't know what she was going to do. In despair, she asked Becky, her prayer partner at work, to pray that God would give her a definite answer by the following Monday.

KINDRA TOOK THAT MONDAY OFF BECAUSE SHE AND BOB HAD moved into a new house over the weekend. She planned to use the day to unpack boxes and settle in. As she moved furniture and hung pictures, put away pots and pans and changed diapers, she prayed and worried over her dilemma at work. By early afternoon, she was exhausted.

Boy, am I tired! she thought as she sank onto the living room floor, stretched out her denim-clad legs, and rested her head against the wall. *Maybe all the stress in my life is finally taking its toll.*

Stifling a yawn, she pulled herself to her feet a few minutes later and wandered downstairs to a long storage closet, where she planned to store her maternity clothes. After some deliberation, she had decided to box them up rather than leaving them on hangers. *I won't need these any time soon. In fact, maybe it won't be long before I'll be wearing my favorite suits again.* Kindra smiled at the thought.

She had just put the last maternity outfit into a box and closed the lid when she felt the room spin. A wave of nausea swept over her, and pressing her arms against her stomach, Kindra went to her bedroom to lie down.

"I'm going to rest for a bit, Eric. I am not feeling well," she said to her son, who was lying comfortably in his crib next to his parents' bed. Wrapping her petite frame in a fluffy comforter, Kindra sprawled out on the bed and tried to sleep.

Suddenly, she sat bolt upright, overwhelmed by a shocking thought. *Could I be pregnant?* But that was impossible! She wasn't used to having one child yet. How would she be able to handle *two?* "There's just no way. This can't be," she said aloud.

She lay back down, her thoughts in chaos. When she glanced at the clock on the nightstand a while later, she realized almost an hour had passed. Bob would be home soon. She got up, lifted Eric out of his crib, and set out in the Honda to pick up some dinner, still unable to shake the hunch that she might be pregnant. Thirty minutes later, she returned with two barbecue chicken sandwiches and a home pregnancy test. Tearing open the box, she walked into the bathroom.

After 20 minutes, the test registered positive. Feeling faint, Kindra sank onto the toilet seat and put her head between her knees. Suddenly, God's peace flooded over her. Today—Monday—was the day she'd asked Him for a decision, and He'd been faithful to answer.

God wanted her to stay home.

A FEW DAYS LATER, KINDRA STOOD NERVOUSLY OUTSIDE THE posh office of the vice president of personnel. Tony was Kindra's mentor and the person who had created the promotion opportunity for her. When she heard that he wanted to see her first thing that morning, her stomach had done a somersault. *Norman must have told him about my decision to resign,* Kindra had thought as she walked down the hall to Tony's office. Her meeting with Norman the evening before had not been easy; the thought of now disappointing Tony was close to unbearable.

Taking a deep breath to calm herself, Kindra knocked on the open office door. Tony looked up from the papers on his desk. "Kindra," he said congenially, "come in, please."

Kindra's knees shook as she walked over to a plush, gray chair in front of Tony's desk and sat down.

"Norman tells me you've decided to stay home," Tony said, leaning forward and looking at her intently. "Kindra, if getting adequate day care is the problem, I know I can find you a great nanny in two days at the most. How about it?"

Lord, help me to be strong, she prayed silently. Then, tugging at the short strand of pearls around her neck, she said, "Tony, I feel strongly that God wants me to stay home with my children. You know I love this job, and I appreciate so much what you, particularly, have done for me . . ." Her voice trailed off as she fought to control her emotions. After a moment, she continued. "This company has been like a family to me, and I know I'll regret leaving. But I can live with that regret. I can't, however, live with the regret of having missed the early years—the most tender, foundational time—of my children's lives."

"Any chance you'll change your mind?" Tony asked resignedly, the expression in his eyes softer.

"None. This is something I have to do."

The next afternoon, Kindra, pale and trembling, stood before her staff. As she scanned their faces, she bit her lower lip to keep herself from crying. *I've already let so many people down,* she told herself. *But the hardest part is having to tell these dear friends that I've resigned.*

She cleared her throat, then said, "I called this meeting to make an important announcement." A tear trickled down her cheek. "I'm leaving," she choked out.

Her coworkers stared at her in stunned silence.

Tears flowing freely now, Kindra said with a shaky laugh, "You may not believe this, but I really am happy about my decision. I'm going to have another baby."

A chorus of congratulations followed Kindra's words. Several colleagues hugged her, promising to keep in touch. Though many of her closest friends didn't understand her decision, they were genuinely happy for her.

Shortly after the meeting, a company-wide memo was sent out to formally announce Kindra's departure. Since her position was so visible, she received numerous calls from coworkers in field offices across the nation. Some calls were disheartening. One prominent company official, a woman, told Kindra, "I just can't believe this. You've devastated us, and you're making a big mistake." Many men, however, told her they wished their wives had stayed home with their children.

These small bits of encouragement comforted her, but

nothing affirmed her decision more than the day Bob stayed home alone with Eric. Kindra returned late from a going-away dinner with her staff.

"Honey, I'm home," she called out teasingly as she closed the front door. When she turned and saw the scene before her, however, her eyes narrowed.

Bob stood at the entrance to the kitchen. He was wearing the same old, gray T-shirt he had worn the day before, his fair skin showed the beginnings of a beard, and his thick, red hair looked as though it hadn't been combed in days. He was holding Eric, who had on dirty clothes—and smelled.

"Did you remember to change Eric's diaper?" Kindra asked, grimacing.

"I changed him an hour ago," Bob said defensively. "I figured the next diaper could wait until you got home."

"Bob, you know better than that!"

She followed him into the living room, which was strewn with toys, unwashed dishes, and remnants of Bob's pizza-delivery lunch.

"Bob, this place is a mess! Help me pick this stuff up," Kindra ordered.

"Hey, I don't report to you," Bob said, putting Eric in his playpen.

Kindra rolled her eyes. "Thank goodness for that," she muttered.

Bob ignored her comment and began putting fire engines, rattles, and stuffed animals into the toy box. Shaking his head, he said grudgingly, "I have to admit I'm not cut out for this. I'm glad you'll be the one staying home."

"So am I," Kindra said as she lifted the pizza box off the couch and tossed it into the trash.

*K*INDRA WAS GLAD TO BE HOME—AT LEAST FOR THE FIRST FEW weeks. She lavished attention on Eric and made a list of what she wanted to accomplish. First, she intended to rest. She had been such a workaholic that she couldn't remember the last time she'd taken two weeks off in a row. She would finally have the time to relax, read, take long, leisurely walks, and catch up on letters to friends and family. After that, she would get some chores done that had been nagging at her for months—cleaning out the closets, rearranging the kitchen cupboards, and putting away the baby clothes Eric had outgrown.

Soon, however, isolation and day-after-day sameness began to take a toll. Kindra felt as though she were fighting the same draining battle over and over. The energy and excitement that had filled Kindra Savage, career woman, were nowhere to be seen in Kindra Savage, housewife and mother. It took a supreme act of the will for her to pull herself out of bed every morning.

One particular morning, after tending to Eric during the night, Kindra had been fortunate enough to get some sleep before the alarm went off at 6:30. Reaching over to shut off the buzzer, she yawned tiredly. *When I decided to stay home with Eric,* she mused, *I thought I'd be able to sleep in later than this.* She got up, rubbing her eyes, and took a quick shower. Throwing on an old, oversized T-shirt and black maternity sweatpants, she trudged down the hallway to Eric's room. He was already awake—of course.

After she'd fed herself and her son some breakfast, she settled on the living room couch with Eric leaning against her very pregnant belly. Her lap had disappeared a couple of months ago.

"Let's read *Where's Baby Jesus?* sweetie," she said, adopting a peppy, baby-talk voice.

Eric delightedly clapped his tiny hands.

Kindra opened the small pop-up book and read, "Where's Baby Jesus? Is He in the tree? No." She dramatically shook her head. "Is He in that car? No," she said, pointing to the page.

Then Kindra noticed Bob in the doorway, ready to leave for work. "Say good-bye to Daddy," she said, taking Eric's little arm and waving his hand good-bye.

They finished the book about 10 minutes later.

"Let's go on our walk now," Kindra told Eric. She strapped him into his blue-and-white stroller and pushed him through the neighborhood.

When they reached their front door again, Kindra looked at her watch and realized, *It's only 9:00! What am I going to do for the rest of the day?*

She spent the remainder of the morning cleaning up after Eric, taking him to the fast-food restaurant for a hamburger and fries, and then walking the aisles of the local department store, hoping to tire her son enough to take a nap.

Hanging out in stores depressed Kindra because she couldn't buy anything. Since they were now reduced to one income, she had to stay on a tight budget. Pushing Eric in his stroller, Kindra walked slowly past the racks of stylish clothes, sighing deeply as she caught sight of her own sloppily clad self in a strategically placed mirror. All she had in her closet were professionally tailored suits—nothing casual or cute that would make her feel like a *Vogue* mom. It was awful having so much time to shop and no money to buy—even the things they needed.

When they returned home, Kindra tried to put Eric down for a nap. He wouldn't sleep, however, so she picked up *Where's Baby Jesus?* again to read to him. She might be tired of the book, but Eric never was. *Thankfully, Bob will be home soon,* she thought.

Kindra gingerly lowered herself onto the couch with Eric at her side. "Okay, now we're going to find Baby Jesus . . . again," she said in a monotone. She began to read rapidly. "Where's Baby Jesus? There He is. Look at Baby Jesus." *I hate this book!* Kindra thought, yawning.

Eric smiled happily, looking intently at the worn pages.

Kindra was in the middle of reading when Bob walked in the door.

"Hey, you two were sitting there trying to find Baby Jesus when I left this morning," he said, laughing.

"Yes, I guess we were," she responded dryly, shooting a

look at her husband that communicated he had said the wrong thing. "Here. Take your son." Kindra handed Eric to Bob, then slumped despondently back onto the couch.

Not only were her days long, boring, and unstructured, but she was lonely, too. The Savages had just moved into a different neighborhood and were looking for a new church, so Kindra had nobody to connect with. When her friends from work gradually stopped calling, the isolation became almost unbearable. Baby talk was *not* enough for the woman who had previously advised top executives and presided over power lunches. And though she hadn't cared about the perks of her position when she'd been working, now she didn't know how she was going to be able to live without them. All along she'd said the power and prestige of her job meant nothing to her, but after they were stripped away, she realized there was nothing left of herself underneath. *I'm a nobody—totally and completely worthless,* she told herself bitterly.

These feelings created sudden, deep insecurities in Kindra. Here she was, a formerly successful career woman, now barefoot and pregnant with only a toddler to talk to all day. Looking for comfort, she turned to food and began to gain weight steadily—more weight than she needed to gain because of her pregnancy. Soon she stopped taking care of herself completely. Many days, she lived in a purple velour robe. *Why should I bother with nice clothes and makeup?* she rationalized. *I've got no one but Eric to impress.*

Kindra also became increasingly sensitive to being "just a mom." When she'd stopped in stores wearing her fashionably tailored suits, the salespeople had been courteous and prompt. Things were different now that she wore only shapeless sweatpants and T-shirts.

One day shortly before Shelby was born, Kindra made a quick trip to a swanky department store to purchase a birthday gift for her mother. Since the errand would take only a few minutes, she had thrown on an old, baggy sweatshirt and hadn't bothered with makeup. Quickly finding the slippers her mom wanted, Kindra, with Eric in the stroller, made her way to the cash register.

The young saleswoman, her blonde hair pulled into a tight French twist and her makeup perfectly applied, looked at Kindra haughtily. "May I help you?" she asked.

Kindra swallowed. "Uh . . . well, I just wanted to buy these slippers."

"Certainly," the woman said. She rang up the purchase while Kindra made out a check.

"Here you go." Kindra tore off the check and handed it to the saleswoman.

"Excuse me, but do you have a work number?" the young woman asked curtly.

"No, I don't have a work number," Kindra said. She was beginning to feel a little sick.

"You don't?" The woman looked smug.

"No."

As soon as the cash register had printed out the receipt and the saleswoman had put it and the slippers into a bag for Kindra, the clerk turned and began folding clothes on the counter behind her. Kindra stared at the woman's brown-pantsuit-clad back and realized, with a sinking feeling, that she'd just been snubbed.

The next time Kindra was asked for her work number, she said, "It's on the check."

The grocer looked puzzled. "Well, where is it? I just see a home number."

In a tone that surprised even herself, Kindra tossed her brown hair and said defensively, "It's right there. I work at home. Taking care of my son is hard work."

Even though Kindra knew that she was no longer a professional—that God had clearly told her to quit her job—she still didn't feel that she fit in with other stay-at-home moms. Though she and Bob had finally found a good church, Kindra couldn't relate to the other mothers she met in the babies' Sunday school class. For one thing, they were all younger than she and had blissfully traded in their careers for motherhood. They couldn't understand her sense of loss.

Another difficulty was that Kindra wasn't as domestically inclined as the other moms. Once she had tried to connect with them by visiting a ladies' Bible study. But when the women were instructed to introduce themselves and then tell the group what their favorite craft or hobby was, Kindra froze. She didn't have a craft or hobby.

After Shelby was born, Kindra's feelings of inadequacy and isolation were magnified by her fatigue. Shelby didn't sleep during the day and was up every two to three hours at night for a year. Kindra spent many sleepless nights running between her son's and her daughter's rooms, on opposite ends of the house. Most days were a blur as she tried to stay alert and keep from erupting into fits of tears. Usually, she found herself alone with her children.

There were some moments of great joy with Eric and Shelby—for instance, when they asked "God questions" or snuggled up to her during thunderstorms—but in the first two to three years, the "bad" days far outweighed the "good" ones.

One Wednesday, Kindra planned to have her children's pictures taken. She woke up early and spent a long time bathing and dressing Shelby and Eric. Finally, by early afternoon, they were ready. One-year-old Shelby had on a new blue-flowered dress, and two-year-old Eric wore a button-down-collar shirt tucked into new khaki pants.

Kindra strapped both children into their car seats and then said, "All right, kids. Now, you need to behave for Mommy today. We're going to get your pictures taken. Okay?" She smiled at them, but her chocolate-brown eyes were serious.

Eric nodded solemnly; Shelby just stared.

When they arrived at the photo studio, they were whisked into a large room at the back. The photographer, a tall man with a bushy beard, turned to Eric and smiled. "Hey, buddy, I'm going to put you on this stage right here," he said as he leaned over to pick up the toddler.

Eric took one look at him and became hysterical. "No! No! Mommy! Mommy! No!" he cried, his tiny, olive-skinned face turning the color of a cherry tomato. He pulled away and ran to Kindra, hiding his head in her long skirt.

Kindra stroked Eric's smooth brown hair and sighed. "I'm so sorry," she said to the man. "It looks as though we're going to have to try this another day."

Driving home, Kindra let the tears stream down her face. *I hate this!* she thought miserably. *I worked all day getting these kids ready, and I can't even get their pictures taken!*

When they arrived home, Kindra gathered her children, still in their little outfits, took them outside, and let them play on the backyard swing set. Leaning her head in frustration against one of the bars, Kindra listened to the planes flying overhead toward the San Antonio airport nearby. She looked up at the clear sky, and directly above was her former employer's corporate jet—the jet she had flown in many times—roaring powerfully through the air. The deafening sound of its engines swallowed up the playful shrieks of her children, as well as her soft pleas to God.

Oh, Lord, why are You doing this to me? she asked, burying her aching head in her hands.

A FEW MONTHS LATER, KINDRA FELT AS THOUGH SHE HAD reached the end of her patience—she couldn't cope any longer. Eric, who was cutting his two-year molars, had been waking up, screaming, in the middle of the night. It was difficult enough that Shelby slept only for short periods of time, but now Eric was up at all hours, too.

"Mommy! Mommy!"

Roused yet again by her son's cries, Kindra shuffled, exhausted, down the hallway to his room. Bleary-eyed, she turned the corner and walked right into the door frame, sharply jabbing her shoulder. "Ohh!" she gasped, wincing in pain. This was too much.

Squeezing her aching arm, she went over to Eric's bed and sat on his navy blue comforter. *God, this life is horrible,* she prayed silently. *I know You called me home, but not to be miserable.* Tears soaked her cheeks. *How am I going to make it through that women's retreat tomorrow? I was nervous and unsure about going as it is, and now I'm an absolute wreck!*

The next day, Kindra halfheartedly decided she would go on the one-night retreat after all, but only because she sensed the Lord wanted her there. He had provided the money—found in the pocket of a jacket she hadn't worn in months—making it possible for her to attend. This would be the first time she had been away from Shelby and Eric.

Through the entire retreat, an exhausted Kindra sobbed unceasingly. While most of the other ladies politely gave her "space," one person did succeed in reaching her: Beth Moore, the retreat's main speaker, who was there by video. Beth talked about praying to God, reading the Bible, and taking one's relationship with Him one day at a time. In short, she taught Kindra about slowly learning to rely on God and letting Him be her source of true fulfillment, rather than trying to make a job or a person meet all her needs perfectly. Kindra couldn't expect Bob to solve her problems, because only God was able to pull her through her crises and make things better. A superficial job title would never give her the fulfillment she craved—only God could do that with His perfect love. Only God would always be present, ready to listen, and eager to comfort and guide her.

When Kindra came home, her perspective had changed, and a new sense of hope began to dawn in her heart. She realized she needed to start studying God's Word and spend more time with Him if He were to help her deal with the hardships in her life. So, knowing she couldn't do it on her own, she began asking the Holy Spirit every day to give her a deep yearning to know God. She also started reading the Bible out of desire and not simply out of obedience. And she prayed about everything. *Lord, teach me how to be a good mother. Show me how to be the wife Bob needs me to be. Help me to keep my family as my top priority after You.* As she learned to rely on the Lord, He began to help her deal with the pain in her life.

During this time, Bob's company relocated the Savages from San Antonio to Charlotte, North Carolina. The prospect of moving from her hometown devastated Kindra. "Bob, my family is here," she told him. "I've lived in San Antonio for more than 30 years. This does not make me happy!"

Even worse, once they arrived in Charlotte, it rained and rained, forcing Kindra and her two toddlers to stay inside their small, two-bedroom apartment while they waited for their house to be built. The movers had delivered the wrong things out of storage, so the Savages didn't have any of the necessary furniture. A card table had to be set up in the kitchen, and packing boxes were positioned at each end of the living room couch.

To add to Kindra's frustration, they didn't know anyone in the city, which caused her and her children to feel more isolated than before. With nowhere to go and no one to see, Kindra picked up the only book they hadn't put in storage, her worn Bible, and she began to read it all day—literally. One particular passage—Genesis 19:26—impressed her: "But Lot's wife looked back, and she became a pillar of salt." After reading this, Kindra realized, *I've spent a lot of time looking back and daydreaming about my previous life, and it's wrong. I've sinned just as much as Lot's wife did.* Dwelling on the past was making her discontented with the present.

Kindra also went through the psalms, studying and underlining characteristics of God. And as she asked Him to be her Comforter, Shield, and Source of Joy—her All—He became real in her life. Soon, instead of turning to food when she was upset or lonely, she turned to God. And He faithfully answered each of her petitions, sometimes by putting people in her life to encourage her, sometimes by pointing her to a Bible verse that applied to her situation, and sometimes simply by giving her a supernatural peace that things were going to work out. She still didn't know anyone in their new city, but that didn't matter as much now. During this period of isolation, Kindra spent so much time with God that she finally began to understand that she was never truly alone. The Lord had shown Himself to be her faithful friend and constant companion.

The lessons God taught Kindra during those few months in Charlotte helped sustain her through several more moves. Soon after she and her family had moved into their new house in Charlotte and become rooted in their church and neighborhood, Bob's business sent them back to San Antonio. Again, Kindra had to go through the process of relocating: packing up, moving into a small apartment, and finding a new place of worship.

Six months after they had moved back to San Antonio, Bob came home with some news. His old company was starting a branch in Charlotte, and, unbelievably, they wanted him to get things going there.

Lord, I know I can trust You to direct my future, Kindra prayed in exasperation, *but at times like this, it seems You can't possibly know what You're doing.* By the time they relocated to Charlotte for the final time, the family had moved six times in little over a year.

$\mathcal{K}$INDRA RUBBED HER SHOULDER AND GAZED WITH satisfaction around Eric's bedroom. Almost everything was finally in place in their new home—the boxes were unpacked, most of the pictures were hung, and the closets and cupboards were organized. This would most likely be the final relocation she would have to endure. The past year and a half had been overwhelmingly hard with all its transitions, but those difficulties had also enriched her life. Kindra's relationship with God wasn't the only bond that had been strengthened. She and Bob had grown closer, too.

These days, she couldn't wait for Bob to arrive home from work. After home-schooling her children all day, Kindra was always more than ready to see him in the evening. Six o'clock could not come soon enough—especially tonight. After months of living out of boxes, the Savage family had finally finished moving into their house, and Kindra wanted to share the satisfaction with her husband.

A few minutes later, Bob's key turned in the lock.

"Your dad's home, kids!" Kindra said happily as she jogged down the stairs to the front entryway. She took Bob's briefcase and gave him a hug at the door. "How was your day? Anything new or exciting happen? Did that meeting go well?" Kindra asked, bombarding her husband with questions. She turned and swept her arms wide. "Look at the house. It's done!"

"It looks wonderful, honey. Thanks for all your hard work," Bob said, looking around appreciatively. "To answer your questions, work was good, nothing new happened, and the meeting went well." He smiled, thankful that Kindra was no longer bossing him around as she had early in their marriage. "I'll tell you more about my day when we sit down for dinner. I'm starving."

A few minutes later, with the family gathered around the table, Kindra served up the chicken and rice. Seeing Bob hungrily eye the steaming bowls of food, she said, only half-jokingly, "I decided that I'd better be good to you. You're my bread and butter now."

At first the knowledge that she was financially dependent on Bob had been difficult for Kindra. She had always been responsible for herself. But slowly, as she got used to needing Bob, and as she let him love her and provide for her, their relationship became more balanced. Now that Kindra's heart had softened, her trust in and esteem for her husband was deep, making their marriage a partnership instead of a one-woman operation.

As she served Shelby and Eric, Kindra looked over at her husband. "So, what are you working on this week?" she asked.

Listening to Bob talk about his day made Kindra realize how little she'd known about his job before she started staying home with the kids. During her working days, she had been too consumed by her own career to pay attention. Now Bob was her link to the world. They discussed current events, politics, friends, and family. Kindra sought Bob's perspective on everything.

As Kindra developed a heightened appreciation for Bob, he became more intent on nurturing her. Often he knew just what she needed. When Kindra heard a radio broadcast about the Renewing the Heart conference in Nashville, Tennessee, he encouraged her to go, so she went, taking her friend Kathy along. The conference affirmed what God had already been teaching her about making her family a priority and raising her children to love the Lord and to be "kids of the King [Jesus Christ]," as speaker Kay Coles James put it. As she gazed around the auditorium at thousands of her "sisters," Kindra was comforted by the thought that she wasn't alone and that God would take any hardships they were experiencing and make something good come from them.

During her years as a stay-at-home mom, Kindra had slowly learned that God, and God alone, could meet her needs for love and significance. He was her source of encouragement, but He often used strangers, such as the speakers at the conference, to give her a boost. Once, after Bob's company had relocated them from San Antonio to Charlotte, God used a complete stranger to give Kindra encouragement. It happened one Monday afternoon shortly after they'd moved back to Charlotte.

Because this move occurred after the registration deadline for their new church's private school, Kindra and Bob had decided she would home-school Eric and Shelby. Although she felt peaceful about that decision, her choice to home-school still made it more of a challenge for her and the children to meet friends in their new community. Most days, Kindra could cope with the loneliness and count her blessings, but this particular afternoon as she was driving Shelby and Eric, now ages five and six, to gymnastics class for home-schooled children, Kindra battled depression.

Lord, I know You're in control, but I'm not happy to be back on the East Coast, she prayed silently. *I thought after we moved again that Texas would be my home forever, that I'd be able to stay put for a while.* As she ushered her kids into the gym, she added fervently, *Lord, help me to see the good in this move. Help me to better trust You.*

After sending Eric and Shelby off to their lessons in the next room, Kindra joined several moms with whom she'd become acquainted. As she chatted with them, she noticed a lady standing to the side, watching her children through a large plate-glass window into the classroom. Studying her, Kindra sensed an inner depth and beauty that drew her to the stranger. She'd always felt awkward about approaching people she didn't know, but after several minutes, Kindra went up to her.

"Hi," she said. "I don't believe I know you. Have you been here before?" She hoped the lady wouldn't notice the nervousness behind her smile.

"No, I haven't," the woman replied quietly.

"I just moved here from San Antonio not too long ago." Kindra wasn't sure why she was telling the woman this.

"So do I."

The lady's gentle spirit compelled Kindra to continue. "You know, I feel so isolated right now, having just moved and all. . . . It's really difficult." *Now, why on earth did I tell her that?* she wondered.

The lady nodded in understanding. "Oh, I know what you mean. My husband and I moved to Kansas City a few years ago, and no matter how hard I tried, I just couldn't meet other women. I didn't make any friends for the entire 18 months we were there. But," she continued, her eyes glistening, "I'm enjoying the benefits of that time right now, because my relationships with my children and with the Lord deepened as a result."

When the gymnastics class ended, the woman left quickly with her children. And though Kindra never saw the woman again, she knew her words would stay with her, because she had been reminded that the isolation she was now experiencing was actually God's gift to her—a rich, productive time in which she was able to give her undivided attention to her family and her God. With her brown eyes wide, Kindra looked up toward heaven and said aloud, "You did it again, Lord. Thank You for encouraging me."

*S*EATED ON THE PASSENGER SIDE OF THEIR SILVER MINIVAN ONE day a few months later, Kindra thought and prayed as she gazed out the window to the ocean beyond. She and the kids had spent four days at Myrtle Beach, South Carolina, with Bob, who had gone there on business. Kindra looked at the road stretching out before them and reflected on the different, sometimes challenging paths on which the Lord had led her since she'd quit her job almost six years ago.

Motherhood certainly hasn't been as easy as I thought it would be, but I wouldn't have traded my time with my children for anything, she mused, turning to look at Eric and Shelby, asleep in the backseat. Pulling down Eric's pants leg where it had hiked up on his calf, she smiled, thinking in amazement, *Boy, they sure have grown—some days have been long, but the years have flown by. How did they get so big so fast?*

Turning around, she gazed out the window again and began thinking about the women's Bible study she had "fallen into" leading. It was sponsored by their church in Charlotte, and the study was scheduled to conclude at the end of next month. Kindra wasn't sure what God wanted her to do after that, but she knew He had something planned. The whole time they had been at Myrtle Beach, she had felt Him nudging her toward some new path. Whatever it was, Kindra decided she would never let her priorities get as messed up as they had been when she was working outside the home. No matter if she stayed at home, worked at an outside job, or volunteered in a ministry, she was adamant that God would remain foremost in her life.

To her surprise, the Bible study had been a real blessing—perhaps her transparency had enabled the women to be open about their own lives as well. Oftentimes the women in the class felt comfortable enough to express their own struggles and heartaches through tears. As she helped them focus on pursuing their relationship with God first, their lives also began to change. Buoyed by this success and her newly found passion and burden for women, Kindra had repeatedly asked God during the four days at Myrtle Beach if He wanted her to start another Bible study.

"Bob," Kindra said, turning toward her husband, "I'm confused. I feel as if the Lord is calling me to do something, but I'm not sure what it is." She spoke hesitantly. "I've told Him that I'm content being a wife and mom, that I don't need to do anything else, but I still think He has something new planned for me."

Bob looked over at her and smiled. "I'm sure He'll let you know soon, honey. He always does."

"Yes, I suppose you're right," Kindra said, gently squeezing his arm.

They arrived home a few hours later, and after Kindra had gotten Eric and Shelby unpacked and cleaned up, she went into the kitchen to sift through the mail and check the answering machine. One of the messages was from Connie, an associate pastor's wife at the church.

Kindra's eyebrows pressed together. *Why is Connie calling me?* she wondered. *We've met only once, and that was months ago.* Puzzled, she picked up the cordless phone and dialed the number.

Connie answered. "Kindra, I'm so glad you called," she said eagerly. "I wanted to talk to you about something."

"Okay. What's going on?" Kindra asked, taking the phone into the living room, where it was quieter.

"Well, we've been trying to start a women's ministry for two years, and we've prayed and prayed to find the right person to chair it. We heard about you and feel the Lord has led us to ask you to chair that ministry. Would you prayerfully consider taking the position?"

As Kindra listened to Connie's request, an overwhelming

sense of peace came to her. Sinking onto the couch, she realized God had just answered her prayer. And she knew, without a doubt, what He wanted her to do.

Kindra Savage lives with her family in Charlotte, North Carolina. She currently works from home as the chairperson of women's ministries at Christ Covenant Church, where she has had the privilege of mentoring numerous women; organizing seminars, social events, and Bible studies; and giving her testimony on stay-at-home motherhood, job relocation, and food addiction. She continues to home-school her two children, Eric and Shelby.

Heart to Heart

Kindra's story reminded me of a time several years ago when I was laid off from a ministry position that I loved. In tears, I told my mother I couldn't believe such a terrible thing had happened to me. I was quite sure that it hadn't been God's will. I expected Mom to cry with me and tell me how sorry she was, but instead she told me to begin studying Isaiah. She said that I should pray for the heart and mind of a blind prophet. I wasn't sure what she meant by "blind prophet," but it didn't sound very appealing. I've always liked to be able to see where I'm going and know what lies around each curve. I like to be in control, to have everything mapped out.

It took me a year to study Isaiah thoroughly, and during that year many of the scriptural truths I learned from that book became applicable in my own life. God reminded me that He leads the blind by ways they have not known and guides us along unfamiliar paths. He turns the darkness into light for us, and He will make the rough places smooth. He reminded me that He stretched out the heavens and laid the foundations of the earth, therefore I shouldn't worry about any part of my life. He reminded me that even when mountains are shaken and hills are removed, His love for me will not falter.

The greatest lessons God taught Kindra and me were during the times our lives weren't going as we'd planned. He showed us that regardless of our shifting circumstances, He remains faithful. And only when we realize that we are the clay and He is the Potter will we experience true peace and security.

Walking by Faith ~

Lisa

Carried by
the Master

*Strengthen the feeble hands, steady the knees
that give way; say to those with fearful hearts,
"Be strong, do not fear; your God will come . . .
he will come to save you."*

—ISAIAH 35:3–4

CATHY CRAFT LOOKED OUT THE CAR WINDOW AT THE LUSH Georgia countryside. The soft October sunlight had sprinkled the rolling, green hills with gold; towering sweet gum trees stretched yellow- and red-clothed branches over the rural road, casting it into shadow. Between the thick tree trunks, Cathy caught glimpses of wide pastures dotted with grazing horses, cows, and sheep. Any other day, the scene would have been breathtaking. But today, Cathy was distraught at the loss of her mother a few days ago, and nothing seemed beautiful.

Cathy leaned her head against the glass and sighed heavily. *How can everything still look so peaceful outside when I've lost my best friend?* she thought numbly. She looked down at the wrought-iron doorstop, a cheerfully painted basket of flowers, cradled in her arms. Her mother had given it to her for her birthday before she passed away. *Mama must've bought it from the hospital gift shop.* Cathy bit her lip. Battling the last stages of breast cancer, her mother certainly wouldn't have been able to go anywhere else those last few weeks.

"Baby, are you doing okay?" her husband, Jim, asked, interrupting her thoughts. He took one of his hands off the steering wheel and placed it comfortingly on her shoulder.

"Well, my heart is breaking, but I believe that God knew best when He took Mama home," Cathy said slowly. "Still, I miss her so much."

She stared quietly out the window. For the last five years, since her mother had been diagnosed with cancer, there had been no such thing as a "normal" conversation with her. Cathy couldn't just call her and say, "Hi, Mama. Are you having a good day?" The shadow of cancer always loomed in the background. Cathy rubbed her forehead tiredly.

"Remember how we used to talk about cancer?" Jim broke in, his normally upbeat voice serious. "How, if the refrigerator broke or both of the boys got the flu, we'd say, 'Well, at least it's not cancer'?"

Cathy nodded.

"I think we'd better quit saying that," he told her grimly, guiding the car around a sharp curve in the road.

"You know what?" Cathy said with sudden determination. "I'd like to avoid the subject completely. From now on, I don't want to hear, see, or discuss the word *cancer.*"

With that, she folded her arms, leaned her head against the seat, and closed her eyes.

*S*EVERAL WEEKS LATER, CATHY, JIM, AND THE BOYS DROVE TO her father's house in Alabama. They went down a road that wound past the graveyard of the small country church Cathy had attended as a young girl. Justin put his nose to the window, eagerly commenting on the numerous bouquets of flowers mourners had left at the gravesites.

"Go see the flowers!" he said excitedly. His "Gran Gran" wasn't buried in that graveyard, but Justin always associated the flowers in the old church cemetery with the abundance of flowers at his grandmother's funeral.

The Crafts pulled into the driveway of a blue and white, country-style house, and the boys jumped out of the van, giggling. They were always happy to see Papa. Cathy's dad, bundled up in a warm wool sweater, met them at the front door.

Cathy shivered in the cold as she walked up the path to the house. "Hi, Daddy!" she said, giving her father a hug.

His lined face crinkled into a smile. "Hi, honey—thanks for coming. I'm so glad my family is here," he said tearfully. Turning to his small grandsons and holding out his arms, he said, "How are my boys?" Five-year-old Justin and three-year-old Jordan gleefully raced into their granddad's embrace. He held them tightly for several moments before releasing them and welcoming them all into the house.

Cathy watched misty-eyed as Jordan helped Justin, who is moderately mentally handicapped, over the threshold. "Be careful you don't trip," Jordan told his brother, protectively holding out his tiny hand. Jordan had developed an intense compassion and patience for his older brother and other children who had disabilities.

As they filed in, Cathy discreetly scrutinized her father. The bags under his eyes and the added silver in his hair showed how deeply his wife's recent death had affected him. Cathy swallowed the lump in her throat. Her parents' marriage—like her own—had been like a fairy tale, characterized by an intense, special, blessed love.

I'm so glad we came to visit Daddy this weekend, she reflected as she walked into the kitchen and began putting the meals she'd cooked for him into the freezer. *He needs us so much right now.*

That night at dinner, her mom's absence left an unmistakable void in the tight-knit family circle. In the past, she would have lit up the room with her gracious smile and servant's heart.

They had just finished dessert and were sitting silently around the table when Cathy's dad pushed back his chair and began studying his rough hands. "You know," he said, twisting the paper napkin on his lap, "your mama had several lumps biopsied, but they were all benign. We didn't expect this last one to be cancerous."

Didn't expect . . . cancer. Her dad's words struck fear in Cathy's heart. She crossed her arms and nervously tapped her foot. She'd found a lump in her own breast just two months before, around the time of her mother's funeral.

Her dad raised the twisted napkin and dabbed at his eyes. "I just don't understand what happened," he said, his voice trailing off. He stared at a framed picture on the wall, looking away from Cathy and Jim. "We always had the lumps checked out right away. We were so careful."

Cathy tried to smile at her dad, but her blue eyes were fearful. "Oh, we know you and Mama did everything you could, Daddy," she said weakly.

Getting up abruptly from the table, she began clearing the dishes, trying to appear more composed than she felt. Until now, Cathy hadn't taken her situation seriously because the lump didn't seem to be dangerous. It was tiny and sensitive, and it came and went with her monthly cycle. *It certainly doesn't feel like breast cancer,* she'd rationalized. *After all, everyone knows malignant lumps aren't painful.*

But now her father's words weighed heavily on her. *What if it is something serious, like Mama's was?* she thought. Her hands trembled as she placed the dishes on the counter.

With her back still turned, she addressed her father. "Daddy," she asked quietly, "did Mama tell you what the lump felt like?"

Her dad paused, then said, "She said it was small and felt tender."

AFTER RETURNING FROM HER DAD'S, CATHY WASTED NO TIME in calling for an appointment with the general surgeon in their hometown of Thomaston. But when she heard that the soonest available date was December 6th, Cathy almost put off the appointment. December 6th was the same date her mother had undergone surgery for her cancer a few years earlier.

The day of the appointment, the general surgeon, after examining the lump and performing the biopsy, told Cathy he didn't think the lump was cancerous and she could go home. That night she and Jim celebrated, believing the worst was over.

The next afternoon, however, they were back in the surgeon's waiting room. Someone from his office had called Cathy at work early that morning, asking her to come in immediately. As she waited for the doctor to see her, she fidgeted on the vinyl waiting-room chair, unable to shake the images of her dying mother lying listlessly in her hospital bed. The cancer and chemotherapy had slowly eaten away at a beautiful, vibrant woman, leaving in her place a stranger. *Oh Lord, I don't think I can go through that,* Cathy silently cried out.

"Mrs. Craft, the doctor is ready to see you," a nurse said briskly, interrupting Cathy's thoughts.

Cathy and Jim followed her down a featureless hallway

and into an even more sterile examining room. After a few minutes, the surgeon entered and sat down in a chair facing them. Seeing his sober expression, Cathy reached for Jim's hand.

"Cathy, Jim, I'm glad you're here together," the doctor said quietly. Turning to Cathy, he took a deep breath and said, "It's cancer."

Feeling the room begin to spin, Cathy dug her fingernails into Jim's hand and closed her eyes. *This is too much*, she thought. *It's just not possible. How can I deal with having the same disease that just took Mama's life?*

Jim, pale with shock, turned to the surgeon and demanded angrily, "How can that be? Yesterday you said it wasn't anything!"

The surgeon sighed and admitted with difficulty, "I know. I didn't think it was. But we got the results of the biopsy this morning, and it's definitely cancer. I'm sorry."

He began to explain Cathy's condition and what their options were, but Cathy couldn't hear him. She felt too numb, too fearful. *This isn't fair, Lord!* she prayed desperately as the blood drained from her face. *Jim and I have already been through so much. Don't You think having a disabled child and then watching Mama die from cancer is enough for anyone? And now You're going to let me have cancer, too? Don't You care, Lord?*

Cathy slumped back into her chair, wishing it would swallow her up.

*T*HE NEXT FEW DAYS PASSED IN A BLUR FOR CATHY. THE general surgeon had given her two options: a lumpectomy or a mastectomy. Removing her whole breast rather than just the lump would heighten her chances of getting rid of all of the cancer, but . . . her absent breast would be a painful, lifelong reminder of her battle with the terrible disease. She had a week to decide.

During this time, their family, friends, and church kept Cathy and Jim going. Countless cards filled with words of encouragement and scriptures of faith and healing were sent to the Crafts. Relatives offered to watch Justin and Jordan, and their pastor fasted often and prayed continually for them— also reminding them of the scriptures that spoke of God's healing power. But Cathy felt depressed and overwhelmed, while Jim was simply angry. Although they believed God was in control of their lives and Cathy's health, they both struggled with prayer. When they did pray, too often they visualized their words hitting the ceiling and falling, unheard, onto the floor.

"Lord, we're here, but we don't know what to say," Jim brokenly told God one night as he and Cathy tried to pray. "We want for Cathy to be healed, but we also want Your will. Please give us the grace to accept it, whatever it is."

In their helplessness, Cathy and Jim clung to encouraging testimonies from others who told of God's physical healing power and recited Bible verses that gave them hope. The book of 2 Kings was especially encouraging to them, as they were reminded that King Hezekiah had fallen ill and God had healed him. Cathy and Jim didn't know if God would choose to heal her, so they also held on to verses that reminded them of God's love and provision for their family. They continued to believe in the Bible's truths, despite how they felt.

Cathy knew in her heart that though she'd failed God many times, He would never fail her—no matter how bad her circumstances appeared or how difficult it was to believe in His faithfulness at any given time. Yes, she had cancer, but as the old hymn often reminded her, all was well with her soul.

Still haunted by her mother's recent death, Cathy opted to have a mastectomy. She didn't think much about losing her breast when making the initial decision—she just wanted to get rid of the cancer. So, a week and a half after her diagnosis, Cathy underwent the surgery. This time, the surgeon brought them promising news.

"You can rest easy, Cathy," he told her as she lay in her hospital bed. "We got all the residual cancer cells, and everything

looks great. You can go home as soon as the incis
healed."

"That's great!" Jim said, smiling widely. "But she'll still
need further treatment, right?" he asked, looking from his wife
to the doctor.

"Yes," Cathy said. "When do I start chemotherapy and
radiation?"

The surgeon pushed his glasses up on his nose. "We don't
recommend that you undergo any treatment," he said patiently.
"The cancer is gone."

"Are you sure?" she persisted. "My mother just died from
cancer." *How can this be right?* she wondered nervously. *Mama
had so much treatment—shouldn't I have at least some? I don't want
the cancer to come back. I don't want to die like she did.*

Jim studied his wife's pale face, and leaning forward in his
chair, he said earnestly, "Doctor, we just want to be absolutely
positive that this is the right thing to do."

The surgeon looked at Cathy's chart again, then set it on his
lap. "I've consulted with a panel of six doctors, and we all agree
that due to the small size and location of your cancer, you don't
need chemotherapy or radiation," he told Cathy. "We'll have
you come in for regular checkups, of course, but I assure you
we've gotten everything."

When Jim and Cathy left the office, they remained uncon-
vinced. Not wanting to take any chances, they went back to the
surgeon several times that month, asking about treatment—just
to be sure. Each time, they were told that nothing else was necessary. Finally, realizing they needed to move on with their
lives, they stopped going.

A S TIME WENT ON, CATHY'S EXPERIENCE WITH CANCER
became little more than a bad memory. She would
have to see the doctor for routine checkups every few months,
but her prognosis remained excellent. The doctors all confidently predicted that she would live to see—and pass—the

five-year remission mark, which usually signifies that a patient has won the battle with cancer and the disease won't recur.

Once again, Cathy and Jim began to fill their world with activity, taking care of their young sons and working—Jim as a transportation superintendent at a Japanese-based music manufacturer, and Cathy as an aide in Justin's preschool classroom. Soon Justin entered a special education program at the local elementary school, and a year later, Jordan started kindergarten.

Once the boys were both in school, Cathy underwent additional surgery. On the advice of her oncologist in Atlanta, she had her right breast reconstructed with her stomach muscle, and her left breast—which had been free of cancer—was stripped of its tissue and also reconstructed with stomach muscle.

"Removing the tissue from the other breast will reduce your chances of having the cancer come back," her doctor explained. "And then, having your breasts back, so to speak, will probably help you feel better about yourself as a woman."

It did help her self-esteem. After the surgery, Cathy no longer had to wear the heavy, hot prosthesis, which had always felt unnatural and uncomfortable—and reminded her of the cancer, causing her to dwell on it even more. Every time Cathy had looked in the mirror and had seen the ugly, flat scar, she had felt unfeminine. Having her breasts reconstructed made her feel more comfortable as a woman. Jim had always told Cathy she looked beautiful, with or without two breasts, but he, too, was happy that she had the reconstructive surgery done, simply because it lifted her spirits and made her more self-confident.

The procedure also made Cathy less fearful that the cancer would come back. Now that she'd had the surgery, the doctors could do nothing more to minimize the risk of recurrence, which now stood at less than five percent. The questions and doubts that had plagued Cathy for two and a half years were finally put to rest.

When Cathy had fully recovered six months later, she decided to return to college to become certified as a special education teacher. Because of Justin's disabilities, she had long felt drawn to other children with special needs.

During this time, Cathy and Jim also immersed themselves in church activities. Jim directed the choir, and they both taught Sunday school. God had strengthened them spiritually during Cathy's illness. With Cathy near death's door, she and Jim had learned to trust God more deeply and appreciate life more fully. They relished their church, their jobs, their children, and each other. Both felt a new peace and joy.

Cathy, who'd never been much of an outdoors person, now loved to take walks with Jim in the cow pastures around their farm. One crisp autumn day, as they strolled in the fields, drinking in the afternoon colors and watching their cows graze, Jim gently squeezed Cathy's hand. "You know, baby," he said, "everything just seems more vibrant. The colors look brighter, the air seems clearer. . . . Walking here with you, I'm totally content."

"Yes," Cathy agreed, smiling happily at her husband, "I think we've learned to appreciate the small things in life. They're truly gifts from God."

Soon another gift came—Cathy's five-year anniversary of being cancer-free. At the morning Christmas service that year, she stood in front of their 40-person congregation at Pine Mountain Church of the Nazarene and waited to testify about her good health. Clad in a new holiday sweater, Cathy looked out at the faces of her church family and thought, *There's no place I would rather be on Christmas morning than worshiping God with my dear, faithful brothers and sisters here.* When Cathy had first moved to Thomaston with Jim almost 10 years before, she'd been homesick for her family in Alabama. But the friends she'd made at Pine Mountain Church had filled that void— now they were truly family to her.

"You know, I just celebrated my fifth year of being free of cancer," Cathy told them joyfully. "I'm still here, and I'm doing well." She caught Jim's eye in the congregation. "But now more than anything, regardless of my health, I just want to be true to

God and do His work, because He has been so faithful to me and has taken care of my family." She paused, thinking, *And I know He always will.*

A few months later, before Cathy had even finished her degree, she was hired as a full-time substitute teacher for emotionally and behaviorally disturbed children in kindergarten through third grade. After she received her credential two months later, her job changed from substitute to full-time teacher.

Most of that year was spent in a whirlwind of activity. So when the summer came, she was more than ready to relax, spend time with Jim and the boys, and focus on God. Hungering to know the Lord more intimately, Cathy read *What Happens When Women Pray?* The book inspired her to spend more time with God, and as a result, she found herself sitting on their front porch many summer mornings, cradled in their chair swing, talking to God.

Lord, I want to be fully committed to You, she prayed silently, gazing out contentedly at their small farm. *I want Your will for my life. Thank You so much for loving me the way You do.* Those summer mornings, Cathy felt closer than ever to the Lord.

She also felt closer to her family. That July, Cathy and Jim took the boys to the Tennessee mountains for a vacation. There, they rode bumper boats, go-carts, and horses, laughing and playing together.

The quality time Cathy spent that summer with Jim, the boys, and especially God revitalized her and strengthened her tired spirits. She didn't realize the Lord was also preparing her for the months ahead.

ONE DAY, ALMOST A YEAR LATER, CATHY STOOD IN THE elementary school gym and watched as the children in her class shouted, laughed, and bounced basketballs on the wooden floor. Her head throbbed with the noise, and she pressed her hand to her neck.

"All right, kids," she called to the 20 children scattered around the gym. "Recess is over."

The students reluctantly put away the sports equipment and lined up at the door. Cathy put her hands on her hips and surveyed the gym, looking for stray children. Her shoulders tightened involuntarily, and she squeezed her blue eyes shut, fighting off a neck spasm. *I need to cut out some stress in my life,* she thought. *That must be why I've been having these pains.*

Or maybe it was just that her students were being a pain in the neck.

She smiled at her own joke, then spotted Mindy, a small kindergarten student, standing at the top of the bleachers.

"Mindy, you need to come down. It's time to go back to class," Cathy called patiently, walking toward the girl.

Mindy, a developmentally disabled child, began to descend with some difficulty. Cathy glanced over at the other students, who were starting to get unruly, then began to climb the bleacher stairs two at a time, intending to carry Mindy down and speed up the process.

When Cathy reached the little girl, she leaned over and placed her hands on her tiny waist, lifting her a few inches off the bench. A stab of pain rushed through Cathy's upper body. "Ohhh!" she groaned in agony, almost dropping Mindy. It felt as though she'd pulled her shoulder out of the socket—she could hardly lift her right arm.

Cathy motioned for an aide to help her, and the woman picked Mindy up off the bleachers and got the class in order, taking them out of the gym. Cathy, still writhing in pain on the bench, slowly pulled herself up and, after informing the aide that she wasn't feeling well, drove home.

She was still lying on the living room recliner when Jim arrived home early from work after hearing about her incident at school. He took one look at her pale, distressed face and began making plans for the boys to stay with their aunt that afternoon and night.

"We're going to the emergency room," he said worriedly.

They spent the evening in the hospital, where Cathy went through a battery of tests. Her blood work showed an elevated calcium level, and due to her history of cancer, the doctors ordered a bone scan and additional X-rays. But nothing else showed up. The doctors, at a loss to diagnose the problem, referred her back to her oncologist in Atlanta.

In the days before her appointment with the oncologist, Cathy's pain continued to worsen. Soon she was unable to ride in their car because whenever Jim accelerated, her neck throbbed unbearably. At night, she slept in Justin's twin bed because her neck had become so sensitive that she couldn't handle anyone even touching the bed. Cathy made it through those painful, restless nights by reminding herself that God would be glorified through her weakness, as the apostle Paul wrote about in the book of Philippians. She didn't want the devil to defeat her, and she was adamant about praising the Lord even through her suffering.

Late one night, Cathy lay on Justin's bed, trying to rest. After about an hour of resting quietly and praying, she decided to get up. As she tried to prop her head up with her hand, she gasped in pain, tears running down her face. Each time she moved, her neck went into violent spasms, leaving her in agony.

I can't lie here forever, Cathy thought frantically. *Lord, please help me get up.* Crying and praying, she clenched her teeth, trying to shut out the pain. She lay motionless for several moments. Finally, gathering all her strength, she pulled herself up and wriggled out of bed. With difficulty, she slowly made her way down the hall to the master bathroom, where she and Jim had a large, Jacuzzi-style bathtub.

If I can just get those jets on my neck, I'll have some relief, Cathy thought. In the bathroom, another jolt of pain ripped through her neck as she raised her arms and pulled her nightgown over her head. She turned on the water and plugged the drain, then carefully lowered herself into the tub. Resting her head against the side, she let the warm water fill up until it had almost covered her; then she reached with her toes to turn off the faucet. But again, each time she tried to move, the pain paralyzed her.

Petrified, Cathy watched the water rise higher and higher. *Everybody else is asleep,* she thought fearfully, *and I'm going to lie here and drown in my own bathwater.*

"Jim!" she called out, hoping her husband, who was sleeping in the next room, would hear her above the sound of rushing water. "Jim, help me!" *Lord, help me,* she prayed.

A moment later, Jim raced into the bathroom and lifted his wife from the tub. Cathy collapsed in his arms, sobbing.

When Cathy and Jim went to Atlanta a few days later to see her oncologist, they brought the boys with them, thinking it would simply be another short appointment. Her doctor would probably tell her the pain was stress-induced and send her home. Though Cathy was experiencing debilitating pain, she refused to believe the cancer was back. She was approaching her sixth cancer-free anniversary, and if the cancer did recur, it would probably show up in her breasts, not her neck. Nevertheless, her doctor was concerned enough to schedule more bone scans, an MRI, and more X-rays.

The technician in the hospital's radiology lab discovered Cathy's problem. Wanting to photograph a different angle on her neck, the young man asked Cathy to hold two heavy jugs during a series of X-rays. When the X-rays were developed a few minutes later, he nervously approached Cathy, Jim, and the boys.

"Uh, Mrs. Craft? Mr. Craft?" he said, his voice shaking. "I hate to be the one to tell you this, but I found a cluster of cancer cells on your neck. The cancer has caused your C-2 vertebra to degenerate almost completely."

"Are you sure?" Cathy asked, shocked. Her blue eyes were wide with fear.

The lab tech nodded. "I photographed your neck in a slightly different position, and this X-ray revealed the cancer. Your neck is very unstable at this time."

Cancer. The word seemed to knock the breath out of Cathy's lungs.

Jim wrapped his arms around his wife, and Cathy numbly covered her face with her hands. Confused, Justin simply stared at his parents—he couldn't understand everything the technician had said. But Jordan began to tremble, and his small face turned white. He knew what *cancer* meant—that his mommy could die.

Her doctor immediately put Cathy in a neck brace and a hospital bed and ordered that she stay the night. Meanwhile, Jim called his sister, Theresa, who lived near them in Thomaston, and asked her to come to the hospital to pick up the boys for a few days.

To make things easier for Cathy and Jim while they waited, the nurses on duty cared for Justin and Jordan, taking them to get snacks and drinks, talking to them about what was going to happen to their mom, and even bringing the hospital chaplain to counsel the boys.

While Justin and Jordan were occupied, Cathy went through more testing. Afterward, she lay helpless and terrified in her hospital bed, clinging to Jim's hand. Today God did not make sense. *Why is this happening to us, Lord?* she prayed angrily. *I'm a good person—I'm faithful to You. And now I probably won't live to see my children grow up. They need their mother.* Cathy's mind flashed to her own mother, weak and sickly, deteriorating in mind and body from the chemotherapy treatments. *I can't go through that*, she prayed, anguished. *I don't want to die and leave my boys. And I don't want to leave Jim.*

Suddenly, their whole life was falling apart before her eyes.

Theresa arrived late that night to pick up Justin and Jordan. Cathy hugged and kissed her boys good-bye, not certain if she would ever see them again. In two days, she was scheduled to undergo radical surgery in which the neurosurgeon would take part of her hip bone and attach it to her vertebrae with titanium wire, hoping it would fuse her neck and spine. Possible outcomes of the surgery were paralysis and even death. Would she live? And if she did, would she have the ability to embrace her family once more?

The next two days were a blur for Cathy. She received phone calls from friends and family all over the United States, and her hospital room soon filled with flowers. Her public school principal even called to say that he'd led all the teachers in a special prayer time, asking God to heal Cathy.

She also had many visitors. Jim and Cathy's pastor, her dad, her two sisters, and Jim's mother and father arrived the day of the surgery to comfort and pray for her and Jim.

At one point, Cathy's father-in-law took her hands in his own trembling ones. "I love you as if you were my own daughter, Cathy," he said to her. "We're praying for you."

"Thank you," she said hoarsely. "I don't know what I'd do without all of you here." Her complexion, once so tan against her short blonde hair, now looked white.

Finally, the surgeon came to wheel Cathy into the operating room. Turning to him, Jim said quietly, "Doc, if you feel someone else's hands on yours during the surgery, know that it's God guiding you. A lot of prayers have been going up for this woman."

The surgeon looked at Jim. "I know," he said seriously, "and I wouldn't have it any other way."

"Good." Jim leaned over and tenderly kissed his beloved wife, then watched misty-eyed as the doctor wheeled her away. While Jim waited with the rest of the family, he prayed, pacing the waiting room floor.

Some time later, the surgeon came to see him. "She's going to be okay," he said, smiling. "The surgery went well. You know, your wife is a very lucky person. It's a miracle that she isn't sitting in a wheelchair right now."

Jim clasped his hands together in relief. "Praise the Lord!" he said fervently. Then he turned to the surgeon. "Thank you."

Two days after Cathy's surgery, it was Jordan's tenth birthday. She, Jim, Justin, and Jordan celebrated with cake and balloons in Cathy's hospital room, thankful that they could be together. A few days earlier, no one had known whether Cathy would even be alive for her son's special day.

Cathy was able to go home from the hospital a week later. As her condition improved, so did her spirits. She felt blessed simply to be alive—and walking. Now that she'd made it through the radical surgery, her fear and sadness dissolved. The Lord had obviously taken care of her and, without her knowing it, had prepared her for this trial she now faced. The time she had spent during the past few years praying, reading, and studying the Scriptures had strengthened her spiritually more than she had realized, allowing her to trust God through this current health crisis.

As Cathy focused on the Lord's love and power, praying and poring over the Bible, she truly learned what the apostle Paul meant when he wrote in the book of Philippians, "I have learned to be content whatever the circumstances. . . . I can do everything through [Jesus Christ] who gives me strength" (4:11, 13). Cathy had hope and peace—not necessarily that she would be healed, but that God was in control of her life, as well as her family's. No matter what her future held, Cathy wanted God to be glorified.

Jim shared the same sentiment about their future, and he faithfully supported Cathy, often reminding her to put her faith in the Lord. He'd say, grinning, "I know how much I love you, and God loves you even more than I do. He'll take care of you."

*O*NE DAY, SEVERAL WEEKS AFTER CATHY'S SURGERY, JIM DROVE furiously down I-75, trying to reduce the hour and a half travel time from Atlanta's Emory University Hospital to their home in Thomaston. He looked uneasily over at Cathy sitting next to him. She had just gone through another day of intense radiation. After each treatment, she became deathly ill for hours—swelling and throwing up, becoming dizzy and frighteningly weak. The whole spell would last for five to six hours, and then she'd go to sleep. The next morning, she'd get up, go to work until two o'clock, then go to the hospital for more treatment and start the process all over again. Knowing that Cathy was comfortable only in her own bed, after each treatment Jim raced to get her home, praying that God would protect them on the road.

One day, after he'd tucked his wife into bed, Jim phoned Cathy's new oncologist. "Dr. Miller? I need your advice on something," he said. He anxiously ran his hand through his dark hair. "I need to know when Cathy's going to get her strength back. We've always wanted to take the boys to Disney World, and I need to find out when she'll feel up to it so I can arrange it," he said.

Dr. Miller was blunt. "Jim, if you're going to take her, you'd better take her now," she said without hesitation. "Her cancer is still spreading. The sooner you go, the better off you'll be."

The next day, Jim approached his boss, Ingram, and told him of his vacation plans. "I'm going right now to find somebody to buy my cow herd," Jim said, putting on his jacket. "I want to take my family to Disney World next week, and the only way we'll be able to afford the trip so soon is if I sell my cows."

Ingram looked compassionately at Jim, knowing that Cathy's health must be precarious if Jim were planning to sell his cows so quickly—he'd bred them and raised them all from birth. Ingram stroked his chin thoughtfully. "Well, that's fine," he said. "But come back and see me in a couple of hours. I want to talk to you about something."

Helpless about what else to do, Jim approached several friends who also owned farms nearby, asking if they would consider buying his cows. When he reentered his office a few hours later, he had a number of offers to mull over. Sitting down at his desk, he decided he'd catch up on a few things before going to see Ingram. He clicked on his computer, pulled up his E-mail, and stared. Countless messages told him not to sell his cows. Jim scratched his beard. *I have to sell my cows or we won't be able to afford the trip right now,* he thought, puzzled.

A few minutes later, a knock sounded on his door frame. It was Jan, the human resources manager. "Jim!" she said excitedly, walking in. "Don't sell your cows." She smiled as she dropped an envelope onto his desk. "Here's Disney World!"

Paper-clipped to the outside of the envelope was a note: "Your friends and family here want to give you a trip, all expenses paid, to Disney World." Company employees from California to Georgia had financed one week of accommodations in a posh hotel located within the park. Inside the envelope was the room confirmation. Seven days at Disney World were all wrapped up and paid for by those who truly understood kindness, compassion, and friendship.

Jim's eyes filled with tears. He opened his mouth to say "Thank you," but nothing came out, he was so overcome with gratitude.

That night, Jim told Cathy the good news as they watched Justin compete in Thomaston's Special Olympics. But Cathy was feeling so low, both physically and emotionally, that she couldn't even get up the energy to be enthusiastic about the trip.

"Oh, that's nice," she said dully. *It's going to take a lot more than Disney World to make me happy right now,* she thought miserably. *I don't know if I'll be able to do all that walking, let alone have the strength to help the boys enjoy the trip.*

Over the next few days, hundreds of dollars poured in for their trip. Jim and Cathy received cash and personal checks given by the employees at Jim's plant and by the corporate office in California. As Jim thumbed through the checks and cash, much of it one-dollar bills, he knew that his friends and coworkers—his other "family"—had dug deeply to help him.

The principal from Cathy's school dropped off more cash for the family. One of the teachers there was married to a coworker of Jim's and had informed Cathy's school about the Crafts' desire to go to Disney World. Teachers, parents, and even students chipped in to help. After only a few days, they had more than $2,000 in spending money for their trip.

Cathy's spirits soon lifted when she realized how much their friends and coworkers had given. Her depression turned to humble amazement. *I can't believe people care this much,* she thought. *It's incredible!*

From the day she'd been rushed to the hospital six months earlier, she and Jim had been surrounded with support and love. Every day during the months following her surgery, the women at Jim's work had brought the family a home-cooked dinner. Each week, these same women had cleaned Jim and Cathy's house. And even now, months later, their mailbox was filled each day with 10 to 20 cards that contained encouraging notes, Scripture verses, and money.

Churches she and Jim had never attended sent checks in the mail just when they needed the money. Their own church fasted often, prayed continually for the family, and sent over food. Friends and family paid for odds and ends and helped around the house during the times Cathy was too weak to work. And just recently, a close friend of Jim's had handed him $400 to buy some much-needed tires for the family van. In countless ways, God showed His love, providing emotionally, financially, and spiritually through the people around the Craft family.

Jim and Cathy were scheduled to leave for Disney World the Saturday before Easter, but they waited an extra day because they didn't want to miss church—God had been so good to them. And they were thankful they had stayed. That Sunday, Cathy, along with several others, went forward to the altar for prayer, as was customary in their small congregation. Those who didn't need prayer that day also came to the front to support the others, and together they all petitioned God, crying and lifting their requests to Him. When the church prayed for Cathy, the voices of her brothers and sisters sounded to her like the rumble of holy thunder. As tears streamed down her face, Cathy intensely felt the Holy Spirit's peaceful, loving presence.

After the service, her prayer partner approached her. "I believe God told me this morning that Pastor Fred should pray for your healing and anoint you with oil," she told Cathy.

Cathy nodded her head. "Well, I'll do whatever the Lord wants me to do," she responded simply. *Lord, just grant me the grace to accept whatever happens,* she prayed.

After Pastor Fred finished praying for her, asking God to stop the cancer from spreading, Cathy cried and hugged him. A little later, both she and Jim left the church feeling more content and joyful than they had in a long time.

*T*HE WEEK AT DISNEY WORLD WAS WONDERFUL. ALTHOUGH Cathy had forgotten her pain medicine, she never needed her doctor in Georgia to call in a prescription. All she required for her pain during those days was an over-the-counter pain reliever. Though she walked for miles, Cathy was unnaturally energetic and only had to rest for short periods of time.

Justin, however, tired quickly. Their second day at the park, he plopped down on the hot asphalt, right in front of Disney World's enormous cardboard 25th-anniversary cake, and folded his chubby arms. Jim, Cathy, and Jordan stared down at him.

"No go, Daddy," Justin said determinedly, looking up at Jim.

"You want to rest for a few minutes, Justin?" Jim asked.

"No. Not going."

Jim knew "not going" meant Justin wasn't planning on walking *anywhere* else that day. He sighed, then bent down and picked up his 12-year-old son, cradling him in his arms.

After two hours of toting Justin around the park, Jim's arms began to get cramped and sore. Fortunately, before Jim's muscles gave out, a Disney official spotted their predicament and found Justin a wheelchair, solving the problem. For the rest of the trip, Justin entered Disney World each morning and expectantly asked, "Where my chair?"

Jim and Cathy smiled at the irony of the situation—*Cathy* should have been the one Jim was rolling around the park, but God had truly given her supernatural strength and energy during that week. All of them returned from the trip feeling rested and refreshed.

A month later, Cathy went to see Dr. Miller. Cathy had had an appointment with her shortly before going to Disney World and had gotten extensive scans done of her abdomen, chest, and pelvis. Despite her intense chemotherapy treatments, Cathy's cancer had continued to spread. Dr. Miller had recommended a new type of chemo, but Cathy hadn't opted to take it—and had been off chemotherapy for two months. The treatments had made her so weak and her blood count so low that, every night, Jim had to give Cathy shots to help build up her bloodstream. The chemo had brought Cathy to her lowest point physically, and she didn't know if she wanted to continue the treatments.

Now Dr. Miller was folding her arms disapprovingly. "Cathy, I'm not happy that you stopped your chemotherapy for two months," she said with a frown. "Without it, your cancer will continue to spread. You must have faith in your doctor." She looked pointedly at the credentials on her wall. "If you don't listen to me, you'll get much worse."

"But I've felt better every day," Cathy protested. "I think you're a great doctor, but I put my faith in God, not people."

Dr. Miller had new bone scans done, and to her amazement, no new cancerous areas could be found—the original ones were still there, but nothing else had developed. Cathy smiled. She wasn't surprised. She believed that God had touched her body on Easter Sunday and, at least for now, had stopped the cancer from spreading.

*C*ATHY SAT ON THE BLEACHERS AT HER NEPHEW'S BASEBALL game a few months later, talking to her sister-in-law, Theresa. She wiped her forehead and squinted in the bright summer sun. "When I get home, I'm going to call Focus on the Family so we can get Renewing the Heart tickets," she told Theresa. "How many do you think we'll need?"

Theresa frowned in concentration. "Well, probably 15 to 20—enough for all those women from our church to go, too," she said.

"Okay," Cathy responded. She hugged Theresa. "Won't this be great?"

As soon as Cathy arrived home, she called the ministry.

Ever since she'd heard about the conference on the radio, she couldn't wait to attend—Focus on the Family had been a part of her life since her children were toddlers. When she tried to order the tickets, though, an apologetic voice came over the line.

"Oh, I'm so sorry but we're all sold out," the woman said. "Maybe you can try again next year."

Cathy gulped. To a cancer patient, that seemed like forever. Her eyes smarting with tears, she hung up and phoned Theresa. Between sniffles, she told her the bad news.

Theresa was heartbroken. But three days later, she called her sister-in-law back and spoke excitedly. "Cathy, you'll never believe this," she said loudly. "Focus on the Family just called, and they have two tickets for us!"

"You're kidding! That's wonderful. But how did you manage that?" Cathy asked, amazed. She'd always been much quieter than Theresa, who was a real go-getter.

"Well, it wasn't easy, but when you called me and were so sad about not getting to go, I decided to contact Focus on the Family and explain the situation," Theresa said happily. "For a few days, it didn't look as if they'd be able to find any tickets. Finally, last night, I stopped trying to explain the situation and prayed about it, putting the conference in God's hands." Theresa took a quick breath. "I asked God to provide the tickets if He wanted you to go to Renewing the Heart. And just this morning, the ministry found two more tickets. We're going!"

Cathy shook her head. Never had she so appreciated her sister-in-law's assertiveness and faithfulness.

SEVERAL WEEKS LATER, CATHY AND THERESA ARRIVED AT the Nashville arena after a six-hour drive from Georgia. Though Cathy's health had been unstable, she felt wonderful all day. Every time one of the speakers finished, Cathy turned to Theresa and said emphatically, "Oh, man, I needed that!"

But Anne Graham Lotz's talk affected Cathy the most

deeply. Her beautiful description of heaven and equally vivid depiction of hell gave Cathy the strength to face her future and the courage to eternally influence other people's futures as well. Impassioned, Anne encouraged the women to get busy and spread the gospel.

Cathy and Theresa talked about the conference all the way home.

"I just want to get out there and lead people to Christ," Theresa said enthusiastically. "Those speakers inspired me to follow through in my faith."

Cathy nodded. "I know so many people at work and in the hospital who don't know God," she said thoughtfully. Her words were tinged with quiet sadness. "This has been such a good reminder to me that I should always do God's work and tell people about Him—no matter how many days the Lord gives me."

In some ways, Cathy had already been doing this by preparing a tangible legacy of faith and love for her family. Since the cancer's recurrence a year ago, she'd been composing love notes for Jim and letters and journal entries to leave for the boys. In the messages to her sons, she told them of the many ways God had answered her prayers; she also composed special thoughts for important occasions in their lives, such as sixteenth birthdays and school graduations. More than anything, she wanted Justin and Jordan to know how proud she was of them and to reassure them that God loved them very much.

It was heartbreaking for her to do this, but she knew she needed to "get her house in order." *I don't want them to forget me,* she often thought mournfully. *I want them to know what I was like—to know that I used to hate the winter and now it's my favorite season, to know that I love waking up in the morning and seeing dew on the grass.* Cathy wanted to leave a record of herself so that her boys would always feel that their mother was present, even if only in spirit. Still grieving her own mom's death, Cathy knew Justin and Jordan needed to be prepared for a potential future without her.

She also had frank conversations with her boys about the possibility of "something happening to Mama." Justin had only a limited understanding of his mother's situation—Cathy knew he wouldn't understand the concept of death. Whenever she returned from the hospital, Justin would happily throw his arms around his mother. "Mom, I found you!" he would say exuberantly, a smile lighting up his face. "Where have you been?"

"In the hospital, Just," Cathy would tell him, gently stroking his light-brown hair. Cathy knew that if Justin didn't realize where his mom was when she stayed in the hospital for a few days, he certainly wouldn't be able to comprehend it if she died. *Justin won't understand my absence if he can't find me again,* Cathy often thought painfully.

Eleven-year-old Jordan was a different matter. He was truly burdened by the cancer. He would often begin crying, seemingly out of the blue. One day, he said quaveringly, "Mama, I hope I die before you and Daddy do." His eyes quickly filled with tears.

Where did that come from? Cathy wondered, startled. *I'm feeling better now than I have in two years.* They had just bought dinner at a fast-food restaurant and were preparing to bring it home. She looked over at her son and saw that he was trying valiantly to control his emotions, so she pulled into a parking space and turned off the engine.

Twisting in her seat, Cathy looked at him. "I understand how you feel, honey," she said seriously. "But you're going to grow up and probably get married and have children and live a long, happy life." She leaned over and ruffled Jordan's dark hair. "And I hope I will, too."

Jordan began to cry into a napkin. "But Mama, I . . . don't . . . want . . . anything . . . to . . . happen . . . to . . . you." He could barely get the words out through his sobs. "It's not fair! I love you so much," he said, rubbing his eyes.

Cathy looked down at her hands. She wished she could reassure Jordan that everything would be fine, but she didn't know what the future held. The cancer was still very present.

"Well, neither of us likes to think about that, but if something does happen to me, you're a lot more prepared now than you were two years ago," Cathy said soberly. She leaned across the seat and put her arms around her son. "Oh, honey," she said hoarsely, "I love you so much." She paused, then borrowed one of Jim's favorite sayings. "But God loves you even more, and He'll be with you—no matter what."

$\mathcal{G}$RIPPING THE MICROPHONE, CATHY STARED NERVOUSLY OUT AT the unfamiliar congregation. She looked over at Jim, who was standing at one side of the stage, singing. Shortly after she'd returned from the Renewing the Heart conference, she and Jim had begun speaking at local churches, giving their testimony—recounting the spiritual growth they'd experienced through their trials. With each talk, they hoped to tell people about God and encourage those who were struggling.

Not that it was always easy. A few weeks earlier, Cathy had learned that her cancer had begun spreading once more, for the first time in a year and a half. She would have to start chemotherapy again, after being off it for almost a year. Sometimes Cathy and Jim would get weepy, but Cathy was quick to tell everyone, "God has given me so much time already. I'm not going to let the devil steal my joy. I'm going to live with my eyes on the Lord and not on my cancer."

Now here she was in another church, giving her testimony. *Lord, let my words be Your words,* she prayed silently during Jim's song. *Speak through me—You know what these people need to hear. Use me to encourage them.*

She closed her eyes, listening to her husband's rich tenor voice, and her mind flashed to the trials they'd experienced and the ways in which God had provided for the family's every need. Despite the medical bills, they somehow always had enough money; despite Cathy's terrible physical condition, she was still teaching school and caring for her family; despite the strain they felt, people were always generously supporting them—praying for them, sending encouraging notes, and helping the family out.

Cathy's throat began to constrict with the weight of tears. *No matter what the circumstances, no matter how hard or scary or uncertain things get,* she again prayed silently, *God, You have shown me that You will always be with us, giving us the grace and strength to face anything.* She was still often fearful about her health, but God had given her a peace that was far more powerful than her worries.

Jim finished his first song, and the room was silent. When the music started up again, Cathy felt a rush of peace. Jim began singing his second and final song, which led into their talk. This song was especially meaningful, as it reflected Cathy's feelings about her health and how her hope was in Jesus Christ. Cathy looked over at her husband. His head was lifted, but his eyes were looking tearfully at something beyond that room as he sang.

The music faded out, and Jim walked to the podium and put his arm around his wife. Facing the sea of unfamiliar faces, Cathy took a deep breath and began her story.

"I'll never forget the day we were driving home from my mother's funeral," she said, speaking clearly into the microphone. "I was cradling a wrought-iron, flower-basket doorstop—the last present she'd given me—and looking out the car window at the Georgia countryside. . . . "

Cathy paused and looked heavenward. Though her life was filled with uncertainty, her future was firmly in the Lord's hands. And since she was being carried by the Master, she knew she'd continue to find the strength to lift her head up, smile during the worst of times, and rejoice in each day that God gave her.

Cathy Craft lives with her husband, Jim, and their sons, Justin and Jordan, in Thomaston, Georgia. There, she teaches special education classes at Upson Lee South Primary School, where she was awarded

Teacher of the Year in 1997, her first full year of teaching. Cathy is still being treated for cancer, but she attests that "prayer is my best medicine." She and Jim speak regularly to church audiences, giving their testimony and telling of God's goodness and grace in their lives.

Heart to Heart

I've been pretty grouchy lately because I'm having some
problems with the little house I bought in Nashville a few
months ago. It's my first home, and boy, has it been a
doozy! It's about 50 years old, and I'm quite certain that
whoever built it is in prison for fraud. He definitely wasn't
a real builder. The walls aren't plumb, the floors aren't
level, the wiring is bad, the plumbing is shot, and the
heating system is illegal. And I'm in debt up to my eye-
balls for this tiny, "quaint" money pit! I was fretting about
how I was going to pay for house repairs when I read
Cathy's story.

Her *faithfulness* reminded me of my *faithlessness*. I
often worry about trivial things that have no eternal
value. Silly things like plumbing problems distract my
heart from the things that really matter—things like trust-
ing in God despite my circumstances, things like taking
the opportunity to talk about Jesus with a friend who
doesn't know Him. Thank you, Cathy, for reminding us
to put our hope in things eternal and to remember that
this world is not our home. But I'll bet our heavenly man-
sions have great pipes!

Walking by Faith ~

Lisa

Freed from the Past

*Therefore, there is now no condemnation for those
who are in Christ Jesus, because through Christ
Jesus the law of the Spirit of life set me free from the
law of sin and death.*

—ROMANS 8:1–2

$\mathcal{D}$ONNA ANDERSON STOOD ON HER HIGH SCHOOL FOOTBALL field in Yorkshire, Tennessee, wearing a long, white, flowing gown. Gazing at the hushed crowd in the bleachers, she nervously tucked her long, straight blonde hair behind her ears. It was the night of Yorkshire High's big homecoming football game, November 1976, and Donna was about to find out if she would be crowned "queen." Most of the community had shown up for the annual event. Homecoming was a special occasion in their small farming town.

Standing on the wet grass next to Donna, the three other nominees giggled and whispered in excitement and anticipation. Donna, however, was silent. With all she had to worry about, homecoming was the least of her concerns. She twisted her shiny, new engagement ring around her finger. Her heart fluttered as she remembered the evening a few weeks before when her long-time sweetheart, Tom, had proposed.

"I love you, Donna," he had said softly, his dark eyes shining in the soft evening light. "You're my best friend, and I want to spend the rest of my life with you." Kneeling, he had pulled a small ring box out of his pocket. "Will you marry me?"

A radiant smile had spread across Donna's freckled face. "Oh, yes!" she'd said immediately, mesmerized by the glittering diamond. As Tom stood up, she had thrown her arms around his neck, thinking dreamily, *I know we'll have the best marriage, the best life together.*

After two years of dating, everyone had expected them to get married, including Donna herself. In their small town, it wasn't uncommon for kids to "tie the knot" right out of high school. Furthermore, Donna and Tom were a perfect match— one of the most popular and visible couples in school. They had recently been voted "Mr. and Mrs. YHS [Yorkshire High School]," an honor for Donna second only to homecoming queen. Tom was the handsome captain of their high school football team, and Donna was a cheerleader, a member of the student council, and a straight-A student.

Always the model teenager, Donna didn't drink, smoke,

disobey her parents, or cause trouble in school. She knew that her parents already had enough to worry about with her older brother, Jeff, doing drugs, disappearing for months on end, and continually creating an uproar in the Anderson household. Growing up, Donna had always tried to compensate for her brother's rebelliousness by being the perfect daughter, girlfriend, student, and friend—and according to her classmates and parents, she was. Because she'd taken the compliant approach, things had generally gone smoothly for her. But now, because of something she had done, rough days lay ahead of her.

Donna bit her lip and shifted uneasily on the wet grass. The night Tom proposed, he'd taken her out to dinner to celebrate the engagement. Afterward, the two lovestruck teenagers had driven his large, burgundy station wagon down a lonely country road a mile from Donna's house. As they sat in the car, talking and kissing, one thing quickly led to another—and before she knew it, Donna had lost her virginity.

Having grown up attending a small Baptist church, Donna had always planned to stay a virgin until she was married, but the magic and romance of the night had intoxicated her. She was engaged! Going to be a real bride! Tom's fiancée! That evening, her youthful head had been so full of romance that nothing else mattered.

Lying in the station wagon beside Tom, Donna had shut out all feelings of guilt. This was different from what some of the other kids in school did. She and Tom were in love. *It doesn't really count*, she'd rationalized. *We're getting married in August anyway. Besides, it's my first time. What could happen the first time?* She truly believed their one evening of passion would be no big deal.

But now, three short weeks later, the consequences from that night were haunting her. Donna shivered in the brisk, damp November evening. *Calm down*, she berated herself. *This should be one of the best nights of your life.* Fidgeting with the neckline on her gown, Donna plastered on a smile, remembering that she was supposed to look happy.

Finally, after what had seemed like ages to Donna, the announcer's voice came over the loudspeaker. "Ladies and gentlemen, the 1976 Yorkshire High homecoming queen is—" The booming voice paused dramatically as a drum rolled. "Donna Anderson!"

Happily surprised, Donna felt her mouth drop open. *I'm homecoming queen!* she thought in awe. It was something the girls from her high school all dreamed of becoming. The crowd in the bleachers cheered wildly, quickly drowning out the disappointed sighs of the nominees next to her. Donna's green eyes widened in surprise as Tom emerged from the rest of the football players, holding a delicate gold-painted crown in one hand and a bouquet of red roses in the other. Handsome in his blue and gold football uniform, he walked over to Donna, gave her a kiss on the cheek, and gently placed the crown on her head.

"Donna, you look beautiful," he whispered in her ear. "I'm so happy for you—you deserve this."

Donna smiled weakly. "Thanks," she mumbled, avoiding Tom's loving gaze. Her heart thudded. *Tom doesn't even know,* she told herself nervously. *And I'm not telling him.* If she told him, the situation would only get more complicated and ugly. By keeping it a secret, their relationship could remain the fairy tale it had been.

The evening dragged on as Donna rode the senior float—a homecoming tradition—and waved halfheartedly to her well-wishers. The looks of happiness and admiration on the faces of her classmates did nothing to lift her spirits. Parading around the football field, Donna could think of only one thing, and it was ruining her magical night. *They all think I'm so wonderful,* she told herself miserably. *But nobody knows.*

After halftime was over, Donna climbed off the float and was quickly surrounded by hoards of students wanting to congratulate her. She painted on a smile and tried to appear excited. What would these people think of her—Donna Anderson, perfect senior and now homecoming queen—if they knew her secret? Donna looked at her admiring friends and took a deep breath, trying to relax. She would try to maintain her flawless image as long as she could.

"This is so great!" one girl told her exuberantly. "You're so lucky!"

"I bet this is the best night of your life!" a cheerleader exclaimed.

"I can't believe you're homecoming queen!" another friend told her in awe. "You must be so happy!"

Donna looked at their envious faces, and her throat tightened. She would have traded places with any one of them in an instant. "Yeah, I feel wonderful," she said weakly, flashing a hollow smile.

Actually, Donna felt sick to her stomach. She didn't belong here tonight, especially wearing a white dress. Though Donna would never tell Tom or anybody else, their fleeting moments of passion in his station wagon had produced a lasting result. What she had reasoned didn't count would, in fact, count forever. Donna had missed her period the week before, and she knew her "clockwork" body well enough to realize that this could mean only one thing:

Donna Anderson, the homecoming queen, was pregnant.

*D*ONNA SAT NUMBLY IN THE BACKSEAT OF HER PARENTS' CAR A week later, staring out the window at the cold November night sky. The Andersons were on their way home from having dinner in a nearby city. As her parents talked quietly in the front seat, Donna turned from the window to discreetly catch their expressions in the wide rearview mirror. Her mother's face was drawn, and her father's forehead was furrowed. Jeff, Donna's brother, was missing again, and obviously his disappearance was causing her parents much grief.

Donna watched as her mother sighed and leaned closer to her father. "Well, at least Donna never gave us any trouble," she said, loud enough for her daughter to hear.

Donna cringed and folded her arms across her still-flat

belly. Always the good girl. Never causes any trouble. It was something she'd heard her parents say a million times. She squeezed her eyes shut. How could she tell her mom and dad that their perfect daughter, the one they always counted on to behave, was pregnant? How could she add to their already heavy burden?

Turning again to stare out the window, Donna felt her stomach churn with anxiety. *Maybe I should just open the car door right now and fall onto the interstate,* she thought wildly. *If I died, I wouldn't have to deal with this.* She shuddered at the idea. She was in a terrible situation, but she didn't really want to die. *Maybe I should run away,* she thought desperately. *I could raise the baby by myself. Or I could tell Tom, and we could elope and pretend the baby was born premature.*

Or she could do the right thing: inform her parents and Tom, stay in school, have the baby, and endure the sneers of her schoolmates. Donna sank lower into her seat. No, that was a terrible option. Teenage girls from Yorkshire weren't supposed to get pregnant. No one would understand. Donna could just imagine how shocked her classmates would be when they heard the news, how they would point and whisper as she walked by.

"Did you hear that Donna Anderson got pregnant?" one girl would say to another. "I didn't know she was so loose!"

"And she always acted like she was such a goody-goody," the other would add, scandalized. "What a hypocrite!"

Donna's schoolmates wouldn't be the only people talking, though. The members of the small Baptist church she attended with her family would be shocked and disappointed as well. Donna cringed as she recalled a girl from her church who'd gotten pregnant a few years back. Lumbering around the sanctuary with her swollen belly, the girl had been the subject of many stares and gossip sessions—and Donna knew she would be, too.

She shook the terrible image from her mind. *No way,* she told herself fiercely. *Having the baby is* not *an option.* At 17 years old, she still had her best school year ahead of her, as well as many other things to look forward to: graduation, her dream wedding to Tom, and college, just to name a few. Donna didn't know exactly what her career plans were, but she did know they didn't include being a teenaged mom.

No, there was no way she could continue this pregnancy.

HE FOLLOWING SATURDAY, DONNA ANXIOUSLY HEADED down to the Yorkshire courthouse with a purse full of change. Folded up in her hand was a newspaper ad that read simply: "Abortion. Call (555) 623-XXXX." The big, black letters had caught Donna's attention a few days before when she'd been looking through the Memphis *Commercial Appeal*, hoping to find a solution to her problem. Seeing the ad, she'd immediately decided to call for an appointment. Memphis was two hours away—and no one knew her there. It was her best bet for confidentiality.

Grateful to see that the courthouse lobby was deserted, Donna entered the enclosed phone booth. The courthouse was the only place in Yorkshire where someone could use a private pay phone. And usually the only people who came there were old men who smelled like stale tobacco and peppermint.

Her hands shaking, Donna dropped several coins into the slot to make her long-distance call. She punched in the number, and a woman answered the phone on the first ring. "Memphis Clinic for Women. May I help you?"

"Uh . . . hi," Donna said nervously. With her mouth close to the receiver, she said in a low voice, "Are you the clinic with the newspaper ad?"

"Yes," the woman said in a soft drawl. "Do you want to make an appointment?"

Donna's heart pounded. "Uh-huh," she mumbled quickly, her knuckles white as she gripped the newspaper clipping. "How much does it cost?"

"Just $200, honey," the woman replied. "And it's fast, safe, and confidential."

Donna got the information she needed, along with directions to the clinic, then made her appointment for the following Saturday. A few days later, she went to the bank and closed her savings account. She had exactly $225, barely enough to cover the cost of the procedure. No one at the bank questioned her need for that much money, and she knew why: Donna Anderson never caused any trouble.

Donna went through the motions that week, never allowing herself to think about the abortion. A good, church-attending girl, she knew abortion was wrong, but the knowledge that she was pregnant overrode everything else. Abortion, in Donna's frantic mind, was the only solution to what would otherwise be a lifetime of shame and hardship.

When Saturday morning finally arrived, she woke up early. She showered and dressed quickly, then hurried downstairs. Her mother was already up and having breakfast.

"Where are you going so early?" her mom asked, smiling as she looked at the clock. It was only 7:30.

Donna's fair cheeks flushed. Turning her back to her mother, she opened the refrigerator door and pulled out a pitcher of juice. "Tom and I are going Christmas shopping in Jackson all day," she fibbed, grabbing a clean glass from the dish rack on the counter, her back still to her mother. "We wanted to get a head start, before all the crowds hit after Thanksgiving."

"That's a wonderful plan, honey," her mom said, returning to her coffee and newspaper.

Donna let out a little sigh of relief, thankful that her mother had accepted her explanation so easily. Because Jeff caused so much trouble, Donna had considerable freedom. Her parents were usually too emotionally worn out from dealing with their son's defiance to keep a close eye on their daughter.

A few minutes later, Donna climbed into her old car and slammed the door shut. Pulling the directions to the clinic from her purse, she tried to ignore the fear climbing up her throat. The farthest she'd driven alone was to Jackson, a trip of 45 minutes. The trip to Memphis would take two hours. If she was going to find the Memphis Clinic for Women, the directions would have to be good.

They were. Two hours later, Donna pulled into the parking lot of a brown, nondescript building in the Memphis business district. Feeling as though her knees were about to buckle, she got out of the car and entered a small waiting room. It was packed wall to wall, mostly with young girls. Donna walked up to the front desk, and the receptionist handed her some forms with the instruction, "Here. Fill these out, and we'll call you in a few minutes."

Donna took the forms and found an empty chair next to an older woman. Staring at the paperwork, she nervously wrote the name "Karen Davis." Never in a million years would she put down her real name. Donna didn't want to risk having anybody find out about this. *I'll just have to remember to turn every time they say "Karen,"* she told herself uneasily. She did, however, give her true age: 17. She knew her youthful looks wouldn't fool anyone.

It didn't take her long to complete the forms. There were no lengthy waivers for her to read and sign, just a few questions to answer. In fact, she didn't have to give much information at all. When Donna finished, she took the paperwork back to the receptionist.

I wonder if she's going to tell me I'm too young to have an abortion, Donna thought nervously as the woman looked over her forms.

But the receptionist merely smiled kindly at the girl and asked her to take a seat. Obviously, the Memphis Clinic for Women routinely performed abortions on minors.

About 20 minutes later, a nurse opened the door to the waiting room and called out, "Karen Davis? . . . Karen Davis."

Donna looked up. *Oh! That's me,* she realized with a start. Swallowing the massive lump in her throat, she followed the nurse down a hallway into a tiny room, where Donna was asked to change out of her clothes and slip into a blue hospital smock. When Donna had finished changing, the nurse led her to another small room and instructed her to lie on the examining table. The room was brightly lit and looked like a typical doctor's office. The sounds, however, were much different. As Donna lay on the table, her feet in stirrups, she winced at the vacuum-cleaner-like noise that came from similar rooms in the building.

The nurse stayed and talked with Donna until the doctor arrived. When he walked into the room, Donna felt even more nervous. He looked like a hippie with his long, scraggly hair and his black, peace sign T-shirt. He grinned down at Donna, revealing a large gap in his front teeth.

"We're gonna put this gas mask on you, Karen," he said jovially, placing a mask over Donna's mouth and nose. "Now, this won't take more than a couple minutes." He smiled again. "You just need to relax."

Almost immediately, Donna fell into a foggy state—but even then, she could still hear the terrible sucking sounds from the machine. About 10 minutes later, the nurse gently nudged her.

"Karen," she said, "you're all done. Come with me."

Stumbling from the effects of the gas but otherwise feeling fine, Donna followed the nurse down the hallway into another, larger room, where a half-dozen girls were lying on cots. Some were vomiting into bedpans.

"Lie down over there," the nurse said, pointing to an empty cot farthest from the door. Donna's clothes were already folded neatly on the edge of the cot. "You can change your clothes and then rest for a while. Oh, and here's some information that you'll need if you have any complications." The nurse handed her a brochure.

Donna took the pamphlet and then changed back into her clothes. The last thing she wanted to do was stay in that tiny, smelly, terrible room. *I just want to leave,* she thought wildly, lying on her cot. *I want to run out of here and go home and forget this day ever happened.* Donna "rested" for about 30 seconds, then sprang up from her cot, grabbed the pamphlet, and walked rapidly out of the room.

The nurse on duty dropped her magazine and widened her

eyes in alarm. "Karen!" the woman called out. "Karen, stop! You really need to rest!"

In an unusual outburst of rebellion, Donna kept walking. She scanned the brochure, memorizing its contents, then immediately dropped it into a trash can outside the clinic door. *I'm not taking any chances by having this around,* she thought resolutely. *Nobody's going to find out what happened today.* Donna quickened her stride toward the parking lot. *I'll be fine as soon as I get out of here,* she told herself as she got into her car and sped off, leaving the clinic behind. She was determined to erase this day from her mind forever.

*D*ONNA WALKED IN THE BACK DOOR OF THE ANDERSON HOUSE A few hours later, hoping to avoid her parents. No such luck. Her mother, a blue apron tied around her waist, was at the kitchen counter, washing dishes. She looked up as Donna entered.

"Hi, honey. You've been gone a long time," she observed gently.

Donna shrugged off the question. "Yeah," she mumbled, tucking a wayward strand of hair behind her ear.

"Well, we're going to have dinner in a couple of hours," her mother said.

Food sounded terrible to Donna. Sick from the anesthetic, she had stopped twice on the way home to vomit. She crinkled her nose. "I'm not hungry," she informed her mom.

Her mother sighed. "Well, okay," she said and returned to her dishes.

Donna's face relaxed, and she quickly left the kitchen, happy to retreat to the comfort of her own room. For some reason, it felt good to refrain from eating, to be alone.

An obsession with food and dieting was triggered in Donna that painful day. The abortion had affected her more than she knew—and without realizing it, she started to numb her emotional and spiritual pain by starving herself. She became increasingly obsessed with her weight and controlling her food intake.

Sitting at the dinner table, she would pick at her meal, subsisting on bites of food. Soon Donna stopped having meals with her parents altogether. And if she ate at all, it was alone, in her room. This was relatively easy for Donna to do, since her parents, especially her mother, never fought her about it.

None of Donna's friends noticed that she had a problem, not even Tom. At lunchtime, Donna would sit and chat with Tom and her friends, ignoring the empty space on the cafeteria table where her lunch should have been. She always claimed that she wasn't hungry, and the others seemed to take her explanation at face value. Actually, Donna was always hungry. But denying herself made her feel less emotionally empty, more in control, and happier.

As her preoccupation with dieting escalated, Donna became almost skeletal. Just eight weeks after her abortion, she had lost 20 pounds. She weighed herself every day, letting the scale determine her mood. If she stayed at exactly 110 pounds, she felt wonderful. But if she weighed even an ounce above that, her day would be spoiled, and she'd starve herself until the weight came off.

The months flew by, and Donna and Tom's wedding day drew closer. By July, she was so thin that her size-5 bridal dress had already been altered twice in an attempt to keep up with her diminishing figure. Finally, Donna's seamstress had had enough.

"Are you dieting or what?" the woman snapped at Donna, who was modeling the loose-fitting dress in front of a full-length mirror. It hung limply around Donna's waist, and the chest was puckered in the front.

"Kind of," Donna said, flushing with pride. *She thinks I'm skinny!* she told herself, taking it as a compliment. In her mind, thinness equaled success.

"Well, I can't keep altering the waist," the seamstress persisted. "If I have to take it in again, it'll ruin the dress!"

"Really?" Donna asked. Not quite convinced, she reinspected the numerous folds in the waistline.

Donna's mom put her hands on her hips and faced her

waif-like daughter. "I agree," she said, unusually firm. Her face was pinched with worry. "Donna, you need to stop losing weight. How many times will we have to adjust this dress?"

A flicker of surprise crossed Donna's face. Her mother had never addressed her obvious eating problem before.

"Okay, okay," she said, trying to placate the women. She looked at her mother. "This will be the last time, Mom. I won't lose any more weight. I promise." The wedding was only a few weeks away. She could stay at the same size until then. After all, Donna didn't want anything—even a less-than-perfect dress— to ruin her dream wedding.

The big day came quickly, and it was everything Donna had hoped it would be. The church was packed with flowers, bridesmaids, and guests. Floating down the aisle toward Tom in her tiny, Cinderella-style wedding dress, Donna's head was full of romance. Tom, her knight in shining armor, was going to be her husband. *I love him so much,* she thought dreamily. *We're meant for each other. I know we're going to have the perfect marriage.*

Just days after they returned home from their honeymoon, Tom and Donna packed up and prepared to move to college in Murfreesboro. Eager for their fairy-tale lives to start, Donna anticipated the change with excitement. She just knew things were going to be wonderful.

They weren't.

*T*HE TRANSITION TO COLLEGE LIFE WAS ROUGH FOR BOTH Donna and Tom. Middle Tennessee State University was a huge school with a sprawling campus. Donna and Tom's rural hometown was only half the size, and they both felt lost in the crowd. Also, unlike during their high school days, Donna and Tom now found it difficult to make friends. Living in married student housing at the outskirts of campus, they were separated from the rest of the freshmen and lacked the social interaction that went on in the dorms. In Yorkshire, Donna and Tom had been the most popular students in their high school. In Murfreesboro, they were nobodies; the university just swallowed them up.

Attempting to get rooted in the community, they had attended one or two services at a nearby Baptist church, but both found it easier not to go at all. Since the abortion, Donna had felt guilty and disconnected from God—and being in church just intensified those feelings. Normally a confident, independent young woman, Donna became insecure and indecisive. She kept to herself in class, turning quiet and withdrawn. Unable even to make up her mind what her major should be, she changed her degree five times before the end of her sophomore year.

Tom, too, felt enormous pressure. He had never excelled academically and found his college courses difficult. Unfortunately, he also struggled under the weight of family expectation. His father and brothers were all doctors or lawyers; but the reality was, Tom wasn't cut out for medicine or law. At home, his family was also falling apart. A few months before Tom and Donna's wedding day, his father had left his mother for another woman, devastating the family. Tom was especially crushed. His father had always been his hero, and Tom didn't know how to cope with his anger and pain.

All this affected him more than Donna first realized. One day after class, she had dropped her books on the kitchen counter and was sifting through the mail when she saw an official-looking blue slip of paper. Donna's brow wrinkled in confusion. On the paper was a printout of Tom's classes, but three of the five listed read "Incomplete." Donna knew Tom had dropped a few classes, but she'd thought he was planning to replace the units. *What's going on?* she wondered angrily.

She turned to Tom, who was sitting in his usual place—on the couch, in front of the TV. "What is this?" Donna asked hotly, waving the paper in front of his face. "Why aren't you taking a full class load?"

Tom's brown hair was still uncombed, and he was wearing the same sweatpants he'd put on the day before. "I told you," he muttered, his eyes still glued to the TV. "I didn't like those other classes."

"I can't believe this," Donna sputtered, her face turning crimson with anger. "First you quit your job at the restaurant, and then you drop so many classes you're practically not even a student! Meanwhile, *I'm* taking 18 units and working 15 hours a week to support us."

"Unlike your cushy job at the bookstore, that busboy job was terrible," Tom retorted, his eyes never leaving the screen. "And like I said, I hated those classes. Besides, I can't register for more units now anyway—the cutoff's already past."

Donna put her hands on her hips. "Well, I still shouldn't have to do everything around here!" she said heatedly. "It's not fair. If you're taking only two classes, you should get a job, too."

Tom grimaced. Wordlessly, he sank deeper into the cushions of the couch.

Donna sighed crossly. "If you would just *do* something . . . " Her voice trailed off in frustration. Tom, his eyes riveted to the old movie on TV, wasn't listening. *I'm not getting anywhere*, she realized with a sick feeling. Her stomach burned. *This wasn't how it was supposed to be for us*, she thought, blinking back tears. *It was supposed to be wonderful and perfect. We were supposed to be madly in love.* She left the room and curled up on their bed, crying softly into the pillow.

Over the next year, Tom became more depressed and withdrawn. Soon he stopped going to classes altogether and stayed holed up in their tiny apartment all day, every day, watching old movies. The little communication he and Donna had shared during their first year of marriage deteriorated even more. Sullen and angry, Tom wouldn't even talk with her.

Tom, who had always been Donna's anchor and confidant, was slipping away from her.

FEELING LOST, HELPLESS, AND ALL ALONE, DONNA BEGAN TO turn to food for comfort. Each night, after Tom had gone to bed, Donna would binge on candy bars and other treats. Her frenzied late-night eating soothed her troubled emotions, but soon she began to put on weight. By the middle of her sopho-more year, she had gained 60 pounds.

Tom never said anything about this change in Donna's appearance, and his silence hurt her. Secretly, she hoped that if she gained enough weight, Tom would notice her. He would realize she was lonely and hurting and would talk to her again, touch her again, love her again—and their life would return to normal. But Tom acted as if Donna were invisible, and that sent her over the edge. She hated herself enough as it was, but to have her own husband refuse to communicate with her or make love to her sent her self-esteem plummeting even further. Sometimes when she pleaded for his attention, he would fly into a rage, beating her up physically and emotionally. Finally, after almost a year of enduring his depression, withdrawal, and verbal and physical abuse, Donna couldn't take it anymore. In June, just two months before their second anniversary, she told him to move out.

Donna was too far from God to seek His comfort and advice about her marriage. Since having the abortion two years before, she'd been afraid of talking to Him for fear of judgment. In her mind, it was less scary to do things her own way than to face a wrathful, condemning God. Being young and naive, Donna never thought about seeking help from a marriage counselor, either. She felt that despite her efforts to work things out, the relationship was doomed. She just wanted Tom gone.

Their divorce was final a year later, and finally Donna was free.

*J*UST AS SHE HAD DONE AFTER THE ABORTION, AFTER THE DIVORCE papers were signed, Donna tried to put the past behind her. She never saw Tom again—and she lived as if he'd never existed, as if she'd never been married. She took back her maiden name, Anderson, and moved almost immediately into another apartment. She also threw herself into her major—music.

Donna had always been a talented pianist and exceptional

singer. Growing up, she had sung solos in her church and been part of the choir. So, after skipping around from major to major, Donna had finally chosen music in her junior year. It was something she knew she did well. What she didn't know, however, was that music was one of the most challenging areas of study at her university. She was up against some stiff competition.

This proved to be good for her. It forced Donna to work harder than before, and she began to channel her energies into singing. She auditioned and performed in musicals, recorded songs, and sang pop music at parties to earn extra income. Since she was so involved, Donna was also able to make friends within her major, and soon she escaped her isolation.

The singing itself was therapeutic for her. When she chose songs for parties, Donna picked music with words that encouraged and uplifted her. She would sit for hours at the piano and sing. The singing comforted her and lessened her preoccupation with food. In time, her weight leveled off.

What Donna found difficult was songwriting. As a teenager, she'd always enjoyed writing poetry and songs because it was a way for her to express her emotions; after the abortion, however, she'd gradually stopped. Writing brought up too many painful feelings. But being a music major, Donna couldn't escape it completely—songwriting was one of her required classes.

For her first assignment, Donna wrote a song about her childhood. The words—which described her living in a world of lies—came to her quickly though painfully. When she was done, she brought the song into class and dropped it on the professor's desk, thankful that the assignment, and her songwriting, was over.

Later that week, however, her professor told her that he was going to include it on a recording project. "You have a talent for songwriting," he said warmly. "I think you should make a career of it."

"Oh, no," Donna said, shaking her head firmly. "I'm definitely not interested in writing music." *I don't want to deal with my pain,* she added silently. It was only her first attempt at writing, and already so much baggage from her past had surfaced.

"I don't understand," her professor said, disappointed. "Not everyone can write music. You can, and you should."

Donna folded her arms. "I want to be a singer, not a writer," she said stubbornly. No one was going to talk her into the latter.

Throughout that semester, her instructor continued to push her to write, but Donna refused. For too long, she'd survived by becoming numb to her past, and in some respects, her method of coping had worked. Donna wasn't about to change her ways now. Why mess with success?

Donna might have stuffed her feelings forever had God not had other plans for her. Slowly, He began to heal her and draw her to Himself—and He did it by bringing Johnny into her life.

ONE DAY A YEAR AND A HALF AFTER HER DIVORCE FROM TOM, Donna walked rapidly to the Murfreesboro theater, across from campus. She checked her watch. It was almost 6:00, time for her to check in with the other performers. If she didn't hurry, she'd be late. Donna had graduated a few months earlier, in December, but she was staying in Murfreesboro, singing in a production that she'd auditioned for a while back. Patting her long, perfectly coifed hair, Donna quickened her pace, running through the lines of music in her head.

"Donna!" A voice cut through her concentration.

Startled, she looked up. Johnny Shearron, whom one of her friends had dated the year before, was walking toward her. Johnny was a senior and would be graduating in May.

"Hi, Johnny," Donna said, smiling in surprise. "It's great to see you."

It was. Johnny was one of those all-around-nice guys. Tall, lanky, and funny, he always made her laugh. In fact, he was so crazy and energetic that Donna and her friends called him "The Tornado."

"It's good to see you, too," Johnny said sincerely. His long legs easily matched her rapid pace, and he began walking with her toward the theater. "So, what brings you so near campus, graduate?" he asked, eyeing her fringed flapper-style dress and heavy theater makeup. A wide grin crept across his face. "Got a hot date?"

Donna laughed. "Very funny," she said, punching his arm. "I'm appearing in a musical in exactly—" She checked her watch. "—an hour. And the director wants all the performers there in five minutes." She stopped in front of the theater. "Why don't you come see the show?" she asked suddenly. "We can go out to eat afterward and catch up on old times."

Johnny's dark eyes sparkled. "That would be great."

They went out that night and talked for hours—and Donna really enjoyed herself. Soon, they began to spend a lot of time together. Though Johnny wasn't a sweet talker, his actions communicated to her that he considered her valuable and beautiful. He was her biggest supporter, encouraging her in her singing career and attending her productions and gigs. At times, he seemed to believe in her more than she did in herself—and this did wonders for her low self-image. At first, Donna tried to brush off the importance of their relationship. *We're just having fun,* Donna reasoned. *It's not serious.* But something continued to draw her to him.

As the months passed, Johnny's unconditional love for her began to change her view of him. She learned to trust him and soon was sharing things from her past that she hadn't told anyone. When Johnny heard about Donna's childhood and her abortion, eating problems, and divorce, he simply put his arms around her and let her cry. Before Donna realized what was happening, her feelings about Johnny had turned from friendship to love.

He proposed a few months later, and a year and a half from the time they'd started dating, they were married. Donna was ecstatic. She knew her relationship with Johnny was healthy and mature—very different from her high school marriage to Tom—and she wanted their wedding to reflect that. So she opted to have a small ceremony, inviting only family members; and rather than wear a bridal gown, she chose a simple street dress. She and Johnny also decided to forgo the flowers, music, and professional pictures; Johnny's parents paid for a huge reception to which all their friends and family members were invited.

After the wedding, the Shearrons moved to Nashville, where Johnny got a job doing real estate appraisals and Donna continued her schooling. Wanting to teach college-level voice, she had received a fellowship to get her master's degree in music at Austin Peay State University in Clarksville.

The intense workload she was carrying, plus the hour and a half commute, made school a full-time job for Donna, and she often arrived home long after Johnny had. Donna's hectic schedule gave him a lot of time alone in their apartment. A few months into her schooling, she began to notice a change in her husband—and she wasn't sure what to make of it.

One muggy summer afternoon, Johnny dropped the first hint. "Have you ever seen that Christian TV show?" he asked casually, putting down his computer magazine. "You know, the one where they interview people?"

Donna shrugged. "Yeah, I think so."

"Well, I was flipping through the channels the other day, and I watched some of it," Johnny said. He ran his hand through his dark-brown hair. "It's pretty good. Anyhow, they were talking about these books that sounded interesting." He paused for a moment.

Donna's eyebrows shot up. *Where is he going with this?* she thought.

"Would you mind if we dropped by that Christian bookstore near the mall?" he continued. "I want to look at those books."

Donna stared in surprise at her husband. Johnny, cynical about religion because of his difficult family background, had always claimed to be an atheist. "You want to go to a Christian bookstore?" Donna asked him skeptically.

Johnny nodded.

"Well, okay," she said, feeling a little uneasy.

Donna had been running from God for almost seven years now, and any mention of Him made her uncomfortable. She didn't think she was ready to go back to Him. If she did, Donna knew she'd have to deal with her past and start making some changes in her life. Since she and Johnny had married, her eating had once again gotten out of control—and because of her own disgust at her lack of willpower, Donna found herself making biting, critical comments to her husband. She realized that the pain she felt inside was spilling out into her marriage, and it bothered her, but she was too afraid to go to God for help. Thus it was with mixed feelings that she witnessed this new spiritual development in her husband.

As the months went by, Johnny began to drop more and more hints, frequently talking about the TV show and making comments about church. One day shortly after Thanksgiving, he shocked Donna. He was lying on the floor, putting their newly purchased Christmas tree into its stand, when he said casually, "You know what I'd like for Christmas?"

"No, what?" Donna asked, looking up from the string of lights she was untangling. "Hey!" she said sharply. "Why are you putting the tree over there? It looks awful, Johnny."

Johnny ignored her comment. "I'd like a Bible," he said.

Donna almost dropped the string of lights. "Did you say 'Bible'?"

"Yeah, that's what I said," Johnny replied with a grin.

Donna eyed her husband suspiciously. *Has he become a Christian?* she wondered. *I'm not sure I like what's happening here.*

Despite her reservations, Donna bought Johnny a Bible for Christmas, and he read it voraciously. Soon he also wanted to find a church. This presented an interesting challenge for Donna. During the last few months, she had already been going to church—but not to worship. She was getting paid to sing in a local, prominent church. The wealthy congregation wanted to have the best choir in the city, so the choir director held auditions and hired singers. As Johnny's interest in the Christian faith deepened, he began to attend with Donna. Neither one of them got much out of the services—the church was too traditional and ritual-bound for them—but God was still working, even in Donna. As she sang and prayed with the congregation, her heart slowly began to soften. So when Johnny decided he wanted to find another church, Donna quit her choir job and began looking with him. *If he wants to go to church, I don't want to tell him no,* she reasoned. Despite her uneasiness, in her heart Donna was thankful her husband was being drawn to God.

They visited a couple of churches in Nashville, but none of them seemed right for them. Just weeks after they started looking, however, Johnny got a job offer in Murfreesboro, and they moved back there. Once the Shearrons were settled in an apartment, Johnny began researching the churches in their area. After trying out a few, he decided he liked Belle Aire Baptist the best. Donna, however, balked at the idea of attending that church. Years before as a college student, she had visited Belle Aire with Tom a couple of times. The thought of going there with Johnny was embarrassing and uncomfortable. Donna did not want to go someplace tainted by bad memories.

"Sorry, Johnny," she said adamantly each time he brought up the idea. "I'll go to any other church but that one."

But Johnny wouldn't be put off so easily. "I really think we should try Belle Aire," he persisted.

Donna finally gave in, and one Sunday in August, they went. That morning a visiting pastor was preaching, and the church was packed. As Donna sat next to Johnny in the balcony, the pastor's enthusiasm captivated her, and she sensed a joy among the congregation that she'd never witnessed before. Suddenly, the wall she had built around her heart crumbled, and for the first time in years, Donna yearned to be back in the Lord's arms, to have a relationship with Him again. Tears began to flow down her cheeks. *Lord,* she prayed, *I've messed up so badly, and I've been running from You for so long. Please forgive me.*

At the end of the service, the pastor gazed out at the congregation. "If anyone wants to dedicate his or her life to Jesus

Christ," he said, his round face glowing, "I invite you to come forward."

I want to go forward, Donna realized. Her heart fluttered as she turned to look at Johnny. Their eyes met, and without a word, they both got up and began walking toward the communion table at the front of the church.

The area was crowded with people crying and praying. As Donna stood quietly next to Johnny, a man motioned for them to join him. He led them to a small room off the sanctuary and waved them toward two folding chairs.

"My name's Charlie," the man said seriously, looking from Donna to Johnny. "Have you accepted Jesus Christ into your hearts as your Lord and Savior?"

"I asked Christ into my heart last September, watching a TV show," Johnny said.

Donna's heart jumped into her throat. *I was right!* she realized.

"I've been wanting to join a church ever since I became a Christian," Johnny continued, his eyes unusually bright, "and I believe this is the right one."

Charlie turned to Donna. "And you?"

Donna nodded. "Yes, I accepted Christ when I was a little girl," she said hoarsely, "but I haven't been in church for a long time." She took a deep, quavering breath. "I want to rededicate my life to Jesus and join this church."

Donna could hardly believe what she was saying as the words flowed from her mouth. But she felt wonderfully at peace. She knew that God had led them to Belle Aire Baptist. More importantly, He had also led them to Himself.

*T*HE SHEARRONS JUMPED INTO CHURCH ACTIVITIES immediately. Donna sang in the choir and worked with children's missions, and she and Johnny both taught Sunday school. Donna truly believed that this was what God wanted her to be doing, and on the outside it appeared as if she'd turned her life around—but her heart was still bitter. No matter how much she read the Bible and prayed, it seemed she couldn't control her overeating or her sharp tongue.

One day several months after rededicating her life to Christ, Donna stood in front of the mirrored closet doors in their bedroom, trying to close the zipper on the jeans she was wearing. After struggling unsuccessfully for some time, she jerked the jeans off in disgust and threw them across the room.

"You're fat!" she said bitterly to her reflection. "Because you pigged out on that popcorn, you can't even fit into your jeans." Last night, after Johnny had gone to bed, she had decided to treat herself to some popcorn as a reward for a long, hard day at work. But that treat had quickly turned into another binge. Now here she stood, feeling bloated and ugly.

I've got to stop doing this, she thought, her eyes filling with tears. *When am I ever going to have some self-control?*

Donna went over to her bureau, jerked open a drawer, and pulled out a baggy blue sweater. She pulled the sweater over her head, then kicked the drawer shut with a *bang*.

"Are you okay, honey?" Johnny asked, coming into the room.

"I'm fine!" Donna muttered angrily. "Just leave me alone." She turned to make up the bed, and as she did so, she caught sight of her husband.

"Why are you wearing that shirt?" she snapped, hands on her hips.

Johnny looked down at the slightly wrinkled, green-plaid shirt and raised his eyebrows. "I thought it looked good," he told her.

"Well, you were wrong," Donna said sharply. She pulled a freshly ironed blue shirt from the closet and held it out to him. "Put this on. It looks much better."

Johnny complied, promptly dropping the old shirt onto the floor.

"I can't believe you!" Donna lashed out. She snatched the shirt off the floor and hung it neatly in the closet. "Why don't you pick up after yourself!"

Johnny threw his hands up in surrender. "Sorry," he said quickly. "I'm sorry." Shaking his head, he left the room.

Donna watched her husband's retreating back and bit her lip. She didn't mean to constantly criticize Johnny, but on days like this, when she was feeling extra insecure, the stinging comments just slipped out. Sinking onto the bed, Donna put her head between her hands. *If I could just lose weight, I'd feel much better about myself,* she thought miserably. *Then I wouldn't be so cranky with Johnny.* It seemed that every day she fought a battle with food, and food always won. *God, why don't You help me?* Donna prayed in frustration. *Why can't I be thin again? And why can't I control my tongue? I pray and pray, but You don't answer me.*

*A*BOUT A YEAR AFTER SHE AND JOHNNY BEGAN ATTENDING Belle Aire Baptist Church, Donna decided she wanted to start a family. At 27 years old, she felt that she and Johnny were ready to have children. Within six months, she was pregnant, and she and Johnny were ecstatic. They called their family and friends, announced it to their church, and made plans for their new addition.

Ten days later, Donna began spotting. *Oh no!* she thought in horror when she saw the blood. *This didn't happen before. Lord, are You going to take this baby from me?* Trembling uncontrollably, Donna called her doctor, who instructed her to lie on the couch with her feet propped up with pillows. All night, Donna stayed put, but the next morning, the spotting grew worse. By the end of the day, she knew she'd lost the baby.

Devastated, she slipped into a deep depression. Now that she had decided she wanted to be a mother, she couldn't think about anything else. For the next two weeks, Donna didn't leave the house. Countless people sent cards and flowers, even stopping by to see her—but Donna couldn't bear to be around anybody. It was too painful. *God, where are You in all this?* she prayed helplessly.

One afternoon, about a week and a half after she miscarried,

Donna was dozing on the couch in front of the TV when she heard something that caught her interest. Sitting up, she gave the screen her full attention. A blonde woman, who looked a lot like Donna herself, was being interviewed on a Christian talk show about her experience with abortion.

"I had an abortion when I was a teenager," the woman said emotionally to the TV host. "Like a lot of girls, I thought it wouldn't affect me, that I could push the experience away and forget about it."

Donna sat up, shivering in her sweatsuit. *So did I,* she thought.

"But it never did go away," the woman continued. "The abortion haunted me. I became bulimic shortly afterward, never realizing that my eating problem was related to the abortion. I began to struggle in my relationships. I became controlling. I felt alienated from God. And still, I didn't know why. Finally, at 28 years old—"

That's how old I am! Donna thought, her eyes glued to the screen. Their situations were so similar it was eerie.

"—I realized I'd never dealt with this," the woman continued. "For so many years, I'd been stuck in denial, and all these problems had surfaced as a result. I didn't begin to heal from the abortion process until I admitted it to God, begged His forgiveness, and started to grieve the loss of the baby."

Donna dropped her face into her hands and began to sob, suddenly hit by the irony of her situation. Here she was, grieving the loss of a baby she'd only known of for about 10 days, when she'd never grieved over the baby she'd aborted more than 10 years before. She had sent what probably was a healthy child home to God because she, a frightened, confused teenager, hadn't wanted it.

For the first time, the aborted baby became real to Donna—and all the pain she had dammed up for 10 years came crashing over her. With tears running down her cheeks, she fell face-down on the floor and began to pray. *Lord, forgive me for taking the life of Your child into my own hands,* she pleaded desperately.

I'm so sorry for all I've done. Forgive me for not controlling my tongue or my overeating. Forgive me for the mess I've made of myself.

Donna spent the next several hours crying, praying, and grieving. When she finally lifted herself off the carpet, she felt a deep peace. God had forgiven her, and He would lift those burdens from her heart.

As Donna read through her Bible in the days that followed, the Lord reassured her of His forgiveness and acceptance by leading her to verse after verse. One in particular comforted her: "If my people, who are called by my name, will humble themselves and pray and seek my face and turn from their wicked ways, then will I hear from heaven and will forgive their sin and will heal their land" (2 Chronicles 7:14).

Finally feeling at peace, Donna thought the healing process was complete. But God wasn't finished with her yet.

FIVE MONTHS AFTER HER MISCARRIAGE, DONNA WAS pregnant again. This time, she and Johnny didn't tell anyone except her parents—they wanted to be sure the baby would survive. Thankfully, the pregnancy was normal, and nine months later, she gave birth to a healthy girl they named Kelsey. Donna and Johnny were overjoyed. Then, almost two years after Kelsey came into the world, Mary Keaton arrived.

The birth of her daughters produced many positive changes in Donna's life. Conscious of being a role model, Donna realized that she needed to get control of her tongue and her overeating. She'd confessed her critical spirit to God, but now she had to do something about it. Thus a few months after Keaton was born, Donna started seeing a counselor.

In counseling, she and Johnny began to deal with issues in their marriage, and Donna worked through some of the pain in her own heart. Her problems with eating also began to slowly heal as she sought out God, rather than food, for comfort. The Lord revealed to her that her preoccupation with food was an idol in her life. He also reminded her of something she had learned in a Bible study: that she should enjoy food and love God instead of the other way around. *I don't care what size you are, Donna,* God told her. *It's not the weight I care about. It's your heart.*

Donna listened. The road to emotional and spiritual well-being would be difficult, but she knew that God would meet her needs—she just had to trust Him.

$\mathcal{A}$LTHOUGH DONNA HAD WORKED THROUGH MUCH OF THE pain that resulted from her abortion, she still hadn't told anyone other than Johnny about her experience. How could she tell her friends and church family? They saw her as a godly, committed woman who led many of the ministries at Belle Aire. What would they say if they knew about her abortion?

She would soon find out.

Almost three years after Keaton was born, Donna's pastor, not knowing her background, asked her to sing on Sanctity of Life Sunday. Donna sang in church all the time, so she immediately accepted, not thinking too much about it. She figured she'd just find a song she liked and sing it.

It didn't prove to be that easy. All week, Donna searched Christian music stores, looking for something on the subject of life and children, but nothing seemed right. Finally, the day before she was to sing, she sat down at the church piano and bowed her head.

"Lord God," she whispered, "please help me find a song. Show me what to do." But Donna never expected what happened next.

Pick up a piece of paper and a pen, God silently directed her, *and I'll give you a song.*

Donna froze in fear. She hadn't written music since college, and doing so had been extremely painful. "I can't write a song, Lord," she protested. "It will be awful! It will sound amateurish."

Donna, the Lord told her gently, *it will be good enough if you let Me write it. I understand how these children feel. And only I could understand the sacrifice it took to forgive you and others like you. Those people need to hear your story.*

With a trembling hand, Donna complied and spent the afternoon writing. It was as if she were taking dictation—the music and words came so quickly and eloquently that she knew God was writing it. When she was finished, she called her friend David, who could play music by ear. He came to the church, and an hour later, they were ready to perform the song before an audience.

That Sunday morning, Donna stood with wobbly knees in front of the 500-person congregation. As she looked at the church body, she suddenly realized that she needed to give her testimony as well. Trembling, she looked over at David, who was seated at the piano. His hands were folded in his lap, as if he knew she needed to say something before she sang. After standing on the platform in scared silence for several moments, Donna started to speak.

"W-when I was 17 years old," she began tremulously, "I had an . . . abortion."

The congregation took in a collective breath and fell silent. Donna's heart fluttered, and the color drained from her face. *Keep going,* she told herself. *You've got to do this.*

"This has caused the most incredible damage in my life," she continued, gathering confidence. "I've had eating disorders, major self-esteem issues, and problems in my marriage. I thought I could erase the abortion from my memory, but it has never gone away—the abortion has poisoned every part of my life." Donna paused, wiping a tear from her cheek. When she continued, her voice shook with emotion. "Fortunately, God forgives, and He has helped me work through much of my pain." Gazing out at the sea of familiar, beloved faces, she smiled. "He's given me this song to sing to you on Sanctity of Life Sunday."

Donna glanced over at David and nodded. Then closing her eyes, she began to sing:

> No one heard her singing there inside,
> Though her heart was beating just the same;
> And all because we thought she was too little,
> She never got a name.

She could have been a poet, or a dancer, or a wife;
She might have taught your Sunday school,
Or simply touched your life.
Her voice too quickly silenced,
Yet Jesus heard her well—
As we pushed her out of this world,
He caught her as she fell.

And I know I hear a choir of children, singing out
    their joy.
In God's arms there's always room for another girl
    or boy.
Each child has a special place,
Because He knows, like them,
What it's like to be sacrificed
For the selfishness of man.

No one saw him moving there inside,
Though his hands were forming just the same;
And all because we thought there was no room,
He never got a name.
He could have been a writer, or a farmer, or a dad;
He could have been your brother or the best friend
    that you had.
He never learned to clap, to drive a nail, or blow a kiss;
When we pushed him out of this world,
Jesus caught him up in His.

And I know I hear a choir of children, singing out
    their joy.
In God's arms there's always room for another girl
    or boy.
Each child has a special place,
Because He knows, like them,
What it's like to be sacrificed
For the selfishness of man.

As Donna finished, a wave of peace swept over her. The lyrics she'd sung were true. God knew what it was like to be sacrificed for her selfishness: Through His death on the cross, He'd paid the price for her sins. And still, God loved her deeply and unconditionally.

At 17, Donna had made a choice that she thought would release her from a burdensome chain; instead, the chain had been wrapped more tightly around her, slowly pulling her into an abyss of self-hatred and despair. But God had smashed that chain with the power of His love and forgiveness, so she could work through whatever consequences remained.

The chain was broken, and Donna was free.

Donna Shearron lives with her family in Murfreesboro, Tennessee. Hearing Bunny Wilson speak about abortion at a Renewing the Heart conference helped Donna realize that her unborn child needed a name, so she named her Sarah. Since she first sang on Sanctity of Life Sunday, Donna has continued her music ministry, performing at crisis pregnancy center banquets and numerous churches in her area, singing and speaking about her experience with abortion. Thankful that God has brought her back to her love of writing, Donna finds great joy in ministering to others through her songs. She's careful to stress, however, that her life does not have a fairy-tale ending. "I still have a long way to go to be completely healed," Donna attests, "but I face the journey with peace and joy, knowing that God will be with me all the way."

Heart to Heart

Donna's story probably resonates in the hearts of most of us. Like her, we often struggle with other people's perceptions and expectations of us. And in our relentless attempts to please and not disappoint our parents, children, friends, and spouses, we end up feeling frazzled and depressed. Our pursuit of perfection is doomed from the outset, because no human being will ever become perfect through his or her own efforts. If any of us could, there would have been no need for the cross.

God did not create us to perform for the praise and pleasure of humankind. He wants us to play the symphony of our lives for Him, and Him alone. Every day we should wake up marveling at His grace—a grace that forgives mistakes and failures, that fills the holes of broken relationships, that heals the wounds inflicted by sin, that binds the brokenhearted with compassion.

Walking by Faith ~

Lisa

STORY FIVE

Loving a Prodigal

*[The LORD] gives strength to the weary and
increases the power of the weak. . . . those who hope
in the LORD will renew their strength. They will
soar on wings like eagles; they will run and not
grow weary, they will walk and not be faint.*
—ISAIAH 40:29, 31

"WHEW! AM I GLAD TO BE HOME!" BRENDA PACKER SAID, ushering her family into the entryway of their house. "That sure is a mean storm!" She pulled the door shut behind her with a sigh of relief, glad to be off the dangerous roads.

Mount Pleasant, Michigan, was experiencing its first big blizzard of the year. Outside, the November windchill was menacing, and the snow was blowing at a furious speed, causing almost white-out conditions.

Brenda; her husband, Chuck; daughter, Stacy; and son Brett had just returned from their oldest son Ryan's varsity football game, where his team, the Shepherd Blue Jays, had won the regional championship. After the game, the football players and many of their friends and family members had gone out to a local pizza parlor to celebrate the team's victory. Because of the poor weather conditions, the game had lasted longer than usual, so Brenda had suggested that the family pass on the pizza and go directly home. She hadn't wanted to get stuck in the raging snowstorm.

Taking off her hat, scarf, winter jacket, and wool sweater, Brenda hung them on a coat rack by the front door, then watched as her husband, daughter, and two sons all retreated to various parts of the house. *I think I'll have a cup of hot cocoa,* she thought, rubbing her hands together. She was still cold. Before she could heat up the water, however, the phone rang. *Who could that be, calling at this time of night and during this storm?* she wondered.

Brenda walked into the dining room and picked up the phone, which hung on the wall. "Hello?" she said.

"You've gotta come get me," a thin, shaky voice mumbled over the line.

Brenda pushed her glasses higher on her nose and frowned. She couldn't understand what the person was saying. "What? Who is this?" she asked.

The voice spoke more slowly. "I . . . I need help. You've gotta come get me." It was a teenaged boy.

I've gotta come get who? she questioned silently.

The caller didn't sound well. "Aunt Brenda, my mom d-died. I'm at the hospital."

Brenda gasped. It was her 15-year-old nephew, Robert. He lived with his mother, Anne, and grandmother in Grand Haven, about three hours away. His father, who had passed away five years earlier, was Chuck's brother. The Packers had a close relationship with Robert; in fact, they were like a second family to the teenager.

"Robert?" Brenda asked worriedly. "Robert, are you okay? What hospital are you at? What happened?" She tugged nervously at a lock of wavy, brown hair.

There was a pause on the other end of the line. Then Robert said with difficulty, "My . . . mom died, and I'm at Ottawa County Hospital, and Grandma's in the emergency room."

Brenda could hear the pain in his voice, and her maternal instincts immediately kicked in. *There may be a blizzard outside, but I don't want my nephew to have to deal with this all alone,* she thought fiercely. *We're going to go get him.* "Robert," she told him decisively, "we're on our way."

She hung up the phone and hurried down the hall to tell Chuck what had happened. Before Brenda was finished talking, however, Chuck held up his hands to stop her.

"We can't drive to Grand Haven tonight," he said calmly. As always, Chuck was rational and unflappable—sometimes so much so that it frustrated Brenda, who was anything but laid-back. "Most of the roads are impassable," he continued, "and it would take us nearly five hours to get there."

"But—" Brenda protested.

"We couldn't do Robert any immediate good anyway," Chuck cut in quietly. He looked at his wife calmly. "We can drive up in the morning, after the roads are plowed. We'll have to think of someone in Grand Haven who can help him tonight."

Frustrated, Brenda sank onto the bed. Robert had other aunts and uncles, but none he was close to—or could rely on.

His father's family had never been an active part of his life, and most likely none of them would drop everything to comfort him in his time of need. Upset at the thought of this, Brenda crossed her arms. *I can't imagine what Robert must be going through right now,* she thought worriedly. *He needs us—we're his godparents.* Brenda cast another pleading look at Chuck, who shook his head.

A few minutes later, the phone rang again. This time, it was the father of Robert's best friend, Rob Christian, calling with more information.

"Mrs. Packer," Mr. Christian said, "Robert is welcome to stay with us this evening. The weather is too treacherous for you to try to make it all the way here tonight. Why don't you drive over in the morning?"

"Thanks. We'll do that," Brenda said gratefully. Her shoulders relaxed a bit. "How's Robert doing?"

"Well, he seems okay, but he's not talking. His grandmother has been admitted to the hospital. She's in shock," Mr. Christian told her gravely.

"What happened to Anne?" Brenda asked uneasily, trying to take it all in.

"She was out delivering care packages from the Boy Scouts in her neighborhood when she had a seizure and collapsed onto the snow. She died from hypothermia." Mr. Christian lowered his voice. "She wasn't far from the house, and I guess another neighbor found her lying there, because someone had called an ambulance. Robert heard the sirens and went outside to see what all the noise was about. That's when he saw his mother lying dead a few feet off their property."

"Oh, that's . . . that's terrible," Brenda whispered. She felt faint.

As children, Robert's parents had both suffered closed head injuries. His father, David, had been hit in the head with a baseball as a young boy, and his mother, Anne, fell out of a baby crib when she was an infant. David and Anne had met in a rehabilitation center, and they had both always been on high doses of medication for their seizures. Unfortunately, their combined medical problems also caused difficulty in their marriage. A few years after Robert was born, his parents divorced. Then, when Robert was nine years old, his father died of a heart attack brought on by his medication. Because of Robert's unstable family history, the Packers had often tried to include him in various family vacations and outings, even though he lived almost three hours away. Ryan, Stacy, and Brett were almost like siblings to him. That was why Robert had called them first—with his mother dead and his grandmother hospitalized, the Packers were now his only real family.

Brenda hung up the phone and sighed. At least the situation for tonight had been resolved. They would drive to Grand Haven in the morning and see Robert. Knowing he was taken care of for the night didn't ease Brenda's mind, though. She still felt a heavy responsibility for her troubled nephew.

*E*ARLY THE NEXT MORNING, BRENDA, CHUCK, RYAN, STACY, AND Brett piled into their four-wheel-drive truck and made the trip to Grand Haven to support Robert. During the next few days, the Packers talked over Robert's options for the future with his grandmother and Robert's maternal aunt and uncle. The moment Brenda saw Robert, she realized it was a good thing they had come. He was an emotional mess beneath his carefully controlled exterior.

"It's my fault my mom died," he said bitterly to Brenda the day they arrived. "I didn't go with her to deliver the care packages. She asked me to go, and I said no." His long face was pinched.

Brenda bit her lip. "Oh, Robert," she said softly, "it wasn't your fault. You were just acting like any normal teenager. I know your mom wouldn't want you to feel so guilty."

"Yeah," Robert said flatly. He turned away quickly.

Brenda eyed her nephew with compassion. His thin body had

broken out in hives from the emotional trauma of his mother's death, and his blue eyes looked puffier than usual. Robert had been born with ptosis, or droopy eyelids, which restricted his vision by 50 percent and made him appear to be drunk or stoned all the time. Brenda knew that Robert's swollen lids had been aggravated by tears, not drugs, and her heart went out to him. *Lord, please give us all the strength and knowledge to do what is best for Robert,* she prayed often over the next few days.

It wasn't going to be easy.

Though Robert had numerous relatives, only a few from his mother's side came to demonstrate their support. Out of 10 pairs of aunts and uncles, only the Packers and Anne's brother and sister showed up to process the situation with Robert's maternal grandmother, with whom he and Anne had lived.

Though his grandmother adored him, she couldn't raise him alone. Florene was too frail and elderly to bring up her grandson. "I can't handle Robert," she told Chuck and Brenda apologetically. "I love him, and it breaks my heart to say this, but I just can't do it."

Brenda patted Florene's wizened hand. "It's okay, Florene. We know you'd keep him if you could." She shook her head ruefully. *Chuck and I might be the only ones who are willing take Robert in,* she thought sadly. *Besides his grandmother, none of his other relatives will volunteer.* As quickly as the notion came into her head, however, Brenda dismissed it. Robert's mother wasn't even related to her or Chuck—Anne was only an ex-sister-in-law. Sure, she and Chuck were Robert's godparents, but what did that mean? They hadn't talked about that arrangement with Robert's parents for years. *Surely Anne would have wanted Robert to live with either her brother or her sister,* Brenda reasoned.

But Brenda's hunch turned out to be right. The day before the funeral, Robert, the Packers, Florene, and Robert's aunt and uncle sat around the kitchen table, discussing where Robert should live.

Robert folded his arms across his thin chest. "Wherever I

go," he said gruffly, "I'm not going to therapy." Because of his many emotional problems, his mother had tried to get Robert to go to a counselor, but he always refused.

Brenda looked at Robert, her eyebrows raised. "I think that any of us would say that therapy will be up to you, Robert," she said. "As long as you're doing well and we don't feel you need to go, you won't go. But that will be your decision."

"Brenda," Robert's aunt said, jumping in, "you should know that we were going through Anne's things and found a note from her. Her request was that Robert live with you and Chuck."

Brenda looked questioningly at Chuck, who nodded. Everyone knew that taking Robert in would be a big responsibility, and though the Packers had many reservations, they were willing to do whatever God's plan was for them. But who knew if such a note even existed? Were they really the family Anne had wanted Robert to live with? Brenda shook her head, trying to clear her thoughts. Robert was sitting at the table with them, and it was important that he feel wanted.

"Well, I guess that's settled, then," Brenda said, looking around the table. Robert's aunt and uncle looked relieved, and Robert, his arms still crossed, said nothing.

Later that night after they'd returned home, Brenda talked the situation over with Chuck. "Wow! What an honor," she said, still sorting through her emotions. "I feel as though we've won the lottery without buying a ticket."

Chuck, his mouth set firmly, poured dish soap into the kitchen sink, then filled it with hot water. Looking over at Brenda sitting at the kitchen table, he said, "Well, I think it's the right thing to do. Robert's dad was my brother, and I feel a responsibility to Robert."

Brenda searched Chuck's eyes before saying worriedly, "I hope our marriage is strong enough to handle this."

Chuck met her gaze for a moment, then turned and started washing dishes. It seemed to Brenda that he never wanted to talk through anything.

Chuck and Brenda had a workable relationship, but it lacked the intimacy Brenda craved. Chuck had grown up in an unemotional family and so had difficulty expressing his feelings. He'd wash dishes and do laundry all night if necessary, as long as he didn't have to deal with anyone's emotions, including his own. Unfortunately, this left Brenda with the burden of caring for their kids' emotional and spiritual needs.

Brenda sighed and rubbed her eyes tiredly. Things were happening so quickly that she could hardly think straight. *I guess this is what You want us to do, Lord,* she prayed. *But will I really be able to handle Robert?* she wondered. *He has a lot of problems, and I know I'm going to be the one who has to deal with him—Chuck certainly won't. Besides, we have three kids of our own, and I work full-time.*

Overwhelmed by the doubts swimming through her mind, Brenda slumped against the back of the kitchen chair. Taking Robert in was a big deal. How would she be able to handle such a heavy responsibility by herself?

On their way to the funeral home in Grand Haven the next day, Brenda felt more confident in their decision to care for Robert. When she saw how little support Robert's other relatives showed him, she was even more certain that their decision was the right one. After placing a bouquet of flowers on Anne's casket, Brenda watched misty-eyed as a pathetic scene took place a few feet away.

Robert had his skinny arms outstretched to his paternal grandparents, who had just arrived. "Hi, Grandma. Hi, Grandpa," he called. Robert looked pitiful in his borrowed "church" clothes—his mother had never bought him dress clothes—with hives covering his thin neck and face.

His grandparents stopped a few feet away and eyed Robert fearfully. "He looks as if he has chicken pox," his grandmother said nervously to his grandfather. "I can't hug him." Addressing Robert, she said coldly, "I'm sorry about your mother, Robert"; then, taking her husband's arm, she walked away.

Brenda's heart sank as she witnessed this obvious abandonment. She quickly walked over to her nephew and hugged him tightly. "Robert, we love you," Brenda told him, "and we're so happy that you're coming to live with us."

Looking up at the dreary funeral home ceiling, she sighed. She could only hope and pray that God would give her the strength to provide the loving home Robert needed.

*B*RENDA SAT ON THE FAMILY ROOM COUCH, SCANNING A LIST of items on a sheet of paper lying on the coffee table in front of her. It was just a few weeks after Anne's funeral, and Brenda and her daughter, Stacy, were discussing Robert's upcoming move into the Packer home.

"We'll need to pull out the kitchen table so there's room for six," Brenda said, writing furiously, "then put together the bunk beds, so Robert and Brett can share a room. We also need to get a new toothbrush holder. The one we have has only five slots." She narrowed her eyes in concentration. "Okay . . . what else haven't I thought of yet?" There was so much to do to get ready, and only three weeks remained until Robert came. The reality of it made Brenda nervous.

Thirteen-year-old Stacy tossed her long, dark-brown hair. "Well, I still don't understand why we didn't bring Robert home with us right after the funeral," she said loyally, swinging a leg over the arm of the recliner she was sitting in. Stacy and her brothers had been upset when Brenda, Chuck, and Robert's grandmother had decided that he should finish the semester at school before coming to live with the Packers.

"You know why we made that decision, Stacy," Brenda said, looking at her daughter across the coffee table. "Robert needs to have some closure at school and at home, with his grandmother."

Despite his cousins' excitement over the situation, Robert had resisted the idea of leaving Grand Haven at first—all of his friends were there—but after three weeks of staying in a house filled with memories of his mother, he'd let Brenda know that now he was more than ready to come live with them.

Stacy shrugged. "Yeah, I know, Mom," she said. "But I still think you should have brought him here sooner. You saw how much he needed us."

Brenda put down the list and studied her daughter for a moment. Stacy was mature beyond her years, but did she realize what a major undertaking this was? "Honey, this isn't just for a few weeks," Brenda reminded her. "Robert's coming to live with us permanently, and we're going to treat him like he's one of the family. That means he'll also get a clothing allowance, rules, and a curfew. In addition, you and your brothers are going to have to share even more than you do now," she explained. "Our money is like a pie. Now that Robert's going to be a part of our family, your slices of the pie will get smaller."

"I know, Mom," Stacy said impatiently, twisting a long strand of hair around her finger.

"Well, I'm just making sure you and your brothers understand this," Brenda said matter-of-factly. She wanted to arrange things so that Robert would feel as important as her own children. *Lord, I want him to feel included and accepted,* Brenda had prayed frequently ever since she had known for certain Robert would live with them. *I don't want him to feel that he's different from my own children.*

Brenda resumed making notes on her list, and for a few minutes there was silence. Suddenly, the phone rang. Stacy jumped up to grab it, but after hearing who the caller was, she disappointedly handed the receiver to her mother. "It's for you," she informed her.

Brenda took the phone. "Hello?" she said.

"Mrs. Packer," came a woman's businesslike voice over the line, "my name is Sandra Lieberman, and I'm the principal at Robert Packer's high school."

"Oh . . . yes?" Brenda said, wondering why the principal was calling her.

The woman continued. "Robert has just been in my office."

"Is everything okay?" Brenda asked as she quickly scribbled another item on her list.

Ms. Lieberman let out a frustrated sigh, then said, "Well, he was just trying to manipulate me. You need to know that Robert is a master of manipulation."

"I do know that," Brenda replied. She had seen Robert's manipulative behavior several times in the past, when he'd spent time with the Packers. "Robert's had a difficult family life, which causes him to have this tendency to—"

Ms. Lieberman interrupted her. "Ma'am, I don't think you really know what a problem he has," she said curtly. "He was just trying to tell me that I should give him credit for his classes so he can leave Grand Haven High School early. He's using the grief issue, trying to take advantage of his mother's death so I'll be sympathetic and pass him. I'm not going to do that. His grades are very low. And his attitude . . ."

Brenda sighed. "What about his attitude?" she asked wearily.

"He never takes responsibility for his actions," Ms. Lieberman said, gathering steam, "and he has a problem with authority. Robert's mother unintentionally fostered some of his problems. She believed everything he said, to the point that she was in my office every week, making a fuss of some sort." Ms. Lieberman paused, then said, "His mother was constantly fighting a battle that didn't need to be fought. Robert made her think he was being victimized at school. And after my experience with him today, I thought I'd better call and warn you about this."

Brenda massaged the back of her neck. She could feel the tension coming on. "Well, thanks for being concerned, but we already know this about Robert," she said.

Robert had some issues; Brenda understood that. But as she hung up the phone, the principal's words echoed in her head: *Ma'am, I don't think you really know . . .*

*C*LUTCHING ROBERT'S CHRISTMAS LIST IN HER HAND, BRENDA resolutely approached the shoe department at J. C.

Penney almost three weeks later. She had to get Robert's shopping done. He was scheduled to move in with them on Christmas Eve, just three days away.

Brenda studied the crumpled paper again and sighed. *Tomac grip cleats? Mario Brothers Original? Clipless pedals? What is all this stuff?* It was as if the list were written in another language. Out of 12 items, Brenda had been able to decipher only two: a GTeen LTS3 Full Suspension Bike and a pair of Airwalk AfterBoots.

The bike was out of the question—it cost $1,200. Brenda's mouth had dropped open when she saw the price tag in the bike shop. She didn't even know it was possible to make a bicycle that expensive. Unable to figure out the rest of the list, Brenda had decided to find the Airwalk boots, which she knew must be some kind of shoe.

Walking with determination to the men's shoe displays, Brenda studied the different brands. *Penney's should have these boots,* she thought hopefully. If she couldn't find them here, Robert would have to settle for something else, because no other department store in the farming community carried that kind of merchandise.

After several minutes of looking, Brenda didn't see anything with the name "Airwalk." Perplexed, she walked up to the counter. "Excuse me," she said to the saleswoman at the register, "but do you have any of these?" She pointed to number 10 on the list.

The clerk furrowed her brow as she said, "Nooo. I don't know what those are."

"Do you know what any of the things on this list are?" Brenda asked, pushing her glasses higher on her nose to once again study the paper. "I sure don't."

The woman looked again. "I have no idea," she said apologetically. "I'm sorry."

This lady probably thinks I'm nuts, Brenda thought. She threw her hands up in the air, half-laughing, half-frustrated at the situation. "Oh, well, I'll just have to ask Robert," she said.

She put the Christmas list back in her purse and left the shoe department.

With the exception of Christmas shopping for her nephew, preparations for Robert's arrival had come together quickly. Someone from the Packers' church had anonymously donated a mattress for him, and last week Brenda's office at the Central Michigan District Health Department had thrown her a "shower." Her coworkers had provided a cake, necessities such as huge boxes of cereal and economy-size laundry detergent, money, and even a knitted slipper—a "baby bootie."

"Now I know why it takes nine months to have a baby," Brenda had joked with her coworkers. "Kids necessitate so much work that you need all that time to prepare." She looked at them gratefully. "Thanks so much for throwing me a shower," she'd said. "Having all of this stuff will really help us."

Snapping out of her reverie, Brenda headed toward Penney's young men's clothing department and surveyed the displays. Maybe she didn't know what Robert wanted, but she knew what he needed—nice clothes. That had been obvious at his mother's funeral. Squaring her shoulders, she began to browse.

But Brenda still couldn't shake the doubts that had been plaguing her for weeks. As she picked up sweaters, slacks, and dress shirts for Robert, she worried, *What if he doesn't get along with Ryan, Stacy, and Brett? What if our kids start resenting him? What if Robert won't pray with us or go to church? What if Chuck and I aren't strong enough to handle him?*

She would soon find out.

*C*HRISTMAS EVE CAME, AND SO DID ROBERT. HE ARRIVED AT the Packer household with only one paper grocery sack full of clothing. The boy had no socks or decent winter coat, but he did own more than 80 video games, many CDs (most with parental advisory labels), and three video-game systems.

Chuck and Brenda warmly welcomed their nephew, but

they wouldn't accept his explicit CDs. Brenda sat on the edge of Robert's bunk bed and watched as he unpacked.

After a few minutes, she said clearly, "Robert, we don't allow CDs like that in our house. You'll have to give them to Chuck and me."

Robert studied his aunt's face and shrugged. "Okay, Mom," he said casually.

Brenda blinked, startled. *Mom?* The word seemed to hang in the air. *I can't believe he's already calling me "Mom,"* Brenda thought. *Anne's been gone for only six weeks.* She swallowed, unsure of what to do. She didn't feel right about telling Robert not to call her "Mom"—Brenda wanted him to feel that he was one of the family. Smiling weakly at him, she simply said, "Well, then, I'm glad you understand."

Besides myriad CDs and video games, Robert also brought some unintentional humor to the Packers that Christmas. The family stared dumbly at the packages Robert handed to Ryan, Stacy, and Brett—presents Brenda had purchased for him to give to his cousins. They were wrapped in white, with the brightly patterned design facing inside, toward the gift.

"That's creative, Robert," Ryan said with a laugh when he tore off the paper on his gift.

"Hey, no one ever told me how to wrap a present," Robert muttered. He gave a half-smile and tilted his head back slightly to look at his relatives.

The Packers just giggled at their interesting new family member.

It seemed to Brenda that every minute with Robert was eventful. Only a few days after moving in, Robert asked if Chuck and Brenda would adopt him. They agreed to look into it, but after seeking the advice of an attorney, Chuck and Brenda decided that adoption wasn't the best option for Robert. Since he was an orphan, Robert would qualify for numerous college scholarships if and when he decided to get a degree. Chuck and Brenda had saved some money for all their kids' college funds, but they were unable to provide much college money for Robert. The teenager would have more opportunities as an orphan than if he were adopted, and since Robert's last name was already Packer, the distinction would only be biological. Fortunately, after hearing the lawyer's explanation, Robert agreed with his aunt and uncle's decision not to adopt him.

A few weeks later, school started up again. As Chuck and Brenda had anticipated, Robert's transition from a large urban school district to Shepherd's small farming district was difficult. Because of his ptosis, Robert quickly found himself attached to the "druggies" and troublemakers, who thought he was stoned. Teachers also believed Robert was either high on drugs, drunk, sleeping, or being disrespectful, so Brenda had to do a lot of explaining to the school faculty.

Robert's mother had never wanted to correct his defect with surgery because any risky operation made her nervous. Just a few weeks after Robert moved in with the Packers, however, he asked if they could look into the option of surgery.

"Definitely," Brenda and Chuck had said. Both felt that no one should have to live with a physical impediment like Robert's if it could be corrected. So when Brenda checked into it and discovered that her health insurance would cover the entire procedure, she arranged for Robert to have the surgery. Afterward, Robert's eyelids were still slightly droopy—if the doctors had done anything more, he wouldn't have been able to shut his eyes at all—but his appearance was radically improved.

Robert's physical issues were only the beginning, though. Within two months after he arrived, it became clear that he had many deep emotional problems as well. Robert had grown up without having any boundaries set for him, so he had a difficult time adjusting to the Packers' curfews, rules, and responsibilities.

One night Robert came in at 3:30 in the morning, three and a half hours past his curfew. Chuck had waited up for him, sitting with the lights out in the kitchen. When he heard Robert sneak in quietly through the back door, he confronted his nephew.

"Robert, what time is it?" Chuck inquired, his voice booming through the quiet darkness.

Robert, having thought he was the only one awake, jumped.

Still in shadow, Chuck continued talking. "Couldn't you have called us?" he asked, frustrated. "We didn't know where you were! Ryan, Stacy, and Brett have to follow our rules. As part of this family, you're not going to have any privileges they don't have."

The Packers grounded Robert for a week, but Brenda soon discovered that Robert's misbehavior didn't stop after he was punished. In fact, his problems worsened. Robert began banging his head against walls, the bunk bed at night, and anything else with a hard surface. Brenda and 10-year-old Brett, who shared a room with Robert, tried consoling him, hoping he would open up and share his pain, but Robert never did.

One night, the racket went on longer than usual, and the sounds seemed to echo throughout the house. As Brenda walked past the closed door to Brett and Robert's room, she cringed and stopped. Tightening her grip on the laundry basket she was holding, she listened.

"Robert, what's wrong?" Brett's worried voice carried through the door.

Bang! Bang! Bang! Robert continued hitting his head against what sounded to Brenda like the bunk-bed post. "Leave me alone!" he yelled. "I don't want to talk about it!"

Brenda closed her eyes, upset. *What are we going to do?* she worried. They couldn't just shut out Robert's behavior—his actions were impossible to overlook, and it wasn't right to ignore him, anyway. She turned the hall corner and walked into the master bedroom, where Chuck was folding clothes on the bed. Setting the laundry basket on the floor, Brenda looked gravely at her husband. "I think Robert needs counseling," she said quietly.

Chuck looked up from the jeans he was shaking out. "Robert's just been through a lot," he said calmly. "Of course he's acting out. He'll get over it." He finished folding the jeans, then picked up an undershirt. Chuck worked at a center for developmentally dysfunctional people, where he saw individuals with far worse problems than Robert's. That and his own emotionally unhealthy upbringing made Chuck less worried than Brenda was about Robert's outbursts.

Brenda's heart sank. *If Robert had a broken arm or leg, we wouldn't hesitate to take him to a professional,* she thought sadly as she pushed up the sleeves on her denim shirt. *Why is it any different to have a broken heart or spirit?*

As Brenda had feared, Chuck turned out to be wrong in his assessment—Robert didn't simply "get over it." He became angrier as time went on. Once or twice, Brenda asked her nephew if he wanted to talk with a counselor, but the suggestion of therapy was repulsive to him. Crossing his arms, he would reply hotly, "I'm not going to go to some stupid counselor! No way!"

But Robert's emotional distress was already affecting everyone else in the family. Robert wasn't just angry—he was also possessive, especially of Ryan. A junior and talented athlete, Ryan was popular at the high school he and Robert attended, and Robert quickly attached himself to the older boy. Robert insisted on sitting by Ryan at lunchtime, and he had even taken Ryan's varsity jacket and worn it around campus, pretending that he actually was the older teen.

Consequently, Ryan had begun hiding under his bed, pushing all of his sports equipment and dumbbells to the outside so his cousin couldn't find him. He was recovering from knee surgery and having problems with his girlfriend, so he felt a need to escape. Brenda was the only one who knew where Ryan disappeared to, and she understood why. Ryan needed space from Robert, and taking cover under his bed was the only way to ensure that he'd get it.

As Ryan continued to feel trapped, his personality began to

change. Brenda was heartsick as she saw her normally outgoing and happy teenager becoming withdrawn and lethargic. *Lord, what am I going to do?* she prayed. *Now I have two potential therapy candidates in my house! Robert needs our love, but he's driving everyone else crazy.*

Stacy had also found a means of escaping the chaos at home—baby-sitting. Wanting to stay away as long as possible, she begged her mother to let her sit past 9:00 on weeknights. Reluctantly, Brenda agreed to let her daughter bend the rule and watched despondently as Stacy took full advantage of the opportunity. Soon she was almost never around.

Brett worried Brenda more than Stacy or Ryan, though. The youngest Packer didn't act any differently, causing Brenda to fear that Brett was stuffing all his emotions. Fortunately, Brenda discovered after talking to him, that wasn't the case. Brett was just an extremely laid-back child who was able to take Robert's outbursts in stride.

Chuck, as usual, retreated from the chaos by working overtime or tinkering in the garage, leaving Brenda to handle her family's unsettled state alone.

"I wish I could go to the garage and hide!" Brenda often told her husband in frustration. "But I can't, because somebody has to deal with Robert and the kids! This whole family would fall apart if I went to the garage like you do every time things get tough around here."

Chuck would simply cross his arms and let his wife vent, which made Brenda even more agitated. "Why don't you ever argue back, Chuck?" she would ask shrilly. "You drive me crazy!" It was impossible to fight with someone who wouldn't fight back, let alone get emotional support from someone who was incapable of giving it.

Already, the stress of caring for her family, working full-time, and dealing with three teenagers—one of them emotionally unstable—was becoming almost unbearable for Brenda. *Lord, You've got to help me,* she prayed in desperation. *I'm going to lose it soon. I'm just Brenda Packer—not Superwoman!* Many mornings Brenda woke up wondering how she was going to get through the day.

Robert's teachers seemed ready to give up on him as well. In the weeks since he'd arrived, Robert had already caused so many problems that Brenda wondered if her work phone number was on the faculty's speed dial. One afternoon she received yet another call, this time from Robert's life-skills teacher, Mrs. Salsbury, one of Robert's only advocates left at the school. Since Brenda worked in the school system giving vision and hearing tests, the teachers all knew her well.

"Brenda," Mrs. Salsbury began, "do you remember how I gave all the kids raw eggs in class, and they were to pretend the eggs were babies?" Her voice shook with anger.

Brenda's stomach did a flip-flop. "Yes." Last week, she'd received a letter from Mrs. Salsbury in which she explained the project. The kids were supposed to learn responsibility by taking care of their fragile egg "babies."

Mrs. Salsbury continued angrily. "Well, moments ago Robert was standing in the lunchroom with egg dripping down his face. He deliberately broke his egg on his head. Of course, when he did that, the rest of the kids all threw theirs, ruining the project." She took a deep breath, then said, "Robert's on his way to the principal's office right now."

After hanging up the phone, Brenda put her head on her desk and closed her eyes. *It seems as if there's a problem every single day,* she thought wearily.

Although he was filthy, Robert stayed at school that day. Late that afternoon, while sitting in the family room, Brenda smelled the rotten egg even before she heard Robert sneak through the back door. "Robert, you can't hide from me—I can smell you," Brenda called out, exasperated. "Come here. I want to talk to you."

Robert sauntered into the family room, looking innocent.

"Mrs. Salsbury called me today," Brenda said. "I can't believe you cracked that egg on your head and got the other kids to break theirs, too! You completely wrecked her project."

himself—and to us. Either we send Robert to counseling or the whole family will end up in therapy before the year's out!"

Chuck sighed. "Okay," he said resignedly. "Take him to counseling."

"BRENDA?" DR. ALLAN SAID A FEW WEEKS LATER, HOLDING open the door to her office. "May I talk with you?"

"Sure," Brenda said, getting up from her chair in the waiting room.

After the school bus incident, Brenda had immediately called to make a counseling appointment for Robert. Though the teenager complained about going, he was never late for his biweekly sessions with Dr. Allan. Brenda usually came in just as the session was starting so that Dr. Allan could get a fuller picture of how Robert was doing. Tonight, however, Robert's appointment was almost over. It was unusual for Dr. Allan to call Brenda in so late.

Brenda sat down in a plush, high-backed chair and watched Dr. Allan shut the office door. She felt it was therapeutic, talking with the psychologist about Robert. Dr. Allan had enabled Brenda to understand more of her nephew's behavior, relieving some of her fears. The psychologist had told her that, though Robert was a very disturbed teen, he wouldn't purposely hurt any of the Packers. All of his actions were directed against himself, acted out in order to get attention.

Unfortunately, Robert's cries for help had recently gotten even more serious. In the few weeks since he'd started seeing Dr. Allan, Robert had talked about death and had made several feeble attempts to cut his wrists with pocketknives.

Now, sitting in Dr. Allan's office, Brenda studied her nephew. Robert was staring out the window, away from Dr. Allan, who had her hands clasped tightly in her lap.

"What's going on?" Brenda asked anxiously.

Dr. Allan cleared her throat. "Robert has told me that he's planning to hurt himself," she said gravely. "To keep him safe,

I want him admitted to the Rivendale Adolescent Psychiatric Center, in St. John's." She looked at Brenda's white face. "I've already made all the arrangements," she told her. "You'll have to be there by midnight tonight."

As Robert's legal guardians, Brenda and Chuck had to follow the advice of his therapist. "Oh . . . okay," Brenda said. Biting her lip, she wondered how she was going to accomplish this. At 5:30 the next morning, she and Chuck were supposed to drive with his sister and brother-in-law to a Triumphant Marriage seminar in Ohio, six hours away.

Sensing Brenda's hesitation, Dr. Allan looked at her sympathetically. "Robert really needs to be in treatment," she said firmly. On the couch, Robert, his arms folded, never looked at Brenda.

After the session, Brenda and Robert drove the icy roads home in silence. By the time they pulled into the driveway, it was already 10:00 in the evening. When Brenda hurried her nephew out of the car, she was surprised to have Ryan meet them at the door. His usually cheerful face looked sullen, and he followed them quietly around the house, watching as Brenda, Chuck, and Robert prepared to leave for the hospital.

"Mom, when will you be home?" Ryan asked gloomily. He shuffled to Robert's bunk bed and sat forlornly on the end of it.

"I don't know, Ryan," Brenda answered. "Your dad and I have to get Robert to the treatment center by midnight, and it's going to take us at least an hour to get to St. John's"—she glanced out the window—"especially in this ice storm. I have no idea how long this will take." She zipped up Robert's duffel bag, then slung it over her shoulder, beckoning for her nephew and son to follow.

"All right," Ryan said resignedly as he got up from the bed.

Brenda knew something was bothering Ryan, but there was no way she could talk with him now—she and Chuck were legally bound to get Robert to the treatment center by midnight.

Ryan will be okay, Brenda rationalized. *Robert's the one we really need to worry about.* However, when she paused to study her son's pinched, disappointed face, her heart sank. *There isn't enough of me to go around,* she thought mournfully as she hugged him. *Everything is falling apart, and there's nothing I can do about it.*

A few minutes later, Brenda, Chuck, and Robert got into the car and prepared to leave. Ryan stood on the porch, his hands shoved into his jeans pockets, watching with melancholy eyes as they backed out of the driveway and drove away.

Ryan's dejected figure haunted Brenda all the way to St. John's. *Ryan needs me, and I can't be there for him,* she thought miserably. *I've failed him.* Ever since Robert had come to live with them, Brenda had tried valiantly to support everyone in her family—and she still felt as if she were failing totally.

Brenda, Chuck, and Robert arrived at the treatment center only a few minutes before midnight. The outside of the building looked like any normal school building, but the inside looked sickeningly oppressive with its white, bare walls and sealed windows. It looked and felt like a prison.

When Brenda and Chuck finished filling out the seemingly endless paperwork, they walked Robert to the room where he'd be staying for the next week. Brenda shuddered as she heard the doors lock in place behind them and saw that all the bed corners were rounded, so the teens couldn't hurt themselves.

Most of the kids there were drug abusers and had attempted suicide. *With everything Robert's been through, now we have to put him here?* Brenda wondered, nauseated. *He's just a sad, confused kid.* The strength of her feelings surprised her. She knew Robert needed to be at the center, but she hated leaving him there.

Brenda turned to her nephew. "Here's our 1-800 number," she said, pulling a piece of paper out of her purse and writing on it. "Ryan, Stacy, and Brett have it, too, and you're allowed to use it to call us anytime."

Robert took the paper wordlessly. He hadn't fought going to the center. "I'm gonna be fine," he mumbled. "I'll probably like it better here, anyway."

But Robert didn't like the facility at all. Most of the kids were worse off than he, and his time there was more like being at boot camp than being on vacation. After seven days, he returned happily to the Packers, more docile and accepting of their rules. Most of the teens at the center didn't have loving families, and Robert must have realized that he was more fortunate than the others. Robert never vocalized these feelings, but Brenda could see the new contentment on his face.

Meanwhile, Brenda continued to struggle to balance her children's needs with Robert's. A few days after she'd taken Robert to the treatment center, she discovered why Ryan had acted so melancholy that night—he'd just broken up with his girlfriend of two and a half years, and he was devastated. But Ryan never told Brenda this news—Stacy did. Ryan, feeling that his mom had enough to handle already with Robert, hadn't wanted to burden her further.

Unfortunately, Ryan wasn't the only one who continually got pushed to the side. Stacy did, too—especially on the night of her fourteenth birthday. That day, Stacy had volleyball practice late in the afternoon, and Brenda had to take Robert to one of his counseling sessions, so they agreed to celebrate her birthday after dinner with a frozen pie and some ice cream.

Brenda and Robert arrived home from therapy around 8:00 that evening, and Brenda immediately put the pie in the oven to heat up. Just as she was closing the oven door, Chuck walked into the kitchen with Robert trailing close behind.

"Robert needs to talk to us, and he needs to do it now," Chuck told her.

"About what?" Brenda asked reluctantly. It was Stacy's turn for attention now, not Robert's.

Chuck's face was serious. "I don't know," he said. "He just said he's got something real important to talk to us about."

Brenda sighed and looked at Robert. "Can't it wait?" she asked.

"No," Robert said quietly. He stared at the kitchen floor, apparently upset.

Oh, boy, Brenda thought anxiously. *I'll bet therapy brought up some huge issue. What if Robert was abused as a child or is on drugs or something?* She turned to Stacy, who had just entered from the family room. "Honey, we need to talk with Robert for a few minutes. As soon as the pie is done cooking, we'll be ready to celebrate your birthday."

Stacy looked skeptical. "Fine," she replied glumly. She was used to having her birthday pushed to the side, because for the past three years, the Packers had chaperoned Ryan's baseball team to Florida for spring training during her birthday.

Brenda felt terrible. This year she'd tried to make a special effort for Stacy's birthday, but now Robert obviously needed them. So a few minutes later, Brenda and Chuck sat down with Robert in their bedroom, anxious to find out what was wrong.

Robert fiddled with the wristband on his watch. "You know when I lived in Grand Haven?"

"Yes?" Brenda asked, leaning forward with concern.

"Uh . . . well . . . the guys and me, we'd ride our bikes," Robert continued.

"What about riding your bikes?" Brenda asked, glancing at Chuck. His dark brows were pushed together, and he looked as confused as she felt.

"You know . . . we'd go down to Front Street . . . and . . ."

"And what?" Brenda asked. This was going nowhere.

"And we'd ride our bikes off the pier," Robert finished undramatically, pushing his glasses higher on his nose. "But then . . ."

For the next hour, Brenda and Chuck continued to drag the details from Robert. During that time Brenda heard the buzzer ring and the oven click off. A few minutes later, she heard Stacy's door shut in the room next to theirs, followed by muffled sobs and sniffles. Brenda was torn. If she left Robert to tend to Stacy, he would get the message that Stacy was more important to her than he was. But now Stacy was crying in her room, because she was feeling that Robert was more important.

Brenda's stomach churned. She felt trapped. *I don't know how to handle this,* she thought miserably. *It seems as though no matter what I do, somebody always gets hurt.*

It took two hours of talking for Robert to divulge that he had consumed alcohol on several occasions and that he had been in a type of gang at his old school—not the breakthrough information Brenda had anticipated. By the time they were done with Robert, the pie was cold and Stacy had cried herself to sleep.

Brenda tried to smooth over the situation and make up for Stacy's terrible nonbirthday by having a big celebration a few days later, during spring break. But by that time, the damage had already been done.

That was just the beginning of Robert's constant manipulation, in which he tried to tear Chuck and Brenda's attention from the rest of the family. It seemed that every day Robert did something to test them. Despite Brenda's efforts to love him and Dr. Allan's biweekly therapy sessions, Robert didn't seem to be getting any better—at times, he appeared to be worse.

After months of going nowhere, Dr. Allan suggested that Robert see a male colleague of hers, thinking he would be more receptive to a man. Amazingly, he was. Robert opened up more in his first session with Dr. Plummer than he had in months of therapy with Dr. Allan. The only glitch was, Dr. Plummer wasn't covered by the Packers' insurance. So Brenda, desperate to keep Robert in therapy, wrote to Blue Cross and asked them to consider covering Dr. Plummer as a one-patient-only provider. Amazingly, Blue Cross agreed.

Brenda breathed a sigh of relief when she received the insurance company's response. Immediately, she remembered, "What is impossible with men is possible with God" (Luke 18:27). She had felt so tired and weak since Robert had arrived that she often felt unable to pray. When she did feel up to it, her prayers were jumbled, frantic cries for help, not the peaceful communion Brenda had experienced in the past. Even so, Brenda knew God would help her through this mess. Wouldn't He?

*A*S TIME PASSED, ROBERT GRADUALLY BEGAN TO IMPROVE. He joined the track team and started getting involved in the church youth group, even attending a Christ in Youth conference. His therapy sessions also helped, and he opened up gradually, as if he were peeling away layers of his onion-skin shell. All of this began to contribute to a slightly less sullen, more active teen.

Though he was making some positive changes, Robert was still far from easy to live with. He continued to test Brenda, challenging every bit of authority she wielded. One evening, he went into a rage while trying to convince Brenda that he should be allowed to get his driver's license so he could drive up to Grand Haven, three hours away, and see his old friends. Brenda immediately said no. She and Chuck had told Robert that he had to pull his grades up to a C average before he could get his license. Brenda's no didn't stop Robert, though. For two hours, he brought up every argument possible.

Finally, he threw up his hands in frustration. "I don't have anything else to say!" he yelled at his aunt. "I've said all I can think of."

Brenda eyed her nephew through her glasses, holding her ground. "You probably have, but the answer is still no," she said, folding her arms. "Sorry, Robert. You're not going to change my mind."

A "no" answer was never acceptable to Robert, especially when it came from Brenda. He angrily stomped his foot. "Fine!" he roared. "I'm going to go live somewhere else! I'll call my other aunt and uncle!"

"Okay, Robert. Go call them," Brenda said tiredly. She knew now that it was better to agree with him than try to shield him from the pain of his relatives' rejection. Still, she felt deeply sorry for him when his other aunt and uncle coldly refused to take Robert in. Brenda knew it was for the best, but she hated to see her nephew go through that pain.

$\mathcal{T}$HE STRESS OF HAVING TO CARRY HER FAMILY'S EMOTIONAL and spiritual problems all by herself soon began to take its toll on Brenda. She and Chuck hadn't been able to get away by themselves for months, and this neglect of their relationship began to affect their marriage. Brenda couldn't bring herself to leave Robert alone with the kids because he was too unpredictable, and she didn't want Ryan, Stacy, or Brett to be responsible if anything happened. Brenda couldn't justify hiring a baby-sitter for her teenagers, either.

Desperate to do something, Brenda pleaded with Chuck to ask his siblings if they could spend an evening with Robert once in a while; she and her husband needed some time alone to reconnect. With seven brothers and sisters, that would mean each would have him only one night every few months. But only two agreed to help, so Brenda rarely got the breaks she needed.

Exhausted, she was constantly on the brink of tears. Church especially released her emotions. It was the only place she was able to sit quietly and not have anyone disturb her or clamor for her time. Embarrassed by her delicate emotional state, Brenda would purposely arrive late for Sunday morning service so that no one would talk to her before the service. Sitting in a back pew, she would weep silently, hoping that her glasses would hide her tears. Then as soon as church was over, she'd rush out the door, praying that no one would stop her.

Please, please don't anybody talk to me today, she'd often think, veiling her tears with her hand. *I don't think I can do that superficial small talk today. I just can't pretend everything's okay right now.*

Though she was surrounded by God-loving people, Brenda had never felt more alone in her life. Even God seemed far away. Her time with Him didn't give her the peace she craved. And her needs so overwhelmed her that many times she couldn't put her prayers into words.

One afternoon, driving home from work, Brenda started to cry as she turned the corner onto their street. *I can't go home,* she thought in despair. *I know what's waiting for me there, and I just can't do it.* She felt as if she were a single soldier having to fight thousands of enemy troops alone. She just couldn't cope anymore. Pulling into the driveway, Brenda turned off the engine, leaned her head on the steering wheel, and wept. *God, where are You?* she cried, tears running down her face. *You promised not to give us more than we can handle—and I can't handle this anymore.*

Brenda lifted her head and looked at the house, trying to muster the strength to go inside. *Good grief!* she admonished herself. *Robert may be causing you a lot of anxiety, but he's still God's child!* Sighing heavily, she opened the car door and trudged inside.

Brenda was certain of one thing: Something had to change—and soon.

*B*RENDA LAY ON THE EXAMINING TABLE IN THE DOCTOR'S office a few weeks later, trying to keep from crying out as Dr. Wahl poked and prodded her belly. It was the summer after Robert had come to live with them, and during the past couple of months, Brenda had been going to her doctor frequently. Her jaw clenched as she recalled the conversations she had had with him about her symptoms—chest pains, swollen glands, and headaches. He insisted that they were the result of too much stress and that she needed to simplify her life. Brenda had wanted to ask him how she was supposed to do that. She had too many people depending on her, both at home and at work, to cut back.

Dr. Wahl pressed her belly one last time, then sighed. "Brenda," he said, helping her sit up and rearrange the sheet around herself, "you have a hernia, probably among other things. We're going to have to schedule surgery." As he left the room so she could get dressed, he told her bluntly, "Enough is enough, Brenda. You need to get your life under control or you're going to end up in the morgue."

Ten days later, Brenda was admitted to the hospital for surgery. Her doctors decided that since they were already opening up her abdomen, they might as well take care of anything else that needed to be done, too. It was fortunate that they examined her further because Brenda had three large gallstones; the surgeons also decided to remove her appendix as a precaution. She'd been under so much stress for so long that she'd gotten used to the pain.

Brenda awoke in a stupor the day after her surgery, and it took some time before she was alert enough to talk. Her surgeon came to see her soon after.

"Brenda," he told her seriously, "your body's natural resources have been depleted by the tremendous amount of stress in your life. Your red blood cells didn't come to fight for you after your surgery because they're all worn out. We had to give you oxygen and two units of blood." Her immune system had become too weak to fight for her.

As Brenda lay recuperating in her hospital bed, her doctor's words pounded in her head: *You need to get your life under control.* But how would she do that? She couldn't just kick Robert, the major source of her stress, out of the house. *Lord, help me find other ways to cut back,* she prayed. *Help me in my anxiety.*

Brenda stayed in the hospital for seven days—four days longer than she had originally planned—and it took her three weeks to recover completely. During that time she needed help doing everything. She couldn't drive, go up or down stairs, sit up or lie down, or even tie her shoes or lift her head. But God was faithful to Brenda's prayers for rejuvenation; and as He slowly began to heal her body, He also started to heal her spirit—first by revealing that she needed to change her focus.

Years earlier, Stacy had encouraged Brenda to start a journal, but she had never been faithful about writing in it. Now that she was lying on her back, unable to do much after her surgery, Brenda began journaling every day. As she prayed and wrote, Brenda realized that her prayers were all one-sided and repetitive. For many months she had been continually asking the Lord to help her and her family, but when was the last time she had prayed for her grandmother, her friends at work, or the people on the prayer chain at church? Brenda shook her head as she realized that all her entries had a "poor me" quality.

You're probably getting tired of hearing the same thing from me every day, God, Brenda told the Lord ruefully. *I've got to let go of my self-ishness and let You work in my life the way You want.*

Seeing her petitions to God on paper helped Brenda remain focused on others and on what the Lord's will was in a given situation instead of on what her own desires were. Journaling also showed Brenda that the Lord was answering her prayers faithfully—just not always in the specific way she wanted.

Brenda started to write down her blessings, too—five each day. It was an idea she'd gotten from a television talk show hostess. It was so easy to be absorbed by her problems that she often forgot to thank God for His gifts. *Thank You, Lord, for bringing us to Dr. Plummer, who's done so much to help Robert,* she journaled one day. *Thank You that Robert just brought home his first A. Thank You for snow. Thank You for the family at our church that donated the mattress.*

As Brenda began to write to the Lord and spend time with Him, quietly listening to what He was telling her to do, the peace she desired seeped into her heart. Her circumstances hadn't changed, but her relationship with God had, and that made all the difference.

The following months of prayer and praise marked only the beginning of Brenda's process of spiritual, physical, and emotional rejuvenation. Almost a year after her surgery, she heard about a women's conference through the Focus on the Family newsletter.

Renewing the Heart? Brenda thought, reading the small blurb at the end of Dr. Dobson's newsletter. It sounded intriguing, like something she needed—to have her heart renewed. More than anything, however, it presented a perfect opportunity for Brenda to take a vacation.

She wasted no time sending in her application, along with those of her mother and sister-in-law Barb, and they soon got their tickets. When the day finally came for them to begin the 10-hour drive to Nashville, where the conference was to be held, Brenda was ready . . . to rest. Barb drove, and Brenda's mother rode in the front passenger seat. Brenda was content to burrow into a nest of pillows and blankets on the backseat. She felt like a battle-weary soldier leaving the front lines for a long-overdue leave.

When the women entered the arena in Nashville, Brenda couldn't wait to hear the speakers. Patsy Clairmont broke through all of Brenda's barriers with her humorous yet poignant message that women are "emotionally wealthy" and when their hearts overfill with their emotions, their mouths speak. Laughing until tears rolled down her face, Brenda wondered how her family members would react if she told them to "bug off in Jesus' name." It was good to laugh away the frustrations of life.

After Patsy was finished speaking, the women broke for lunch, and Brenda, her mother, and Barb went to the Hard Rock Café. The restaurant was noisy and packed with tourists and women from the conference. Suddenly, a small group of women began to sing "Amazing Grace." As more women from the conference joined in, the raucous restaurant music was turned off and the room grew quiet as everyone listened. Brenda closed her eyes, letting the women's rich voices soothe and refresh her. It was an incredible moment she knew she'd never forget.

Back at the conference, Eva Self was the next speaker, and she proved to be the one who made the most impact on Brenda. As Eva spoke about the difficulties she'd experienced with her mother, and the emotional problems, including suicidal thoughts, that her disability had caused her, Brenda sat transfixed. She felt as if Eva were speaking directly to her, as if she were the only one in the auditorium.

God prepared her message just for me, Brenda thought in awe. Turning to her mother, who was sitting next to her, she whispered emphatically, "Mom, Eva's talking about Robert!"

Brenda saw many similarities between the beautiful woman on stage and her nephew. Like Eva, Robert also had a disability, only his wasn't as visible as Eva's. Like Eva, Robert had attempted suicide. Just as Eva's mother had struggled to raise Eva, so Brenda struggled with Robert. It was encouraging for Brenda to realize that Eva's mother had nurtured her daughter and set boundaries in her life—and as a result, Eva had become a gracious, eloquent, God-fearing woman.

Would Robert one day blossom and mature the way Eva had? Brenda wasn't sure, but Eva's testimony gave her the hope she desperately needed that eventually he could.

"*H*EY, BATTER BATTER, HEY, BATTER BATTER, HEY!" BLUE JAYS fans hollered from the bleachers in their attempt to make the opposing team strike out. It was a warm spring day in Shepherd, Michigan, and Brenda and her family were lined up in the stands eagerly watching the game. Clasping her hands tightly together, Brenda prayed that the visitors would strike out soon, because Robert would be the first of his team to bat.

After much hard work, Robert had made the varsity baseball team as a junior and had earned what he'd been longing for ever since he'd moved in with the Packers almost three years before: a varsity jacket.

Robert had made some marked improvements in the past year. He and Chuck had similar interests, and Robert had begun spending time with his uncle in the garage, working on cars and fixing things. Robert's therapy sessions, in particular, were also productive. Just last week, he'd admitted that since he'd come to live with Chuck and Brenda, he'd probably grown up five years. When he'd moved in with the Packers, his emotional state had been that of an eight-year-old. Brenda had hugged him after that breakthrough comment, saying warmly, "Now we've got to grow you up five more years in the next year, Robert." They had only one year left until Robert would graduate from high school and go to college, should he choose that route.

Shading her eyes with her hand, Brenda spotted Robert in the outfield, his slight frame shifting nervously back and forth.

Robert still wasn't perfect. He continued to bring in poor grades—right now he was barely passing English simply because he wouldn't hand in his homework. A solid C student, Robert had the ability to do better but lacked the discipline.

Brenda had learned to cope more effectively with her nephew since her time at the Renewing the Heart conference. She didn't try to fight the battle alone anymore. When she returned from Nashville, she had started a women's Bible study in her church, and the ladies prayed for and supported one another. This encouragement had enabled Brenda to help others, too—particularly women sitting in the back pews who tried to hide their tears behind their glasses and who exited early. She wanted to comfort those who felt as if nobody cared.

Brenda cupped her hands together and yelled, "Go, Blue Jays!" The other team was finally out, and in a few minutes, Robert would be up to bat. She watched, smiling, as he ran in from the outfield and picked out a bat. His pale face, as always, was serious as he completed his practice swings. His sober countenance had presented a problem for him when he'd recently gone out looking for jobs. At the end of the first day, Robert declared that he didn't want to work anywhere that required him to act cheerful or smile. Brenda had teased her nephew, saying that those requirements would limit his future to being a mortician or an IRS agent.

The baseball crowd, however, didn't mind Robert's solemn attitude. As he walked to the plate, the stands went wild with cheering and applause. Many of the moms and dads had "adopted" Robert as one of their own, taking every opportunity to pump him up.

Stacy put her fingers in her mouth and whistled loudly. "Go, Robert!" she shouted.

Brenda leaned forward and concentrated on her nephew as he took the first swing. His bat made a loud *crack* as it connected solidly with the ball. Robert dropped the bat and began running to first base. The crowd cheered loudly. Suddenly, Brenda squinted in surprise. If she wasn't mistaken, there was a hint of a smile on Robert's usually grim lips.

Brenda felt a wave of peace come over her. Robert still had a long way to go—but she could see a considerable change in him for the better.

And God would take care of the rest.

Brenda Packer lives with her family in Mount Pleasant, Michigan, where she works for the Central Michigan District Health Department, conducting vision and hearing tests in the schools. Her nephew Robert continues to mature. He has joined a debate team, is an active member of their church youth group, and is working at a local fast-food Italian restaurant. Robert hopes to go to college and live at home with either the Packers or his maternal grandmother. Brenda attests that though the road has been bumpy, Robert is now an integral part of the Packer family—and for that, she's extremely thankful.

Heart to Heart

The verse that kept coming to mind as I read Brenda's story is Galatians 6:9: "Let us not become weary in doing good, for at the proper time we will reap a harvest if we do not give up." The most difficult aspect of that verse for me is the "at the proper time" part. Sometimes I think things would be so much easier if God would accomplish His will according to my timetable. If it were up to me, trials and tribulations would be much shorter and less painful. My idea sounds good until I realize that with my timetable, there would be no need for faith, and the subtle lie of self-sufficiency would quickly poison our hearts. "When a good man is afflicted, tempted, or troubled with evil thoughts, then he understandeth better the great need he hath of God, without whom he perceiveth he can do nothing that is good" (Thomas à Kempis, *The Imitation of Christ* [Chicago: Moody Press, 1980], p. 43).

Walking by Faith ~

Lisa

STORY SIX

Holding on to Hope

May the God of hope fill you with all joy and peace as you trust in him, so that you may overflow with hope by the power of the Holy Spirit.

—ROMANS 15:13

"*N*ICKIE!" B<small>ETH</small> R<small>OBISON</small> <small>CALLED OUT, OPENING THE DOOR TO</small> her stepdaughter's room early one February morning. "Nickie, are you up and ready to go?"

Twenty-year-old Nickie had her long, blonde hair flipped over, and she was blow-drying it. She stood up quickly, and the blood rushed to her face, coloring it the same hue as her pink, embroidered angel sweatshirt.

"Oh, I'm up," Nickie said hurriedly. "I've got to be at the bookstore before 8:00 this morning to do inventory." She raced around the room, humming as she put on her gold cross necklace, angel earrings, and watch.

Beth smiled as she studied her daughter. Nickie, who had been on the dean's list all through college, had taken the spring semester of her sophomore year off to plan her wedding, which was in April, only two months away. She'd gotten engaged two years before to Rob, a youth pastor, and now was working at the local Christian bookstore.

"Well, I need to be leaving with the boys soon myself," Beth said, checking her watch. Her southern accent was thick. "I just wanted to make sure you were up—I know how you like to sleep in."

"That's for sure." Nickie looked up from tying her tennis shoes. "Oh, Beth, by the way—happy fortieth birthday!" she said joyfully, a twinkle in her blue eyes.

Beth flushed happily. "Why, thank you, Nickie," she said warmly. "You're the first person who's said that to me today." The Robisons would be celebrating that night as a family, but it still made Beth feel special that Nickie had made a point of remembering.

Beth left Nickie's basement room and walked back up the stairs. *Lord, You have blessed me to be Nickie's momma,* she told God gratefully. *Thank You for that girl.*

Beth and her husband, Donnie, had gotten full legal custody of his daughter, Nickie, when she was 12 years old. Nickie had grown up moving from place to place with her mother, and because she wanted and needed stability, she had always begged to come live with her dad and stepmom. Kentucky law dictated that once a minor turned 12, the child could give input about whom she wanted to live with. So when Nickie turned 11, her mom allowed her to move in with Beth and Donnie. Nickie's mother had been ready to move again, and she had known that in a year Nickie would ask to go live with her father anyway.

Beth poured herself a cup of coffee and sat at the kitchen table, reflecting. For the first few years, it had been difficult for Beth to suddenly have a teenager in the house. For one thing, her eldest son, Matt, was only five years old, and Beth was pregnant with her second son, Luke. Soon after she and Donnie got custody of Nickie, Luke was born, and all of a sudden Beth went from being the mother of one to being the mother of three.

At the same time, Nickie hadn't been used to the strict rules in her father's house, and she often put up a fuss about doing homework and obeying curfews. But as Nickie got involved in school activities, she matured. She discovered that she was talented at playing the flute, and she joined the band. The discipline of practicing and the group of friends she became involved with had a positive influence on her, and Nickie began to blossom.

It's amazing how much she's developed, Beth thought, sipping her coffee. Now Nickie was always asking Beth questions about the Bible. And as she strove to grow in her own faith, she unknowingly challenged her stepmother to dig more deeply into God's Word. Nickie was also a good influence on her brothers. Beth knew she didn't need to worry about Matt and Luke getting into trouble because they both idolized Nickie and wouldn't do anything that would displease her. Everyone in the family agreed that Nickie was a joy, and they couldn't imagine life without her.

Suddenly, Nickie rushed up the stairs and into the kitchen, breaking into Beth's reverie. "Oh, I've got to get going!" Nickie said breathlessly. She flung open the refrigerator, gulped down a glass of orange juice, and took a sweet roll for the road. Nickie flashed a wide smile at Beth. "Have a fun day!" she said, grabbing her winter coat. "I'll see you later tonight at dinner, when we celebrate your birthday." Her blonde hair streamed out behind her as she ran out the door and closed it behind her with a *bang*.

Twenty minutes later, Beth gathered 14-year-old Matt and nine-year-old Luke into their white Jeep Cherokee and prepared to leave for school, about eight miles away. Beth worked as a speech pathologist for the local school system, and conveniently, the elementary and middle school buildings where she worked and where the boys went to school were located on the same campus—allowing her and the boys to ride together.

Inside the Jeep, Beth turned on the heater. Her fair, round cheeks were rosy from the cold. As she waited for the car to warm up, she gazed out the window, drinking in the beautiful scenery around her. Patches of snow covered the 40 acres of land around the Robisons' log-cabin farm, located outside of Harrodsburg, Kentucky. Beth could see the sky lightening toward the east through the branches of the trees lining the property.

"Did you guys get enough to eat this morning?" Beth asked Matt and Luke as she drove down their long gravel driveway through the woods.

Both boys nodded.

Beth turned the Jeep onto the main road, then braked at a stop sign. The wheels slipped a little on the ice. She shuddered as she clicked on her turn signal. "The roads are frozen from the rain we had last night," she said, looking in her rearview mirror at Matt and Luke. "Are you boys buckled up?"

"Yeah, Mom," Luke said, his face ruddy under his winter hat.

As Beth pulled onto Highway 152, the rear end of the Jeep slid. She cranked the steering wheel in the opposite direction and quickly regained control of the vehicle. She realized the highway was covered with black ice.

"Oh, gosh!" she said nervously. "It's very slick. I'm going to have to go really, really slow."

Hunched over the steering wheel, Beth inched along the

road, going only about 20 mph. *We'll be fine as long as I'm careful,* she told herself. *We're just going to creep into town.* As she slowly made her way around a bend in the road, she spotted flashing lights. Beth caught her breath. "Somebody's been in a wreck!" she said to the boys.

A blue car was crunched up against a tree, and a wrecker was trying to wrench it free. Beth could see only the passenger's side, but it looked as if the impact of the crash had crumpled the driver's side all the way to the steering wheel. Glass had showered the highway. A sheriff's car was parked in the middle of the road, its lights blinking in the early morning sun.

Matt stared out the window, his blue eyes glued to the accident scene. "Mom, is that Nickie's car?" he suddenly shouted. "Is that her car?" He looked wildly at his mother.

"Oh, no, Matt," Beth told him calmly. "It couldn't be." *Nickie's car doesn't look anything like that,* she thought. But as she inched the Jeep closer to the accident, her heart stopped. On the top of the backseat by the rear window lay a tiny red fire bucket. Beth gasped. Rob, Nickie's fiancé, had teasingly given her that fire bucket because her old car had caught on fire. Fortunately, Nickie had been all right, and now it was one of her and Rob's inside jokes.

Beth shuddered, her eyes fixed on the red bucket. "It *is* Nickie's car!" she said aloud. *But where is she?* she thought, panic rising in her throat. *Where is my daughter?* Nickie was nowhere to be seen, and the only cars on the road were theirs, the sheriff's, and the wrecker's.

When he heard his mother confirm what he'd suspected, Matt screamed, "No!" and jumped out of the Jeep while it was still moving. Skidding on the ice, he ran over to the patrol car, which was trying to turn around to leave the accident.

"That's my sister's car!" Matt cried frantically, waving his arms to stop the officer. "Oh my gosh! That's Nickie's car!"

Inside the Jeep, Luke sat whimpering in the backseat as he stared at the scene unfolding before him.

Feeling as if she were in a terrible nightmare, Beth pulled

alongside the sheriff's vehicle and rolled down her window, looking past a wildly pacing Matt to the sheriff.

"Are you Mrs. Robison?" the sheriff asked through his open window.

"Yes," Beth said hoarsely. Even under her bulky wool sweater, she was shaking.

"Is this your daughter's car?"

"Yes," she said, trying to swallow the lump rising in her throat. "Where is she?"

"She's been taken by ambulance to Haggin Memorial Hospital in town," the sheriff said, his expression serious. "Ma'am, we've already had numerous accidents on this road this morning—it's a solid sheet of ice. Please be careful trying to get to the hospital."

"Okay," Beth whispered, then waved her son back into the Jeep.

Matt climbed into the car, next to Luke. Tears streamed down the boys' white, fear-stricken faces as they huddled together, praying.

"Lord, please help Nickie," Matt prayed, his lips quivering. "God, please take care of my sister."

Luke sobbed, clutching his older brother's arm. "Don't let her be hurt, God," he whispered. "Please don't let Nickie be hurt."

Beth drove cautiously along the slick highway. *The doctors will take care of her at the hospital,* she told herself. *They'll fix Nickie up in no time.* She glanced at Matt and Luke huddled pathetically in the backseat.

"Boys, everything is going to be fine," Beth said, trying to reassure herself as much as them. "Nickie's going to be okay— just wait and see."

ETH PARKED THE JEEP AT HAGGIN MEMORIAL HOSPITAL AND then, trailed by Matt and Luke, ran into the emergency room. They were met by the paramedic unit that had brought Nickie into town.

Beth approached the head paramedic, who was the father of one of her speech students. "Mike, where's Nickie?" she asked worriedly. She tried to read the man's face. *They're probably getting ready to fix her up,* Beth thought. *I'm sure Nickie just has a couple of broken bones.*

Mike cleared his throat and looked solemnly at Beth. "We're getting ready to airlift her to the University of Kentucky Medical Center in Lexington," he said gravely. "There's no need for you to rush into the hospital. It'll be a while before the doctors can tell you anything or let you see Nickie. You might want to make some phone calls."

"Oh." Beth felt as if the floor had dropped out from under her. *Airlift her? To Lexington? That's 40 miles away.* Beth felt her heart begin to pound and sweat start to trickle from her armpits. *Nickie must be in serious condition,* she realized.

Beth numbly walked over to a hospital courtesy phone, only a dozen feet from the emergency room, where the paramedics were preparing Nickie for transport. Shaking, she leaned against the wall and dialed her husband at work. "Donnie?" she said quickly when he answered.

"Hi, honey. What's wrong?"

"Nickie was in a bad car accident," she explained. "We're at Haggin Memorial Hospital right now." Beth closed her eyes, gripping the receiver. "I haven't seen her, Donnie, and they haven't told me anything about her condition yet."

Donnie's voice was reassuring. "Don't worry—Nickie'll be fine. I'm leaving the office right now. I'll be there in 15 minutes."

After Beth hung up, Wendy, an ER nurse she knew, helped her make phone calls to Nickie's fiancé, Beth's church and school, and the bookstore where Nickie worked.

As Beth talked on the phone, a paramedic pulled Luke over to the side and gave him a teddy bear, trying to calm the boy down. For several minutes, Matt stood alone, watching his mom make phone calls and whisper to the nurse. His knees shook as he began to pace the hospital floor.

Another ER nurse noticed the situation and approached

Matt. "Excuse me, but is that your sister they're talking about?" she asked gently.

Matt looked at the nurse with anguished eyes. "That's not just my sister," he told her, blinking hard to keep from crying. "Nickie's my best friend." With a choked sob, he turned away and pressed his face against the wall.

Several minutes later, the paramedics brought Nickie out of the emergency room to board the helicopter.

A doctor came over to Beth. "Ma'am, Nickie has severe head and possible chest injuries and some broken ribs," he said. "We can't have you ride in the helicopter with her—there isn't room. But you can see her briefly right now."

Beth nodded, her voice sticking in her throat. *Head and chest injuries? It must be really bad.* Things were happening so fast, she could hardly take them all in. She pushed past the doctor and ran over to Nickie. Matt and Luke watched motionless as their sister was wheeled out on the stretcher.

"Oh my goodness!" Beth gasped upon seeing her daughter.

Nickie was covered with a sheet from the chin down. Several IVs and monitors hung from her body. Her face was scratched and sallow, and blood trickled from her right ear. *Oh, that doesn't look good,* Beth thought as she saw the blood. *Nickie must be so scared. I need to reassure her that everything's going to be okay.*

"Nickie honey," Beth said tremulously, "hang on. You'll be all right. You're getting into a helicopter, and Daddy and I will come straight to Lexington to meet you at UK." Beth didn't know if Nickie could hear her—her big blue eyes were shut, and her face showed no signs of understanding. Beth leaned over and carefully kissed Nickie's cool cheek, then backed away from the stretcher and watched as the paramedics loaded her into the helicopter.

Stunned, Beth wiped the tears from her eyes. *I can't believe this,* she thought in despair. *How can this be happening to Nickie? She's such a servant. She's done so many wonderful things—and I love her so much. Why are You allowing this, God?* she prayed, looking heavenward. *Why?*

Beth could only hope and pray that God would give Nickie the strength to hang on to life until she got to the hospital.

ETH, DONNIE, AND MATT ARRIVED AT UK MEDICAL CENTER a few hours later—Luke had decided to stay with Nanny and Pa, Donnie's parents, who lived in Harrodsburg. When the Robisons checked at the desk and identified themselves, a hospital chaplain pulled them aside and brought them to Nickie's room.

Nickie lay motionless on a hospital bed with dozens of tubes and monitors hooked up to her. Beth felt sick to her stomach as the chaplain began to pray over her daughter.

His prayer was devastatingly final. Touching Nickie's forehead, he rested his hand on her temples and said, "Lord, we thank You that Your infinite wisdom is best. May Your will be done, Father. No matter what the outcome, Lord, be with Nickie Robison's soul. Amen."

As Beth watched, she felt the blood drain from her face. Feeling faint, she grabbed Donnie's arm. The doctors obviously didn't think Nickie was going to make it or they wouldn't have sent the chaplain there. *We've lost her,* Beth thought numbly. *But we need Nickie here! How will we go on without her? What will we do?* She knew that if Nickie died, their family would never be the same.

After the chaplain left, Beth walked over to Nickie and touched her cheek softly. "Nickie honey, we love you," she said. "And we'll be with you through every minute of this."

"You can make it through this, baby," Donnie said, looking lovingly at his daughter.

A few minutes later, a nurse came to the doorway. "Mr. and Mrs. Robison," she said kindly, "you and your family will need to leave now. You'll have to wait in another room." She motioned for them to follow her.

The room to which they were led was even smaller and more stark than the one they had left. The nurse asked them to wait there for the doctors to update them on Nickie's condition. They weren't alone long before the pastors from their church, Southside Christian, showed up to wait and pray with them.

After the group had spent an hour or so sitting, praying, and staring at the walls, an ER doctor came in. He greeted everyone before sitting on a metal folding chair. "We don't know if Nickie will make it," he told Beth and Donnie quietly. "She has severe head trauma. We're doing all we can, but we'll just have to wait and see. The first 72 hours are critical because her brain could swell. If it does, she'll probably die." He stood up, nodded to the family, and left the room.

Beth was speechless. *I can't deal with this, Lord,* she told God silently. A sob caught in her throat, and she buried her face in her hands.

Donnie put his arm around her. "Honey, Nickie's a fighter," he reminded her. "The word 'quit' isn't in her vocabulary. She'll make it."

"She has to," Matt whispered, speaking for the first time in almost an hour.

Beth simply closed her eyes, wishing she could wake up from this nightmare.

After a few minutes, Sam Stow, the youth minister, broke the silence. "Why did Nickie leave for work so early this morning?" he asked. "She doesn't usually have to be at the bookstore until much later."

Beth swallowed before saying, "For inventory—"

"No, Beth," Donnie interrupted her. He put his hand on her knee. "We just told you that," he said gently, "because she was going to your school this morning to deliver some doughnuts. She'd planned a surprise birthday party for you, and all the teachers were going to be there."

"Oh my goodness!" Beth said hoarsely. "If Nickie hadn't gone out for my birthday . . ." Her voice trailed off as the horrifying thought sank in: *It's all my fault. This happened because of me.* "I need to get out of this room," she said. Dizzy with an almost physical pain, she walked back into the waiting room. Donnie, Matt, and the ministers followed.

But God's mercy rested on the Robisons. Over the course of the day, almost 200 people from Harrodsburg dropped by to support the family and pray for Nickie. People Beth didn't even know came to the hospital with gifts for Nickie and the family. Many times that day, Beth greeted someone and wondered, *Now, who is this?* Twenty-year-old Nickie had made a powerful impression on countless people in their community. Family members, church people, friends, school personnel, ministers from their church, and several other pastors whom Nickie had known through her work in the bookstore came to the hospital.

Maryann, Nickie's close friend and the owner of the Christian bookstore at which she worked, brought the Robisons a journal from the store. "Beth, there have been so many people here for Nickie, it's unbelievable," she said. "When Nickie recovers, she'll want to know who came to support her. I think you should have each person who visits write something to her."

Beth agreed to the idea. The journal quickly began to fill up with touching notes to Nickie. When Beth read the following entry from a friend of Nickie's, she wept:

> Nickie,
>   I miss you so much. I keep thinking of all the great times we had together and the wonderful things you have done for other people. You are an angel on this earth. Thank you for all the love and care you have shown my family. Believe it or not, I am praying for you.
>
>   Love,
>   Brian

Beth clutched the journal to her chest. The words Nickie's friends, family members, and nurses had written were priceless to her. She could only hope that her daughter would one day be able to read these tributes herself.

Rob arrived that afternoon from Paoli, Indiana, where he was a youth pastor, to stay with Nickie and the family. As always, he was upbeat and optimistic.

"Nickie's going to be fine," he told Beth and Donnie fiercely, pulling his California Angels baseball cap over his brown, curly hair. "I'll push her down the aisle in a wheelchair if I have to, but we're getting married in two months."

"I hope so," Beth said, her voice shaking. *I wonder if she'll be alive in two hours,* she thought, *let alone be able to walk down the aisle.*

Rob and the five other ministers—David Upchurch, Sam Stow, Gary Powell, Dave Miller, and Dave Scalf—stayed at the hospital in shifts, so the Robisons continually had at least one pastor to sit, cry, and pray with them as they waited to see if Nickie would live or die. Beth found great comfort in having the various ministers by their side. Their presence reminded her that God was in control of Nickie's condition, even when Beth didn't feel that He was. The ministers prayed that God would do what was best for Nickie—whether it was to take her home, bring her back to them, or sustain her.

Late in the evening of the day of Nickie's accident, after the Robisons had been at the hospital for more than eight hours, Nickie's doctor came into the waiting room and sat on a bench across from Donnie and Beth. "Good news," he said. "Since Nickie's made it this far, we're going to transfer her to intensive care. This is a step up for her."

Grateful sighs erupted from the friends and family surrounding the Robisons.

"I knew she'd keep fighting," Donnie said forcefully.

"Oh, thank the Lord," Beth murmured.

The doctor looked wearily at them. "As I told you before, the first 72 hours are critical. We'll have to wait and see what happens."

Around midnight, Beth, Donnie, and Rob got ready for

bed. The rest of their family and friends had all gone home. Beth washed up in the hospital bathroom and shuffled to her "bed" on the floor. She and the others slept restlessly that evening, wrapped with blankets and leaning against the pillows their friends and family members had brought them.

Around 7:00 Saturday morning—the day after Nickie's accident—the head of neurology brought more promising news.

"Mr. and Mrs. Robison, your daughter is still alive," he said, shaking his balding head in amazement.

Rob broke into his characteristic lopsided grin, his dark eyes showing his relief. "See?" he said joyfully. "Nickie's going to be okay."

Donnie let out a huge sigh, then tearfully hugged Beth. "That's wonderful!" he said, his deep voice cracking. "How is she doing?"

The neurologist frowned. "Well," he said, "she's barely hanging on at this point. She has some brain damage, and her brain is swelling rapidly—a development that we're trying to avoid." Then he told them bluntly, "We need your permission to put Nickie in a drug-induced coma to slow down brain activity and stop the swelling. If we don't do it, she'll die within a few hours." He looked from Beth to Donnie, waiting for their reply.

Beth turned her tearstained face up to Donnie and nodded her approval.

"Of course you can induce the coma," Donnie said, pulling Beth close to his side. "We'll do whatever it takes to save Nickie."

Beth buried her face in her husband's broad chest. *Nickie's in critical shape,* she thought, *but she has only 48 more hours to go until she's passed the 72-hour mark. Lord,* she prayed, *please let Nickie make it.*

Beth and Donnie called their church and informed the pastor of Nickie's latest development. Pastor Upchurch assured the Robisons that the following morning, Sunday, the entire congregation would get on its knees and pray that Nickie's brain would stop swelling.

That Sunday morning, during the middle of Southside's second service—two days after the accident and one day after the doctors induced the coma—Nickie's brain stopped swelling. By Monday morning she had passed the critical 72-hour mark. Donnie and Rob excitedly went to call the church with the good news, and Beth slumped, relieved, into a waiting-room chair. So many people had been praying for Nickie that Beth knew her daughter's progress was the result of divine intervention.

After more than 48 long, difficult hours, Beth and Donnie felt it was important that Luke and Matt resume their normal activities, particularly school, as soon as possible. Beth knew it would be hard for the boys to be at home, not knowing what was going on with their sister, but she wanted them to get on with their lives. Beth's parents, who had moved into the Robisons' house until the crisis passed, planned to bring the boys up to Lexington twice a week to visit Nickie.

Beth was truly exhausted, both emotionally and physically. She, Donnie, and Rob hadn't left the hospital once since they'd arrived two days before. Nickie's condition was so serious that they hadn't want to risk making the 40-mile trip home, even for only a few hours. Donnie's twin brother, Tommy, had noticed their predicament, and that afternoon he approached them.

"You guys really need a place to rest up," he said. "Why don't you let me call the Campbell House, and I'll get you a room there?" He was referring to a nice hotel about two blocks from the hospital. Putting his hand on his brother's back, he continued. "Donnie, you, Beth, and Rob go freshen up and take a nap. I'll stay right here and call you if anything changes."

Beth gave her brother-in-law a quick hug. "Oh, thank you, Tommy!" she said. "We really appreciate it."

That afternoon and evening, Beth, Donnie, and Rob went to the hotel in shifts to rest and clean up. Having the room available was wonderful for Beth, who'd been washing up in the hospital bathroom for two days. Their hotel was so close to Nickie that Beth felt she could leave to go take a bath, wash her hair, brush her teeth, and sleep for a few hours—without worrying that she'd miss some important development in her daughter's condition. She knew that if anything happened, someone at the hospital would call her.

The next morning when Beth went to the front desk to check out of the room, the clerk refused to accept her key. "Mrs. Robison, you don't need to check out," he said with a smile. "You're paid up for a week."

"Really?" Beth asked, surprised. *I'll have to thank Tommy for this when I see him,* she thought. When she returned to the hospital, she dialed her brother-in-law's number. He and his wife had gone home late the night before. "Tommy," Beth said, "Donnie, Rob, and I are so grateful for the room. I can't believe you paid for a week. You've been so kind to us! Thank you."

"Don't thank me," Tommy said with a laugh. "Someone else must have found out you needed a place to stay and covered the room for a few more days."

Beth hung up the phone, shaking her head in amazement. *Wow!* she thought. *I just can't believe how wonderful people have been to us. Thank You, Lord!*

God continued to take care of the Robisons through the generosity of His people. Each time Beth tried to check out of the hotel at the end of a week, the clerk told her the room fee was covered for another week. She never did find out who was paying for it. And the room wasn't the only thing provided. People offered to do chores, and Donnie's dad and friend David fed the livestock back on the Robisons' farm. Friends and family also brought flowers, cards, books, food, coolers of soda, Christian music, and money for the Robisons. Beth often found cash stuffed into her coat pockets or purse. After a while, she stopped keeping track of who had given what. There was too much money pouring in, and half the time she didn't know who it was from. People loved and sympathized with the family, and as Donnie summarized, adversity had rallied their friends, family, and community together.

Beth was extremely thankful for everything, especially the

extra cash. Donnie would have to return to his job as a leadman in a factory welding shop as soon as his four weeks of vacation were used up, and Beth knew that when her three weeks of accrued sick time ran out, she would be taking unpaid time off from work to be with Nickie. She was thankful that the school system was letting her take a leave of absence, but it also made finances tight.

"You know, Donnie," Beth tearfully told her husband one day after finding another $20 bill stuffed into her coat pocket, "if it weren't for everyone's generosity and prayers, I don't think I'd be able to keep going." People were truly sustaining her—when Beth felt unable to pray, the ministers of her church petitioned the Lord for her.

No one at the hospital, however, ever held out much hope. During the week after Nickie's accident, Beth, Donnie, and Rob met with the neurologist early each morning for an update on Nickie's condition. The doctor always reminded them that Nickie wasn't doing well and made dire predictions about her prognosis.

One morning, four days after the accident and three days after Nickie had been put in the drug-induced coma, the neurologist tried to take her off the drug. Again, her brain began to swell. When Beth heard this news, she was terrified. *Put her back under,* she thought desperately. *Put her back under or she might not live.* She pulled distractedly at her closely cropped, black hair. *Dear God, will I ever have my daughter back again?* she prayed.

Donnie, seeing the fear in Beth's soft brown eyes, drew her closer to him, inviting his wife to rest her head against his shoulder. "Honey, it'll be okay," he said reassuringly. "We'll just start the process again. God will take care of Nickie—and Nickie won't give up. She'll be weaned from the drug just fine."

Three days later, the doctors tried once again to wean Nickie from the drug. It had been one week since the accident and six days since Nickie had been put in the coma. Beth was prepared for the worst. The longer Nickie was in the coma, the harder it would be for her to come out of it; yet without the drug, Nickie's brain could swell again. This time, however, Nickie's brain didn't swell, and the hospital staff was able to take her off the drug. The next day, Saturday, the ICU nurses tried to awaken Nickie by pinching her and giving her response tests to see if she could squeeze their hands or move her head.

On Sunday, nine days after the accident, the neurologist approached Beth and Donnie in the waiting room. "Nickie's in a stage two coma," he said dispassionately. "That means there's only a slight response to pain stimulus." Clasping his hands in front of him, he looked directly at the couple. "Nickie's not brain-dead," he said, "but we don't think she'll ever be able to carry on normal functions like breathing and coughing. You should get ready for organ donation."

Organ donation? Beth thought, horrified. *Lord, what are You doing?* she prayed.

Donnie remained optimistic. "Well," he told the doctor, "we have faith that God can heal Nickie. The Lord has brought her this far already, and we know He has a purpose for her life. We believe we're going to see a miracle."

A flicker of impatience passed over the neurologist's face. "I know what you believe. I believe, however, that she'll probably never be weaned from a respirator." Immediately he sighed, as though regretting his outburst. Looking at the floor, he said tiredly, "I'm just trying to prepare you folks for the inevitable." Then he got up and abruptly left the room.

A week and a half after the accident, the neurologist began to wean Nickie from the respirator to see if she could breathe on her own. Beth, Donnie, and Rob sat nervously in the waiting room, fidgeting on the plastic-covered chairs.

This is it, Lord, Beth said silently to God. *Please make Nickie breathe.* But her prayer was hollow because she didn't really believe that Nickie would make it. After all, that's what the neurologist had said, and he knew more about these things than she did. Beth closed her eyes and tried to control her anxiety. The doctor had said it would take three days for them to know for certain if the process had been successful.

Despite the neurologist's gloomy predictions, Nickie soon surpassed his expectations. To the doctor's disbelief, three hours later, Nickie was off the respirator and breathing by herself.

"I knew she'd do it!" exulted Rob as he jumped up from his chair. "That's my Nickie!"

Beth looked over at her gregarious future son-in-law and smiled for the first time in days. *Nickie's going to be okay,* she told herself, relieved. *Now she's not hooked up to any machines except the feeding tube.*

Although the neurologist continued to minimize Nickie's chances for resuming normal activities, Beth finally began to feel hopeful. For the past 10 days, Nickie's condition had been life or death. But now she was breathing on her own. *The Lord has brought Nickie this far,* Beth thought. *He can totally heal her if that's His will.*

For the first time since arriving at UK Medical Center, Beth believed her daughter might be healed. She conceded that things would probably never be the same with Nickie—she might have to learn to speak or walk again—but Beth now trusted that God would restore Nickie to them.

Determined to trust in God's healing power, Beth and Donnie wouldn't allow the neurologist's grim prognosis to take away their hope. Whenever they couldn't visit their daughter, they went to the chapel to pray, listened to praise music, or talked about the Lord to other families in the hospital. They also read their Bibles and pored over their book of couples' devotions, all brought from home by friends on the day of the accident.

The tragedy hadn't torn the Robisons' marriage apart, as often happens in crises. Rather, Nickie's accident had brought them closer together. True, Beth's naturally pessimistic perspective on life sometimes clashed with Donnie's optimism, but they had learned to support each other instead of arguing about Nickie's condition. Often while sitting anxiously in the waiting room, Beth thanked God that Donnie was with her.

As they encouraged each other and prayed together, some of the people they'd befriended at the hospital showed interest in what they were doing. Experiencing traumatic circumstances themselves, these individuals desired the faith and hope Beth and Donnie displayed. When they began to ask if they could sit in on the Robisons' devotions, Donnie and Beth welcomed them warmly, thankful that God was using Nickie's accident to allow them to tell about His power, hope, and love.

In her own way, Nickie was also a witness for the Lord, even as she lay motionless in her hospital bed. The number of people who came to visit her, bringing gifts and praying, did not escape the notice of Nickie's nurses. As cards, flowers, money, and people poured into her cubicle, her nurses commented that they'd never seen anyone receive as much love and support as Nickie had. They were overwhelmed by the kindness, encouragement, and assistance that people gave the family.

Three weeks after the accident, Nickie was moved from the intensive care unit to a semi-private room on the eighth floor of the hospital, where a staff of nurses again tried to awaken her. Though Nickie yawned, sneezed, and showed some response to pain stimuli, the neurologist said those were only reflexive actions—not enough to move her from a stage two (response to pain stimulus) to a stage three (response to verbal command) coma. Three more weeks went by, and Nickie still showed no progress. Finally, the hospital recommended that she be transferred to Cardinal Hill, a rehabilitation facility across town, where she could continue her recovery.

When Nickie was moved to Cardinal Hill, Beth and Donnie decided they'd better check out of their hotel for good. They needed to return to their jobs, and the rehabilitation staff had made it clear that they were not to stay in the facility with Nickie. "You cannot spend the night here," the head nurse at Cardinal Hill had said to Beth. "Don't you worry—we'll take good care of Nickie. But you need to go home."

"All right," Beth had agreed reluctantly, her throat tight.

She hadn't been away from Nickie since the accident occurred six weeks before. It was hard for Beth to let go and leave her daughter in the care of strangers, but rules were rules. She and Donnie would have to be content driving up to see Nickie after work and on the weekends. They also decided that Rob, who'd taken a leave of absence from his church, would live with them in Harrodsburg until Nickie recovered.

After Nickie was settled at the rehabilitation facility, Beth, Donnie, and Rob prepared to leave Lexington. With her duffel bag over her shoulder, Beth walked to the front desk at the Campbell House and handed the clerk their key. She still couldn't believe they hadn't had to pay for even one night of their stay there.

"Mrs. Robison," the clerk said warmly as he took her key, "I just want you to know that in all my years in the hotel business, I've never seen anything like your situation. Your family has received so much love, it's incredible."

"I know that," Beth said softly.

The clerk opened the cashier's drawer, counted out several bills, and handed them to Beth. "Ma'am," he said, "I've got to give you a refund because you have several days left. People have paid for you to stay here through next week."

"You're kidding!" Beth said, raising her dark eyebrows in surprise as she took the money.

After shaking the clerk's hand and bidding him good-bye, Beth left, her heart filled with gratitude. *Lord*, she prayed, *You have provided so much for us. Thank You.*

*F*OR ALMOST EIGHT WEEKS, NICKIE REMAINED AT THE Cardinal Hill rehabilitation facility in Lexington. With the staff of skilled and caring nurses, Beth and Donnie felt confident that Nickie would regain consciousness quickly. They believed Nickie had improved so much since her accident that God would eventually heal her completely—that He wouldn't stop working until He'd restored her mind and body. Maybe she wouldn't be exactly the same, but with some therapy, Nickie would be able to live a normal life and get married.

But that didn't turn out to be the case.

Nickie and Rob's wedding date came and went while she was still at Cardinal Hill. Rob had learned all of Nickie's therapy exercises and knew all the nurses there. Sensitive to the engaged couple's circumstances, the nurses dressed Nickie up on the day she and Rob were supposed to be married: April 22. They put makeup on her, curled her hair, and dressed her in one of her prettiest nightgowns. Beth and Donnie and Rob's parents came to the facility that day, and it was a bittersweet time for all of them. Rob sat at Nickie's bedside, lovingly holding her hand.

"There'll be another wedding date," he told her, still unable to think his sweetheart of five years might not recover. "You'll get better, Nick. I know you will."

*N*ICKIE'S EYES SLOWLY OPENED AT CARDINAL HILL—BUT that was about the only progress she made in therapy. It was still impossible to tell if she had an awareness of the people around her, since she couldn't communicate in any way. Eventually, the nurses suggested that the Robisons take Nickie home to continue her therapy.

"Many head injury patients do much better in familiar, more comfortable surroundings," the head nurse told Beth, Donnie, and Rob. "Try it out for one day, and see if it's a possibility. If you can handle it, Nickie might recover much more quickly at home."

The Robisons readily agreed to this, and Rob even offered to take care of her as well. By the end of the day, however, Beth was emotionally and physically exhausted. She was forced to concede that she and Donnie were not equipped to care for Nickie by themselves. *What if we give Nickie the wrong medication?* Beth thought worriedly. *Or accidentally hurt her when we rotate her to keep her from getting bedsores?*

The next day, Beth and Donnie brought Nickie back to

Cardinal Hill. "We can't take care of her at home," Beth told the head nurse, her voice trembling with tears. "It's just impossible." Beth hung her head in shame. *I've failed,* she thought. *I can't even care for my own daughter.*

"Oh, Beth, I'm so sorry," the head nurse said sympathetically. "We're going to have to transfer her, then," she added with a sigh. "To stay here, Nickie has to make substantial gains."

Beth nodded, biting her lip. Nickie had undergone two months of intensive therapy, and she hadn't progressed much. The reality was devastating.

A week later, Beth and Donnie moved Nickie to Pathways, another facility in Louisville that cared for severe head injury patients. This move was extremely difficult for them because Pathways was even farther away from Harrodsburg than Cardinal Hill—almost two hours' driving time. Also, Nickie had received excellent care at Cardinal Hill, and Beth had become friends with many of the nurses there.

At this time, Rob decided to move out of the Robisons' house and into his parents' home near Louisville so he could be close to Nickie. When Rob moved out, the Robisons felt an additional void. Rob had been such a part of Nickie's life that his presence had comforted Beth, Donnie, and the boys. Now he was gone. For a few weeks, he continued visiting Nickie at Pathways, but slowly his visits became less frequent, until he almost stopped going to the facility altogether. When Beth and Donnie saw the hope fade from Rob's eyes and his smile gradually disappear, they knew that Rob had finally accepted that Nickie might never get better and that he needed to move on with his life.

The transition was excruciatingly hard for everyone, but it occurred at just the right time. School was out, so Beth was able to drive up to see Nickie almost every day during the summer. She and Donnie made sure one of them visited their daughter every day so that she would never be left alone—and neither would Matt and Luke at home.

Being at home without Nickie was emotionally wrenching for Beth, who cried constantly. It was hard not to set five places at the table, and Beth missed the way Nickie used to light up the room with one of her boisterous stories or generously help one of the boys with his homework. Lying in her bed at Pathways, Nickie was alive physically, but her personality was gone—and, at times, the memory of how her beloved, charming daughter used to be was too painful for Beth to bear. The day she moved Nickie's wedding invitations and bridal dress into the attic, she passed by Nickie's empty basement room several times. At one point, she went into the room and looked at several family photos Nickie had placed on her dresser. As Beth traced Nickie's smiling face in one of the photos, a heavy sadness consumed her. *Will I ever have a reason to laugh again?* she thought dismally. *Will this family ever be happy again?*

She knew that Donnie and the boys were trying to deal with their pain, and she didn't want to add her own suffering to theirs—so she prayed constantly. *Lord, help me through this,* she often pleaded with God. *I know You can do anything. You could heal Nickie if that's Your will. I don't know what Your will is, but I do know that I need Your love and comfort right now.*

Donnie didn't express his pain as openly as Beth did. In fact, often he seemed simply to go through the motions of life. Almost every day during the summer, he got up, went to work, and then drove straight to Louisville to visit Nickie for a few hours. By the time he got home, it was 10:00 or 11:00 at night, and he would just fall into bed, exhausted.

Matt and Luke went through difficult adjustment periods as well. Matt, the mature, quiet one, grieved silently. If he ever questioned God or had bitter or angry feelings, he never expressed them.

"This is God's will, Mom," he would tell Beth when she had had a particularly hard day accepting Nickie's situation. "This is the way God planned it. Sometimes things like this just happen." Frustrated, he'd look at his mother and say, "I wish you wouldn't cry anymore."

Luke, on the other hand, was very open with his emotions, even in front of his parents. During the summer after Nickie's accident, he often sat in his room with the photo album open, weeping over his sister's pictures.

"God *has* to heal Nickie," he'd say, his blue eyes filled with tears. "He wouldn't let her stay in a coma forever!"

"You just keep praying for your sister," Beth would tell Luke, smoothing down his dark hair.

Even as the Robisons struggled to handle their grief, God continued to remind them that He did, indeed, have plans for Nickie's life. The Lord was still using her to affect the people around her.

One summer day, when Donnie had driven to Louisville to see Nickie, a nurse in the facility stopped him in the hallway.

"Donnie," she said, her brown eyes wide, "Brian Coleman's father is in with Nickie right now. He said he wanted to thank her for saving his family."

Donnie stared at her, dumbfounded. "You're kidding!" he said.

Nickie had dated Brian in high school before she met Rob, and they had remained good friends after they broke up. At that time, Brian wasn't a Christian, and neither was anyone else in his large family. Nickie had always tried to keep Brian accountable for his actions and tell him about God. *How could his whole family have been saved?* Donnie wondered. *Nickie hasn't been able to talk with Brian or the Colemans in months.*

When Donnie walked into Nickie's room and saw Larry Coleman, he was amazed. Larry's entire countenance had changed. It seemed as if the lines in his face had been erased and replaced with a peaceful, joyful expression. He smiled when Donnie asked him about the strange news.

"Yep, you heard right," he said in his southern drawl. "Just last month, my whole family accepted Jesus as our Savior, and now we're going to church every Sunday." Larry looked sympathetically at Donnie. "Nickie was always so genuine," he said. "She witnessed to us all the time. We could tell that she lived all those things she talked about. Her example changed our lives. She's the reason we all became Christians."

"That's great!" Donnie said happily. He turned to Nickie, who was lying motionless on the hospital bed. "Did you hear that, baby?" he asked. "Isn't that terrific?"

"I wanted to make sure I told Nickie about it, and I also wanted to tell you or Beth. Nickie did so much for us," Larry continued. "I figure the least I can do is visit her in Louisville once a week." And he did. Every Saturday afternoon that summer, Larry made the hour trip into Louisville to see Nickie.

Yet sadly, by Labor Day, Nickie's condition still hadn't improved, and the facility recommended that she be transferred to a nursing home. This was heart-wrenching for Beth. She felt as if moving her daughter into a nursing home would be admitting defeat. *Nickie's not getting better*, Beth realized despondently. *And we all need to accept it.*

Never had Beth entertained the thought that Nickie might need to receive around-the-clock care. In fact, sometime after Nickie's accident, one of Beth's friends who was a nurse had mentioned the possibility to her, and Beth had immediately dismissed the idea.

"Are you kidding?" she'd said to her friend months ago. "Nickie's going to make a full recovery! She's going to get married soon! You'll see—she'll be back to normal in a few months!"

And at UK Medical Center, after Nickie had gotten through the critical stages in her condition, the Robisons had all believed she'd recover completely. It had been beyond their comprehension to think that God would bring her from the brink of death and then leave her in a comatose state.

But now Nickie was going to a nursing home. The stark reality of it made Beth feel sick. *My once healthy, vibrant daughter is going to be in a nursing home, Lord,* she told God miserably. *Why is this happening?*

To make things even more difficult, Nickie was covered by Medicaid and had to be placed somewhere that accepted that particular insurance. The only guarantee Medicaid offered was that Nickie would be put in a home within a 100-mile radius of Harrodsburg.

One hundred miles! Beth thought weakly. *How can we do this? How can we let Nickie move to some strange place where she doesn't know anybody?*

Feeling utterly powerless, Beth and Donnie went down on their knees and asked God to intervene in the situation and place Nickie somewhere close to home. At least if she were nearby, they could see her frequently and still continue living their lives, as they knew Nickie would want them to do.

Two weeks later, on a Friday afternoon, God gave them their answer.

 $\mathcal{T}$ HAT FRIDAY, SHORTLY AFTER SHE ARRIVED HOME FROM WORK, Beth pulled out the vacuum cleaner and began to clean. She had left the vacuum cleaner humming noisily while she put Matt's football jersey and Luke's tennis shoes back in their rooms when she heard the phone ring.

Racing back into the family room, Beth turned off the vacuum cleaner and grabbed the phone on the end table next to the couch.

"Hello?" she said breathlessly.

"Is this Beth Robison?"

"Yes," she replied. *Who is this?* Beth wondered, contracting her dark brows.

"Ma'am, this is Carol from the Harrodsburg Health Care facility," the woman on the other end of line said, referring to their community's local nursing home. "We have a letter here from one of our employees, Vickie Caudill, telling us about your daughter, Nickie, and her condition. We have a bed to offer her if you're interested."

Beth's mouth dropped open. Vickie was a member of Southside Christian Church. Though she didn't know Vickie well, Beth was aware that she had been praying for Nickie—

and now Vickie had been her daughter's advocate once again. Beth's eyes filled with joyful tears. "We certainly are interested," she said, trembling with excitement.

"Well, we're going to be closing to visitors in a little while. But if you want to see if the room meets your standards, you're welcome to come," Carol said brightly.

"Thank you, Carol," Beth said. "Donnie and I will be there as soon as he gets home from work." Hanging up the phone, Beth fell to her knees, weeping with gratitude. *If Nickie's in Harrodsburg,* she thought, *we'll be able to see her all the time. Lord,* she prayed, *please let this work out.*

Donnie arrived home from work an hour later, and Beth met him excitedly at the door. "Donnie," she cried after greeting him with a big hug, "we have to run up to the nursing home. They've got a room for Nickie!"

When Beth and Donnie walked through the doors of the Harrodsburg Health Care facility, Beth began to weep again. The rooms were clean, bright, and cheery, and from what she saw, the patients were well cared for. When she and Donnie talked to Carol in person, the woman told them more about Vickie's letter.

"Vickie wrote a beautiful tribute to Nickie, describing her character and her Christian faith," Carol told them. "When we read it, we had our admissions director go to Louisville to evaluate your daughter. He approved her to come." Smiling broadly, she added, "We're so glad we can offer Nickie a room."

"So are we," Donnie said happily, a smile lighting up his face. "We'll take it."

They filled out the Medicaid paperwork the next afternoon, and the matter was settled. On the drive home, Beth, her heart filled with thankfulness, gazed out the window. Their lives had been so unsettled for so long. Because she and Donnie had continually been driving up to see Nickie, it had been months since they had both been at the supper table with Matt and Luke. *Now we can run by and see Nickie after school and work, just to give her a hug,* Beth realized happily. *Then, if we want to go back later that night, we can do that, too.*

For the first time in six months, the entire Robison family would be in the same town again.

❧

"HI, NICKIE," BETH SAID, WALKING INTO HER DAUGHTER'S room several weeks after Nickie had been moved to the Harrodsburg facility. "It's good to see you." She bent over and kissed Nickie's pale forehead.

It was just a year after the accident, and Nickie's appearance had changed. Her blue eyes, once so clear and full of life, now darted aimlessly around the room from under half-closed lids; her confident, wide smile was now slack and twisted; and her strong, shapely body was soft and round from lack of use. Her beautiful blonde hair had been pulled back in a ponytail. Gently stroking Nickie's hair, Beth remembered how scrupulously her daughter had cared for it.

"How would you like a nice French braid?" Beth asked, sitting down by Nickie's wheelchair. Taking a comb from the drawer of the nightstand, Beth released Nickie's hair from its clasp and, supporting her daughter's head, began to braid it. It was one of the many things Beth did that she knew Nickie would appreciate. She also often played praise music, sang to Nickie, or filed and painted her nails.

Today, however, Beth wanted to talk with her daughter. Holding Nickie's dark-blonde locks with one hand while she combed through them with the other, Beth tried to swallow her emotions. Sometimes it was difficult for her to see Nickie and not be bombarded with memories of how their relationship had been before the accident. *I remember when we were planning her wedding,* Beth thought sadly. *Everything was so exciting, and we were always discussing the invitations or flowers or cake.* Coming to the end of the braid, Beth fastened it with the clasp and then laid it gently over the edge of Nickie's wheelchair. *If only I could chat with her again,* she thought dismally.

Beth shook her head, trying to clear away the poignant memories. Turning to Nickie, she began to speak. "Nickie honey, I saw Brian Coleman the other day, and he said to tell you hi and that you need to get better. He misses you. Can you believe his whole family got baptized? And that his daddy is a lay preacher now? Honey, it's all because of you!" Beth said it emphatically, hoping to elicit a response from Nickie.

Nickie didn't move a muscle.

Beth continued talking. She tried to keep Nickie updated on everything—from her friends and family to happenings in the community—but she was never sure if Nickie could hear her. Sometimes Nickie would twitch, cry, sneeze, cough, or slightly move her arm, but her responses were never consistent.

For the next hour, Beth read to Nickie from her student Bible and talked to her. Some days it was comforting to visit Nickie, but today it tore at Beth's heart to see her youthful daughter in a nursing-home bed. She placed Nickie's hand in hers and held it for a few moments, looking at her through a veil of tears.

"Nickie darling, if you can hear me, squeeze my hand," Beth said urgently. It was a technique the family had often tried.

Nickie's blue eyes were focused on another area of the room, and she gave no response.

Beth let out a choked sob. "Dear God, what is Your purpose for my girl?" she whispered, looking up at the ceiling. "Lord, please help me to accept Nickie's condition. Sometimes I don't think I can go on like this." She knew she was fortunate to have Nickie nearby, but that didn't make Nickie's condition any easier for her to accept.

OVER TIME, THE ROBISON MEN BEGAN TO HEAL. MATT AND Luke spent a lot of time with Sam, Southside's youth pastor. Sam had been a good friend of Nickie's, and his counsel and attention helped the boys deal with their grief. Donnie started going to Promise Keepers conferences, and Matt and Luke began attending Christ in Youth conferences with their church youth group each summer. These conferences made a significant impact. Beth noticed that all three of them had become more patient and emotionally stable and less irritable. Things that had bothered them before, such as Matt's losing a baseball game, Luke's getting into a disagreement with a friend, or Donnie's car breaking down, were taken in stride. Their newfound calmness extended to Nickie's situation, and Beth sensed a refreshing peace in them.

Seeing the difference in her husband's and sons' lives, Beth decided that when she had an opportunity to go to a women's conference, she would attend. Two and a half years after Nickie's accident, Beth heard about the Renewing the Heart conference through her church. Desiring to be encouraged and revitalized, she immediately sent in her registration. *Maybe Renewing the Heart will help me with my grief,* she told herself.

A few months later, Beth made the six-hour drive to Nashville with a group of women from her church. The conference turned out to be just what she needed. Beth was energized by the presence of so many God-fearing women, but when Dr. James Dobson made a special guest appearance, she was especially thrilled—Dr. Dobson had always been one of Nickie's favorite speakers. Nickie had listened to him on the *Focus on the Family* broadcast and had read many of his books. Beth felt blessed to hear him speak, and she wished Nickie could be there with her.

When Eva Self was wheeled onto the stage to give her testimony, Beth's heart stopped. Eva had been in a car accident as a teenager and was paralyzed from the waist down. *That could be Nickie someday,* Beth realized, her soft brown eyes moist. *Nickie could speak at conferences, too. She's got something to tell and something to share.* Eva's presence was comforting to Beth—a reminder from God that Nickie's life in the nursing home wasn't in vain. As Beth listened to Eva speak about how God had worked through her own difficult experiences, Beth realized that the Lord could work a miracle in Nickie's life, just as He had in Eva's.

Beth returned from the Renewing the Heart conference late

that night, eager to tell Donnie about her time there. She sat down on the bed and poked her husband in the arm. "Donnie," she whispered, "are you awake?"

Donnie groaned and pulled the covers more tightly around himself.

"Donnie!" Beth whispered, louder this time. Pushing against his back, she rocked him gently. "Wake up!" she insisted. "I have to tell you about Renewing the Heart."

Finally, Donnie rolled over and looked dazedly at her. "Huh?" he said.

"Renewing the Heart!" Beth emphasized. "It was amazing."

As Donnie tried to focus on what his wife was saying, she began to tell him about her exciting day. When she got to Eva Self's testimony, Beth began to cry. "Donnie, Nickie has such an incredible story, just like Eva does. She's changed so many lives—the Colemans; the nurses from Cardinal Hill, who still send us Christmas cards telling us to hug Nickie for them; the children from church, who still tell me they pray for her . . ." Beth trailed off, wiping her eyes. "God is still working through our girl," she said softly.

Donnie pulled himself up and leaned against the head-board. "I know, honey," he said. "If we had buried her three years ago, no one would be mentioning her name now, and nobody's prayers would be going up for Nickie Robison." He stroked his chin contemplatively. "And if that's the only reason people are praying, at least they're praying."

"Donnie, hearing Eva's story today reminded me that God has a plan for Nickie," Beth said eagerly. "I know He hears all those prayers for her. For some reason, Nickie has her ministry in a nursing home right now, but it's exactly where God wants her to be." She grabbed a pillow and leaned against Donnie's broad chest. "Nickie's story needs to be heard, too. She could encourage others with her testimony."

"Honey, if God wants her story to get out, it will," Donnie told her simply.

"Oh, I know," she agreed.

And after seeing Eva Self at the Renewing the Heart conference, Beth really believed it to be true. She knew God could do anything—if only it was His will.

"*S*ILENT NIGHT, HOLY NIGHT, ALL IS CALM, ALL IS bright. . . ."

On Christmas Eve one year later, Beth and her family were gathered at the Harrodsburg Health Care facility, as they had gathered the past two Christmas Eves, to celebrate the holiday with Nickie. Clad in a new Christmas sweater, with her blonde hair pulled back in a ponytail, Nickie sat passively in her wheelchair. Her head was tilted back, as though her neck muscles were too weak to support it; and her blue eyes, under half-closed lids, darted restlessly around the room. She seemed oblivious to the family members singing around her.

Beth bit her lip as she surveyed her daughter. *If only Nickie could talk again,* she thought, her eyes filling with tears. *I wish I knew that when I tell her I love her, she really hears me.* As her family continued singing, Beth looked heavenward and silently pleaded, *Lord, if You're not going to heal her, take her home to You.*

Beth uttered that prayer often. Although she had healed a great deal since attending the Renewing the Heart conference, she still struggled to accept her daughter's condition. She continued to feel as if the Robisons were in a long, dark tunnel, and the light at the end would be either Nickie's physical healing or her going home to God. Only when she looked at the big picture—what God's purpose for Nickie might be—was it easier to handle the possibility that her daughter might remain in a coma for the rest of her life. Since Nickie had touched so many people's lives in her current state, maybe that was God's plan for her. But life in a nursing home wasn't what Beth desired for her daughter—so she continued to pray for a miracle.

It hadn't been easy for any of the Robisons to handle Nickie's condition. But they had all been faithful to her, coming to see her often. Luke had recently given a school report on his

"Most Prized Possession" and had brought a photo of Nickie taken before the accident. This photo, which he kept in a prominent place on his desk at home, was his dearest treasure.

Matt had organized a prayer group that went to the nursing home every Tuesday night—rain, snow, or shine. Each week, the group would hold hands around Nickie as she lay on her bed, and they would pray for God to heal her.

Nanny and Pa, Donnie's parents, had been a godsend. Beth's heart overflowed with gratitude as she looked at the frail couple sitting in chairs near Nickie's bed and singing. Ever since their beloved granddaughter had come to stay at the nursing home, Nanny and Pa had come to visit her every afternoon from 12:30 to 3:30. They lived only two blocks from the Harrodsburg Health Care facility, so no matter what the weather conditions, they still came. In fact, the nursing-home staff had told Beth that if Nickie's grandparents didn't show up one day, they would call 911. Only an emergency would keep them from visiting Nickie.

Every day, Nanny and Pa made sure Nickie was taken out of bed and washed and dressed, and then had her lungs suctioned to keep her from getting pneumonia or other respiratory illnesses. Because of Nanny and Pa, Beth and Donnie didn't have to worry about Nickie's well-being. The elderly couple had truly made taking care of their granddaughter their ministry. Beth smiled tearfully at her in-laws. *I don't know what Donnie and I would do without them,* she thought. The time they'd spent with Nickie had given Beth the freedom to pour more time and energy into Donnie and the boys.

Beth looked around the room from one beloved face to the next. *Lord, You have truly given me a wonderful family,* she told God. Grabbing Donnie's hand, she resumed singing Christmas carols and let God's peace fill her in the sacredness of the night.

A few days before, Beth had been reading to her daughter from her student Bible and found a quote Nickie had written in the margin. It said, "If you don't see a miracle, expect a blessing."

For almost three years, the doctors had told the Robisons

that there was no hope for Nickie. But Beth believed they were wrong. She knew that where there is faith, there is always hope. If Nickie Robison isn't healed on this earth, she will be in heaven.

Beth Robison lives with her family in Harrodsburg, Kentucky, where she is a speech pathologist for elementary and middle-school students. Her daughter, Nickie, remains at the Harrodsburg Health Care facility in a semi-comatose state, and the Robisons visit her several times a week. Slowly, Beth and her family have learned to accept Nickie's condition by relying on God's grace and goodness. Beth attests that "the Lord will see you through anything if you just depend on Him." ·

Heart to Heart

A woman in our church recently had a baby girl. There are many babies born in our congregation every month, but this one was extra special because her mom and dad, Nancy and David, had been praying for another child (they have a little boy) for eight years. Everyone was overjoyed at this little girl's long-awaited arrival, especially her parents. They named her Hope. However, within a few days of her birth, Hope was diagnosed with a rare metabolic disorder for which there is no treatment. She will not live to see her first birthday.

I can't imagine the anguish and sorrow Nancy and David are experiencing. Yet, they wrote in their Christmas newsletter, "We know that God has a purpose for Hope's life that will be completely accomplished during her days on this earth." In the face of heartbreaking loss, they cling to their faith. They are sure of what they hope for and certain of what they do not see.

I don't understand why bad things happen to good people. Young women shouldn't be in devastating car accidents, and babies shouldn't be born with terminal illnesses. When tragedy strikes the innocent, life seems particularly harsh and unfair. But I am comforted by the knowledge that my finite mind cannot comprehend God's omniscience. I know that His ways are beyond my ways. And like the Robisons and Nancy and David, I firmly believe in God's sovereignty despite our circumstances and that His providence will not allow us to go where His grace will not meet us.

Walking by Faith ~

Lisa

Becoming Your Mother's Mother

*Dear friends, since God so loved us, we also ought to
love one another. No one has ever seen God; but if
we love one another, God lives in us and his love is
made complete in us.*

—1 JOHN 4:11–12

"*THIS IS AWFUL!*" JEANNETTE WIGGIN MUMBLED TO HERSELF, shaking her white, fluffy-haired head. "I looked in the filing cabinet, and the report's not there. Now, where could it be?" She held a pile of papers and a clipboard against her tiny, frail frame as she nervously paced the living room carpet. "I've got to find it," she mumbled distractedly. "I've got to find it."

Judy looked up from her fourth-grade students' English essays and raised her eyebrows, surprised to see her elderly mother in such a frantic state of mind. Judy had just driven up from Massachusetts, where she was a public school teacher in Lexington, to her childhood home in Sanford, Maine, for the Memorial Day weekend. Being an only child and unmarried, Judy usually spent the weekends and summers with her widowed mother, Jeannette. Judy's father had died almost 20 years earlier, but her mother, at 85 years of age, was unusually healthy and energetic, and Judy enjoyed spending time with her—they had a close relationship. They spent summer vacations together at their lake house, just seven miles outside of Sanford, and shopped, entertained, and went to church together. Jeannette's quick wit and engaging personality were refreshing to Judy.

"Judy, what am I going to do?" Jeannette repeated anxiously. Her knuckles were white against the papers she gripped.

Judy put down her pen. "Mother, it's almost 10:00 in the evening. What are you doing?" she asked, perplexed.

"I have to find the report for the women's club. We're being audited, you know," Jeannette informed her, her cheeks pink with frustration. As the treasurer for the Sanford Women's Club, she had to provide the IRS with an accounting balance. Jeannette had been the treasurer of her club for 20 years, but she'd never had to provide the IRS with information, and it was causing her great distress. Suddenly, a strange glint appeared in her eyes. The papers she was holding fell to the floor as she cupped her mouth with her hands. "Oh my!" she exclaimed through her fingers. "I've got to get the payroll ready for the insurance company! They're waiting on me."

Judy ran her fingers through her short, blonde hair. *Mother*

217

retired from the insurance company almost 20 years ago, she thought
worriedly. *What is she talking about?* It wasn't like her mother to
be muttering strange things. Concerned, Judy pushed her chair
back from the table.

"Mother, I'll help you look for the report," she said, ignoring
Jeannette's last comment. "We'll figure out the balance together."

Her mother's frenzied behavior had come on so quickly.
The sooner I can help her find the information, Judy thought resolutely, *the sooner Mother will be back to her normal self.* She followed Jeannette into the study and began searching the room,
pulling files out of cabinets, rummaging through drawers, and
scanning obscure folders.

Nothing turned up.

Finally, several hours later, Judy threw her hands up in the
air. "Are you sure we're looking in the right place?" she asked
her mother, yawning. She checked her watch. "Maybe we
should quit for the night. It's two o'clock in the morning. . . ."
Her voice trailed off as she gazed around the room. "Mother?"
Judy called out, frustrated. Jeannette had left the study.

A few minutes later, her mother returned, joyfully clutching
a roll of toilet paper in her small, wrinkled hand.

Judy stared at her. "What in the world are you holding that
for?"

"Here it is!" Jeannette exclaimed happily, clasping the toilet
paper to her chest. "I found it. It's $1.59! Now we can go to sleep."

Judy's mouth dropped open. *What's going on with Mother?*
she wondered nervously. *She's acting crazy.* Judy looked at her
mother holding the blue-flowered toilet paper, then answered
haltingly. "That's . . . good, Mother. Now, let's get you to bed."

Judy could keep looking for the missing report in the morning. By then, hopefully, Jeannette would be back to normal.

"*J*UDY, I DON'T HAVE THE TIME FOR THIS!" JEANNETTE
protested anxiously one morning a week later. She
stopped walking toward the doctor's office and peered up at

Judy through her spectacles. Her tiny feet were planted firmly on the parking lot asphalt. "I've got to find the balance. And do the payroll."

Judy gently pulled on her mother's arm, nudging her toward the office. "Now, Mother, you remember why I told you I made the appointment," she said calmly. "You've been complaining about not feeling well, and I wanted Dr. Frank to look at you." Judy had discussed her concerns about Jeannette—that she seemed to be out of her mind, and she wasn't getting better—with Dr. Frank, so he knew why they were really coming.

"Oh, yes," her mother said absently. Her brown eyes were glazed with confusion, but she walked obediently alongside her daughter.

Her heart in her throat, Judy glanced sideways at Jeannette. The day after the toilet-paper incident, she had taken her mother to the local IRS office to straighten out the accounting problem. Fortunately, they'd discovered it was an error—the IRS hadn't realized that the Sanford Women's Club was a nonprofit group and had mistakenly sent a notice to Jeannette. The agency apologized and assured them that Jeannette didn't need to provide the IRS with any information.

Afterward, Judy had left for Lexington, confident that things were okay. Jeannette was still talking to herself and acting distressed, but Judy had thought her mother would settle down after she caught up on her rest.

Yet as the week progressed and Judy talked with her mother on the phone, she realized that Jeannette was not doing well. Even though the situation was now resolved, Jeannette had continued to fret about finding the report for her women's club and preparing the payroll for her old insurance company—often staying up all night in a frenzy. Judy decided that the next time she was in Sanford, she would take Jeannette to the doctor.

I hope Dr. Frank can help Mother, Judy thought nervously as they headed toward the medical building. *Her delusional thoughts and constant chatter have gone on long enough.*

They were almost to the door when Jeannette suddenly halted and peered at something on the sidewalk. "Oh, look at that!" she said, stopping just outside the door to Dr. Frank's office. Feebly, she bent down and picked up a pebble.

"Mother, what are you doing?" Judy asked, confused. She gently pulled on the older woman's arm. "We're going to be late for our appointment."

Jeannette wasn't listening. She stroked the tiny stone with her fingers, staring intently at it. "That's the answer to the question," she said, gazing at Judy in wonder.

"Let's go inside," Judy said firmly. Not knowing what else to do, she simply guided her mother through the door, protectively pulling Jeannette's short form close to her tall, willowy one.

A few minutes later, Judy and her mother sat in a tiny room, waiting to see Dr. Frank. Jeannette was perched on the examination table, mumbling to herself. "Well, now, isn't this wallpaper nice?" she said softly, gazing around at the blue, patterned paper. "I'd really like to get some for my house. . . . Things are so expensive these days, though. . . . I remember back when your father and I were young . . . "

I can't believe Mother has gotten so bad, Judy thought, frightened. *I'm glad I brought her to the doctor.* She picked up a magazine from the rack next to her and absently flipped through it. *What if she's got Alzheimer's?* she thought, fighting back tears. *Why did this come on so suddenly? What's going to happen to her?*

"Good morning, Jeannette. Hi, Judy," Dr. Frank said, interrupting Judy's thoughts. He nodded to both women as he walked into the room.

Judy abruptly put down her magazine and greeted the doctor, then detailed her mother's strange behavior. The doctor listened, and after he examined Jeannette, he sat down in a chair, facing Judy.

"You'd better prepare for her to have long-term care in a nursing facility," the doctor told Judy quietly. He looked sideways at

Jeannette, who was off in her own world, quietly babbling to herself. "But for now, I want to hospitalize her for a diagnosis. I'd like her to be tested in Portland, where they have better equipment than we do here in Sanford."

"All right," Judy whispered, stunned. *Mother in a nursing home? In the hospital?* The thought made her stomach flip-flop. Her mother had always been bright, witty, competent, fun, and active in various clubs and women's groups. Now she was going to be placed somewhere unfamiliar because her mind wasn't functioning properly. It just didn't seem fair.

Judy turned to Jeannette. "Mother," she said.

Jeannette looked past her daughter, a fog in her eyes.

"Mother, Dr. Frank wants to have the doctors at the hospital check you," Judy continued, her voice choked with emotion. "I'm going to take you there now," she said with finality.

"Oh, okay," Jeannette said simply. She didn't appear to know what was going on.

The rest of the day passed in a blur. Judy gathered some of her mother's belongings together and checked her into the Sanford hospital that afternoon. The following day, Judy drove Jeannette to the Portland clinic. After a series of tests, the doctors could only tell Judy that her mother had suffered a manic-psychotic episode, a vague term that only told her what she already knew—that Jeannette was experiencing periods of paranoia, incessant talking, and hallucinations. No one could be sure when or if Jeannette would return to her normal self or even if medication would help her. Fortunately, however, the doctors informed Judy that her mother's condition wasn't related to Alzheimer's, because Alzheimer's disease didn't come on that rapidly.

The neurologist suspected that Jeannette's thyroid medicine might be causing her confusion and anxiety. He suggested that she return to Sanford, where Dr. Frank, who'd prescribed the medicine, could monitor her health. So the next day, Judy drove her mother back to Sanford, to the hospital there.

A thousand worries racing through her mind, Judy again

sat fretting in the waiting room, wondering what would happen to her dear mother. Jeannette had literally become a different person in the space of one week, and Judy was at a loss as to how to handle the situation. *If she needs to be institutionalized*, Judy thought, biting her lip, *how will we pay for the expenses? We'll probably have to sell the lake house, and maybe Mother and Daddy's home, too.* She and her mother had so many memories, both back home and up at the lake. The summer house, in particular, had been in her father's family for almost 80 years. Selling either home would be heart-wrenching.

Judy got up and began to pace the waiting-room floor. Memories of her mother flooded her mind. Jeannette had always been so hospitable, loving, and cheerful. In fact, she'd spent her life volunteering and counseling people. She had advised a sorority for 25 years, had been involved in the Sanford Women's Club for more than 40 years, and worked with numerous church committees. It didn't seem right that she was now losing her mental faculties.

Later that day, a hospital social worker approached Judy. "Hi, I'm Sue," the woman said brightly, smiling sympathetically. "I've been assigned to you and your mother. My job is to help you through this process, in case you need assistance in making decisions about Jeannette. If the medication they're going to try on her doesn't work, I can recommend some residential homes for you to check out."

"Oh," Judy said, still dazed. *I can't believe this is happening,* she thought numbly. *My mother is practically the only family I have.*

Sue toyed with a tiny gold cross necklace she was wearing. "Do you have a minister to talk to?" she asked, concerned.

The fog cleared from Judy's head. *A minister?* she said to herself. *Why didn't I think about calling ours?* She and Jeannette had gone to church faithfully every Sunday, and Judy had been baptized as a young girl, but that was about the extent of her Christian faith. The most she ever prayed was for a few minutes before bedtime—Judy hadn't often thought of leaning on

God. But never had she needed the Lord—and her pastor—as much as she did now.

Judy nodded at the social worker. "Yes," she told her, "we do have a minister. I'll call him right now."

Her pastor, Reverend Robert Stuart, agreed to see Judy that day, so when she left the hospital she drove to First Baptist Church in Sanford. Reverend Stuart had recently gone through a similar situation with his own mother, and his counsel was a comfort to Judy. He prayed with her, asking God for wisdom about what to do. He also reminded Judy that Jeannette's health was in the Lord's hands. Over the next two weeks, Reverend Stuart visited Jeannette in the hospital and encouraged her and Judy, praying for them and talking them through the crisis.

Through her minister's example and counsel, Judy was reminded to start calling on God. In the past, she'd sporadically told the Lord what she wanted, giving Him her list of requests. But now, for the first time, Judy felt nothing was in her control—she could only trust that God would hear her prayers and take care of her mother. Slowly, Judy learned to listen to what the Lord was telling her to do, and He started to guide her.

One prayer that Judy began to pray often was, *God, show me what I need to do. Also, please take care of Mother and do what's best for her, and help me to hear and understand what You're telling me.*

It was a relief for Judy to trust that the Lord would take care of the situation after she'd relied on herself for so many years. In doing so, she found God's peace.

Her minister's counsel and her own prayers helped sustain Judy through the next few days, while the doctors tried out many different medications on her mother, who was steadily getting more paranoid. Since Jeannette wasn't improving, Judy felt she couldn't leave her alone, even for short periods of time. The minute she left her mother's side, Jeannette got into trouble. The third day at the hospital, for instance, after Judy left to get some lunch, her mother picked up the phone in her room and dialed the police station.

"Hello?" Jeannette said loudly into the receiver when someone answered. "I want to report a crime. A man who calls himself 'Dr. Frank' has kidnapped me—and now I'm in a strange place." Her voice began to tremble with panic. "I need you to help me!"

"Ma'am," the voice on the other end of the line said, "can you hold on for a minute? I'm going to have an officer check out this situation."

The police sergeant put Jeannette on hold and informed his chief of the strange call. The police chief phoned Dr. Frank, who happened to be across the hall from Jeannette in the nurses' station.

The doctor got an earful. As he listened, he looked across the hall into Jeannette's room. She was sitting rigidly on her bed, with the phone in her lap.

When Judy returned from lunch an hour later, Dr. Frank pulled her aside and explained the situation to her.

Judy's mouth dropped open. "Oh, my!" she exclaimed. "My poor mother!" Rushing over to Jeannette's bed, Judy took the woman's small hands, saying, "Mother, you don't have to worry. Everything's going to be okay. These people are going to help you!" Her eyes filled with tears.

Jeannette just stared blankly at her daughter.

Dr. Frank, who'd been watching them from the corner, walked up to Judy and comfortingly put his hand on her shoulder. "You should go back to school," he told her quietly. "You're not helping your mother by being here—it's just hurting you to see her like this."

"Okay," Judy agreed reluctantly. Dr. Frank was right. She wasn't keeping her mother out of trouble or helping her state of mind.

Judy went back to her teaching job after three days at the hospital. The morning after she left Maine, Dr. Frank called her at her school, Harrington Elementary.

"In a few days, we're going to transfer Jeannette to another hospital, in Biddeford, Maine," he informed her. He paused, then said, "It has a good psychiatric facility, and that's where I think your mother needs to be. I've ruled out the possibility of the problem being her thyroid medicine, and I can't do anything more for her. The doctors there will be able to give her better treatment."

"Thanks for letting me know," Judy said despondently.

She hung up the phone and slumped into a chair in the school secretary's office. Covering her face with her hands, she thought, devastated, *My smart, kind, capable mother is going to be in a psychiatric ward! What if she doesn't get any better? Lord, help me*, she prayed. *I don't want to see Mother in a place like that.*

A few minutes later, Judy went to the rest room to try to pull herself together. The school bell would ring at any moment, signaling the beginning of the day. She needed to gather her emotions quickly. It wouldn't do to start weeping in front of a roomful of fourth-graders. Fortunately, Judy had many good friends among the faculty there, and by the time she left at the end of the day, she was feeling better.

When Judy got home, the phone was ringing. Ignoring it, Judy dropped her schoolwork on the counter and made herself a cup of coffee. She didn't feel like talking to anyone right now. What if it was more bad news again?

Ring . . . ring . . . ring . . .

The caller wasn't giving up, so Judy picked up the receiver and said hello, trying not to sound as tired and depressed as she felt. It was Gez, a close friend. In a quavering voice, Judy unburdened herself to her, explaining her mother's situation.

"Judy," Gez said resolutely, "I'm going with you to the hospital on Friday. I've been through this with a member of my own family, and I don't want you to go alone into a psychiatric ward. I know what it's like."

"Thank you," Judy whispered.

Friday afternoon, Judy left school early and, with Gez following in her own car, drove back to the hospital in Biddeford, where Jeannette had been transferred that day. Judy and Gez signed in at the front desk and then walked tentatively down the hall to Jeannette's room. As each door locked into place behind them, Judy's fears began to mount. *What will Mother be like? Will she even know us?* she wondered nervously. *Please, Lord,* she prayed quickly, *please let her get better.*

When Judy walked into Jeannette's room, she caught her breath. Her mother was sitting upright in her bed, scrutinizing a sandwich on her lunch tray. "I know they put something in here," she said, looking up at Judy. Jeannette picked up the bread and sniffed it, then began pulling apart the sandwich, layer by layer. "They want to poison me, you know."

"Mother, that's not true," Judy said, trying to calm her down. "The people in the hospital are trying to help you, not hurt you."

"Humph." Her mother folded her arms. She looked disdainfully at the tomato, turkey, lettuce, and cheese spread out on her tray.

When Judy beckoned Gez into the room, things got even worse. Jeannette didn't recognize her daughter's friend, whom she'd recently visited. She stared quizzically at Gez, then turned her attention to her nightstand. In the middle of the small table stood a bouquet Jeannette had received, and a dozen photographs were fanned out around the flowers.

"One . . . two . . . three . . . four . . ." Jeannette counted the pictures, from time to time sneaking a mistrustful glance over at her elderly roommate on the bed next to hers.

Judy found her voice, and she clutched Gez's arm, drawing her forward. "Mother, Gez and I have come to visit you. What are you doing?"

Her mother didn't even look up. ". . . five . . . six . . . seven . . ." she continued, ". . . eight . . . nine . . . ten . . . eleven . . . twelve." She sank back into the bed and clasped her hands together in relief, then looked up at her daughter and her friend. "They're all here," she said, childlike. "She"—Jeannette gave her roommate a dirty look—"will take my things if I don't count them every moment."

Gez looked sympathetically from Jeannette to Judy.

"Oh," Judy said hoarsely. Maybe it would be best if her

mother took a break from her roommate. "Well, Mother, why don't we get you out of this room and go sit in the dining area? That might give you a nice change of scenery." She closed her eyes, trying to regain her composure. *Don't let her see how upset you are,* Judy told herself firmly. *She won't understand.* Though she was able to hide her feelings, she couldn't push away a haunting thought: *Will Mother ever get well again?*

Jeannette stayed at the hospital for two weeks, and though the doctors couldn't find the cause of her illness, after several days they did find medication that helped her. Slowly, the paranoia and hallucinations stopped—but she was heavily medicated and would remain so. Even after leaving the hospital, Jeannette would have to stay on medication for about six weeks to control the dementia.

Fortunately, her mother's release from the hospital coincided with the end of the school year, and Judy was able to live at their lake house and care for her that summer. Jeannette's medication had to be monitored, which required trips back to the hospital every two weeks for blood tests. She also had to see the psychiatrist once a week. These regular visits to the hospital, along with her mother's foggy state, kept Judy busy. The medication made Jeannette dopey—she couldn't do her regular household chores, let alone take care of herself, and so Judy became her full-time caregiver.

By the middle of the summer, her mother had been weaned from the medication and was able to stay by herself during the day. Noting Jeannette's improvement, Judy began to talk with her about what they would do when school resumed.

"Mother, I have to go back to school in about six weeks," Judy told her one day. "What do we need to do to make you comfortable?"

Jeannette put down her crocheting. "Oh, I'm fine during the day," she said. "But I'm afraid to be alone at night."

"Well, then, we'll find someone to stay with you at night," Judy decided, "and I'll continue to visit you on weekends and holidays."

Judy prayed about the situation constantly. She called around and interviewed a few potential caregivers, but she didn't hire anyone right away. God hadn't given her peace about any of the prospects so far. A few weeks later, close to her departure date, Judy found out why. She was in the grocery store in Sanford, picking up a few necessities, when she spotted a familiar face in the produce section. She finished bagging the apples she'd picked out and dropped them into the cart before approaching the woman.

"Teresa?" Judy asked. She hadn't seen this friend for almost 30 years. As a teenager, Teresa had taken care of Mother after she'd had gallbladder surgery.

"Judy! How are you?" Teresa said, breaking into a warm smile. "How is your mother?"

"Actually . . ." Judy's voice trailed off. "Actually, she's not doing so well," she continued after a moment. "She's been in the hospital and on a lot of medication this summer." She rested her arm on the handrail of the grocery cart.

"Oh, I'm so sorry," Teresa said sympathetically. "I've got to come visit her."

The next day, Teresa showed up at the door, her arms filled with ears of corn that she'd just picked from her garden. Judy greeted her heartily and thanked her for the corn. When they sat down to talk, she told Teresa that she was looking for someone to stay nights with Jeannette.

"Mother's afraid to be alone when it's dark," Judy explained.

"Well, I could take care of her," Teresa responded immediately. "I've been looking for a job like this."

"Really?" Judy said. "That's wonderful!" She shook her head in amazement. *Thank You, Lord,* she prayed silently. *You've led me step by step through this whole process, providing for me and Mother.*

Teresa stayed with Jeannette for a year, enabling Judy to go back to teaching in the fall without worrying too much about her mother's well-being. As before, Judy called Jeannette throughout the school week, and she came to visit her on weekends, giving Teresa a couple nights off. The setup worked well, but after a year, Teresa decided to go back to school and become a nurse. Teresa's time spent caring for Jeannette over the past year had confirmed that nursing was the right field for her.

Judy pondered how she would handle her mother's care once Teresa was no longer available. After much prayer, Judy decided to move Jeannette to Lexington to stay with her during the week while she taught school, and then the two of them could drive home to Sanford on the weekends, so Jeannette would be in familiar surroundings for at least a few days. Judy had seen how difficult it was for her mother to be on her own—Jeannette was getting more and more frail—and she wanted to be closer to her. So Judy hired a caregiver to come to the apartment and stay with her mother for a few hours during the weekday afternoons so she could visit, have tea, or go for a walk. But it was still lonely for Jeannette, who wasn't doing much better. Although she didn't experience any more manic-psychotic attacks, she slowly became more and more forgetful and anxious.

She began to demand that Judy pull the shades down in the evenings so "people wouldn't see in." Then names of acquaintances began to slip her mind, and she began to forget to turn off appliances. Judy spent many days worrying that her mother would leave the stove on and burn the house down. At the same time, Jeannette became much slower at cooking. She couldn't figure out where things were, and she didn't understand how to follow basic recipes she'd used all her life. Soon Judy took over the cooking, and Jeannette washed the dishes.

Jeannette developed esophagus trouble as well, which often made her unable to swallow. Judy took her mother to a gastroenterologist, but the first medication the doctor gave her didn't seem to help. Several times Judy was called to the school secretary's office to answer a frantic call from Jeannette.

"Judy . . . my . . . food's . . . stuck," her mother would say over the line, crying and gasping for breath. "It . . . hurts."

"Okay, Mother," Judy would say quietly. "I'll see if I can get away and take you to the doctor in Sanford."

Fortunately, Judy had a wonderful, caring principal and an understanding co-teacher, Ellen, who tended to her students with special needs. Both of them made it possible for her to leave and tend to her mother. But it was still difficult for Judy to desert her class. She realized that she couldn't take proper care of Jeannette as well as give her students the attention they needed and deserved. One of these responsibilities would have to go.

Judy decided it was time for her to retire from teaching. On the day she gave her notice, she told her principal she would finish the six months remaining in the school year, but she wouldn't be back, because she was moving to Maine to care for her mother. Although he was disappointed, Judy's principal understood why Judy had to retire; he, too, had struggled with caring for his aging mother. As Judy left his office, a tear trickled down her cheek. *For 35 years my whole life has been wrapped up in this school,* she thought sadly. *All my good friends are here. The faculty, my students—they're my family.* She knew leaving her career at Harrington Elementary would be the hardest thing she'd ever done. Judy had planned to retire in a few years anyway—she was 58 years old—but she never thought she'd be forced into it. Teaching had always been her passion.

The rest of the year flew by, and soon she was down to the last two weeks of school. The faculty threw Judy a farewell party at a posh country club, and she said many tearful good-byes. Judy could hardly believe she was retiring. She had taught grades third through seventh, where she'd worked with a special program for students who were "bright underachievers." *Thirty-five happy years, and now it's all over,* Judy told herself sadly.

Not only had she loved the art of teaching, but she had also loved her students. The last week of school, the PTA threw her a huge open-house party in the auditorium, and students of all ages poured in to say one final good-bye. Since Judy had been in the same school for so many years, she had begun having her students' children in her classes. It was enjoyable for her to see parent and child standing side by side and realize that she'd taught both of them.

O NE AFTERNOON A FEW DAYS AFTER HER RETIREMENT PARTY, Judy stood surveying her mother's dining room. It looked strange to see her own dining room table and china cabinet in her mother's house. Jeannette's had been there for so many years.

The two women had decided that they would split up their furniture—half of Judy's things would go to their summer home, and half of her mother's would go there as well. That way both women would still have some of their belongings in each house.

Placing her hands on her hips, Judy looked around at the familiar rose carpet and cream walls, then sighed deeply. She remembered her mother and father having guests around the old dining room table. It had seemed they were always having someone over for dinner. *It just doesn't seem right to see my dining room set standing here instead,* Judy thought, overcome by memories. She perched on one of the chairs and closed her eyes. *I'd always wanted to come back to Sanford, but not under these circumstances.* She already missed her friends and school in Massachusetts. *Lord, help me to be content and use my time wisely,* Judy prayed. *Help me to move on and get involved in church and social activities. Help me to care for Mother the way she cared for me growing up.*

Judy knew that full-time caregiving was not going to be easy for her. Her mother had always been much more nurturing by nature than she was—and Jeannette constantly wanted to be hugged, kissed, and complimented. Judy had a lot to learn.

Soon Judy was busy taking Jeannette to the psychiatrist every week and joining various women's ministry groups and committees in her church. These social outlets were a lifesaver for Judy because they allowed her to be with independent, mature adults who affirmed and encouraged her. She needed their support and friendship because life was not easy at home. Not only had her mother become more forgetful over the past year, but after Judy moved back in and took over the older woman's domain, Jeannette had also turned cantankerous.

One night a few weeks after Judy moved home, she walked into the living room, where her mother was sitting contentedly in her favorite chair, watching television.

"Hi, Mother, how are you?" Judy asked.

Jeannette looked up sharply. "Oh, it's you again!"

Judy gulped. *I can't believe she said that*, she thought. *That really hurt.* She took a deep breath and tried again. "Are you tired, Mother?" It was already 9:00 in the evening, Jeannette's usual bedtime.

"Only of you. You never do anything for me," her mother replied. She primly smoothed down her skirt, then turned her attention back to the TV.

Judy turned white and said indignantly, "How can you say that, Mother? I just gave up my job to stay with you!"

Jeannette clasped her hands in her lap and got very quiet.

That was just the first of many incidents in which Jeannette made spiteful comments about her daughter's character, appearance, and actions. Her mother's jabs cut Judy's heart. *Lord, why is she suddenly so mean?* Judy would silently ask God. *Please give me patience and understanding. Help me to deal with this.*

Jeannette continued giving her "zingers," and Judy soon found out why. About a month after she retired, Judy took her mother to one of her psychiatrist appointments.

"Your mother is in the early stages of Alzheimer's disease," the psychiatrist told Judy after counseling with Jeannette. "Has she been forgetful? Has she become more childish? Is her personality changing?"

"Well . . . yes," Judy said numbly. She turned to look at her mother, who was sitting in a cushioned chair, staring into space. Her mother had become very forgetful and more childish lately— but Judy hadn't wanted to believe she was suffering from any kind of dementia. It was too scary. She took a deep breath and asked, "What are my mother's prospects?"

The psychiatrist looked at her quizzically, then said, "Why do you want to know?"

"Because I need to know if I'm going to find her curled up in a fetal position on the floor someday!" Judy said quickly, her voice shaking.

"Given Jeannette's advanced age and the early stage of her disease, she probably won't die from Alzheimer's," the psychiatrist said, folding his hands. "Just keep bringing her here once a week, and take care of her as you normally would." He looked at her more sympathetically. "Don't worry yourself sick about this."

Judy nodded. It made her feel better to know that Jeannette probably wouldn't die from the disease. Judy had known people who suffered from Alzheimer's. She'd seen their minds deteriorate until they were totally different from the people they once had been. *I don't want that to happen to Mother,* Judy thought sadly.

One day about six months after Judy's retirement, she and Jeannette left the doctor feeling particularly encouraged. Her mother had just had a positive appointment, and the physician had said she was in excellent health. In good spirits, they stopped at the grocery store to get a gallon of milk, then drove home. When Judy pulled the car up to the curb and put it in park, she looked over at her mother.

"Wait for me, Mother," she reminded her. "I'll come around and help you get out of the car and into the house."

"Okay," Jeannette said simply. She looked cozy in her blue winter coat.

"Let me just grab the milk," Judy said. She turned from her mother and reached for the grocery bag in the backseat.

But when she had grasped the milk and looked up, Judy froze. "Mother?" she said.

The passenger door was open, and Jeannette, who'd forgotten to stay put, was already making her way up the front walk and heading for the steps.

"Mother, wait!" Judy called loudly, trying to get her mother's attention.

But Jeannette kept going. Gingerly, she put her foot on the first concrete step and tried to pull herself up. But she couldn't reach the railing, which extended only to the edge of the second step. Suddenly, her arms flailed and she lost her balance.

"Ohh!" Jeannette shrieked, her shaky voice piercing the quiet of the neighborhood as she fell to the sidewalk.

Judy rushed over to her mother, who lay whimpering on the concrete. "Mother, I'm here with you," she said, her voice shrill with anxiety. "I'm going to pull you up on the step to sit, okay?" Shaking in the cold, Judy boosted her frail mother into a more comfortable position. *What am I going to do?* she thought, flustered. *I can't leave her alone outside, but I need to call 911.*

"Judy . . . it hurts," Jeannette gasped, writhing in pain. Her usually pink cheeks appeared blanched against her blue coat.

Judy looked around the neighborhood. It was wintertime, so all her neighbors' doors were shut—there was no one around. "Help!" she yelled frantically. "Somebody help us!"

Finally, after several minutes of yelling, a couple from down the street—people Judy had never met—came running up. They retrieved a wool blanket to put over Jeannette and stayed with her while Judy called the paramedics. Within a few minutes, an ambulance had arrived. The paramedics carefully placed Jeannette on a stretcher and raced her off to the hospital, with Judy seated by her side.

It didn't take the doctors long to figure out that Jeannette had broken her hip, but she recovered quickly. Rather than giving her a hip replacement, the doctors put a stainless steel joint in her hip. Within a few days, her mother was able to move with a walker, something that often took many elderly patients weeks to do. So after only a week in the hospital, the staff released Jeannette to go home.

"She's done so well that we don't need to send her to a

nursing home for two more weeks of physical therapy," the doctor told Judy. "You can do the exercises with her. Your mother will be better off at home."

During the next two weeks Jeannette managed well, but Judy almost reached the end of her rope. Her mother was now completely dependent on her. Judy had to sleep on a cot next to her because Jeannette required aid to get in and out of bed, and she went to the bathroom several times during the night. Her mother needed help in every conceivable way—getting dressed, bathing, walking, using the toilet, and doing her physical therapy exercises.

The exercises were supposed to be done every day. At first, Jeannette had to lie on the bed and raise her leg, then stand at the kitchen sink and move her leg from the right to the left. After she mastered that, she had to learn to get up the stairs. The exercises were painful, and Jeannette often complained.

"It hurts! It hurts, Judy!" she'd say to her daughter.

"Mother, the doctor says you still have to do this," Judy would tell Jeannette wearily. She didn't like watching her mother do the exercises, either. It was difficult for Judy to see Jeannette in pain. "Come on, you can finish them," she'd encourage her.

"No!" Jeannette would say, feisty as ever. "I don't want to do this anymore."

"Okay," Judy would say, giving in reluctantly. She couldn't force her mother to do the exercises.

Taking care of Jeannette was exhausting—and humbling. Overwhelmed both emotionally and physically, Judy could only utter frantic prayers to God. *Lord, what am I doing?* she often asked Him, distraught. *I can't help Mother. It's too hard. Why am I even trying? God, please give me strength and guide me. I need You.*

One particularly difficult evening, after four weeks of 24-hour care, Judy broke down and flung herself onto a bed, sobbing into the pillow. Her mother had been especially cruel with her zingers that evening when Judy had given Jeannette her nightly sponge bath. Her mother's words echoed in Judy's head: *What are you here for? You're not needed. . . . You just like to show off. . . . Get out and leave me alone!*

Judy pulled a blanket tightly around her and cried out to God, *Lord, I can't do this anymore. I can't. . . . I can't.*

Suddenly, she became aware of the phone ringing. Reaching for the receiver, she took a deep, shaky breath and said, "Hello?"

It was Lillian, a close family friend and contemporary of her mother's. "I'm worried about you and Jeannette," Lillian said gently. "I know you're spending a lot of time caring for her. Are you getting enough rest, Judy?"

Judy closed her eyes. "No," she answered wearily.

"You need to get someone to help you!" Lillian told her. "You shouldn't be trying to do this all alone. I'll call the hospital and get a name for you, okay?"

Lillian called back a few minutes later. "Joanne, a certified nursing assistant, just finished her last assignment," she said. "She'll be arriving at your house in an hour so you can rest."

"Thank you," Judy told her friend gratefully. Finally, she'd be able to sleep through the night.

True to Lillian's word, an hour later Joanne walked up the front steps, ready to care for Jeannette. When Judy opened the door to let her in, she paused in surprise. The woman's kind eyes and her tentative smile were unmistakable. *I know this woman!* Judy realized. They had been in high school together.

"Joanne Gray?" she asked with delight.

Joanne looked equally pleased. "Judy Wiggin!" she said.

Judy smiled widely and wrapped her arms around her old friend, fighting back thankful tears. The Lord was taking care of her and her mother.

O NE SUNDAY MORNING SEVERAL MONTHS LATER, JUDY SAT with her mother in church, saddened by Pastor Stuart's news. After 10 years at First Baptist Church, he and his wife, the church secretary, were retiring at the beginning of the summer.

"The pulpit committee is interviewing for a new pastor, but we still need to find a secretary," Pastor Stuart said. "My wife has agreed to continue working until we find someone to replace her. So if you're interested in the position, please pray about it and then call the church office for a job description and interview."

Judy's ears perked up. *I'd love to do that if I didn't need to be home with Mother,* she thought. Joanne now stayed nights with Jeannette, and Joanne's friend Claire, a home health aide, had started to come during the day to help, but Judy still didn't like the thought of being out of the house frequently. True, she was already involved to some degree in church activities as a deacon, a member of the Ladies' Aid, and on the board of the finance committee. But even these responsibilities were hard to juggle, because they took her away from home. In fact, she'd recently asked the finance committee if they would meet at her house so she wouldn't have to worry about Jeannette.

The secretary job really interested Judy. Sitting in the church pew, her mind continued to spin plans. *If I could do it at home,* she thought excitedly, *or split the duties with someone, that would be ideal.*

For several months, Judy prayed over and thought about the idea. In order to be a secretary, she would need a computer. *Maybe I could ask the finance committee to purchase one for me,* she thought hopefully. *Our committee could use a computer of its own, anyway.* Judy never got around to asking the finance committee about the possibility, but she did mention the idea to her friends Fran and Nick a few weeks later.

Fran and Nick were teacher friends of Judy's, and they had come from Massachusetts to spend time with her and Jeannette at the lake.

"You need a computer?" Nick asked. "We just bought a new one. The old one is in the garage, collecting dust. I didn't know what to do with it." Nick looked questioningly at his wife, who nodded. Turning back to Judy, he asked, "Do you want it?"

Judy was taken aback. "Oh, that's so kind of you to give it to me!" she said, her eyes shining. "But are you sure?"

"Of course," Fran told her.

Fran and Nick gave Judy their computer, printer, and monitor a few weeks later—everything she needed in order to be the church secretary. *Lord, You sure are providing for me,* Judy thought gratefully. *You are incredible.*

It was obvious to Judy that God was working in her situation, but she still felt unsure about how she would take the job in light of her mother's frail condition. Yet Judy soon discovered that the Lord had that figured out as well.

A month later, Judy was at a Ladies' Aid meeting chatting with some women around the punch bowl when Charlene, another member of the society, pulled her aside.

"Judy, I heard that you were considering taking the secretary job," Charlene said. "I thought about doing it, too, but I wasn't sure about the time commitment. Would you be interested in splitting the position?"

Judy's eyes crinkled with pleasure. "I'm definitely interested," she said, smiling. "Let's pray about it."

They agreed to take a few weeks to pray. Later, when the women met again to talk about the job, both felt that God was leading them to take the position. So Judy and Charlene both became church secretaries and relieved Mrs. Stuart, who had been filling in for the last few months. Since they knew their church budget was tight, they decided to do the job on a volunteer basis, considering it part of their tithe. Judy would work at home, primarily typing the bulletins, newsletters, and other notices, and Charlene would be responsible for outside duties such as getting the mail, ordering supplies, and manning the church office. Then, on Fridays, the two of them would work together at the church.

The job was a blessing. Being able to serve the Lord through her work in the church and seeing Charlene's wonderful

Christian example strengthened Judy's faith immensely. Charlene was so warm and hospitable with everyone—and she always had a thankful attitude. Judy watched her friend struggle with debilitating pain in her knees and other trials, but Charlene's faith in God remained steadfast and joyful. She encouraged Judy to read her Bible and do her devotions more regularly, and the two friends read and discussed the spiritual growth materials that passed through the church office.

After a year and a half, the pulpit committee finally found a new pastor, and this minister's explanations of the Word, teachings about Christian growth, and personal example and witness affected Judy powerfully. The sermons and illustrations helped Judy understand the Bible more fully, and that, in turn, enabled her to better enjoy reading the Scriptures. For the first time in her life, Judy felt the Bible come alive.

Several months after the new pastor arrived, Judy rededicated her life to God during an altar call. Her deepened commitment drew her even closer to the Lord, helping her understand His character better as well. Before, she had known God's majesty and power, but she didn't have a good sense of His grace and love. Now her relationship with the Lord became more personal and exciting.

Judy's strengthened faith soon became vital, as her caregiving responsibilities increased. Her mother was slowly slipping away, becoming more forgetful and childlike. It was extremely difficult for Judy to see her mother, once so intelligent and strong, regress to a child right before her eyes. Jeannette would often sit for hours in her chair, cradling, talking with, and singing to her teddy bear, Peter.

Wanting her mother to have some small luxuries, Judy hired a hairdresser to come in every week to do Jeannette's hair and a manicurist to do her nails biweekly. Her mother was ecstatic, like a little girl. Whenever anyone came to visit, she would show off her brightly painted fingernails.

"One, two, three, four, five," Jeannette would say, waving her hands in front of the amused visitor. "I have five of them!"

Also sensitive to her mother's confused state of mind, Judy took Jeannette through the same ritual every night to provide her with some stability. Joanne cared for her mother at night, but Judy wanted to have a special time alone with Jeannette each evening. First, Judy would put her mother into bed, then together they would say the Lord's Prayer. Afterward, Judy would pray special words over her mother.

"Lord, thank You for my dear mother," she would say, squeezing Jeannette's hand. "Give her a restful, peaceful night's sleep. Watch over her, Lord. Show her Your love." Judy would then stroke her mother's white, wispy hair back from her forehead and kiss her. "I love you, Mother."

Jeannette would always reply, "I love you, too, Judy. You are the only child I ever had."

"And you are the only mother I ever had," Judy would say, concealing a smile. Then she'd leave the room, keeping the door halfway open.

Those pleasant times helped Judy endure her mother's nasty spells. Jeannette was always very polite, funny, and cooperative with Joanne and Claire—but not with her own daughter. The psychiatrist had told Judy that her mother had been raised to be polite to strangers, and, as the old adage says, she consequently hurt the person she loved the most—Judy. Although it helped to hear the doctor's explanation, it was still difficult. Judy had been learning to rely on God's strength to get her through the emotional stress of Alzheimer's, but she hadn't yet been able to brush off her mother's barbs.

One evening, as Judy was getting her mother ready for bed, she suddenly became aware of how cold the house was. Shivering and rubbing her hands together, she looked at Jeannette, who was sitting on the bed bundled up in her flannel nightgown and cradling her teddy bear.

"Are you warm enough, Mother?" Judy asked, concerned. Her own hands felt like ice cubes. "I sure am cold!" She guided her mother under the covers and pulled a thick blanket up to her chin.

Jeannette stared at her daughter, her small, wrinkled hands poking out from under the blanket. "What? A big elephant like you, cold?" she said tartly.

Judy blinked, her eyes smarting from her mother's verbal blow. "Mother, do you know how much that hurts me? Do you enjoy hurting me?"

"Well, you hurt me!" Jeannette said quickly. Her lower lip stuck out in a pout.

Judy turned quickly from her, wiping her eyes. She knew Alzheimer's affected short-term memory but was slower in diminishing long-term memory, and that concerned her. *Has Mother always thought of me like this?* Judy thought, feeling sick. *Is this how she really sees me—as a big elephant? Does she really not like having me around?* They were devastating thoughts.

Burying her face in her hands, Judy prayed, *Lord, help me deal with her insults. They hurt so much.*

And just as He had all along, the Lord pulled Judy through—this time, in a completely unexpected way. One Friday afternoon a few weeks later, Judy and Charlene were working in the church office when they came across an ad in *Focus on the Family* magazine. It announced the first Renewing the Heart conference in Nashville, Tennessee.

"Patsy Clairmont is a speaker!" Charlene exclaimed. Her blue eyes danced. Patsy was her favorite author.

Judy and Charlene looked excitedly at one another. "We have to go!" they said simultaneously.

They called to order tickets, and suddenly they were on the list to go. When the women got their confirmation, however, Judy's head began spinning with doubts. *How can I leave Mother?* she thought. *And how can I afford to go, having to pay for plane tickets and hotel reservations?* Her mother's medical expenses had put Judy on a tight budget.

Over the next few days, however, all the details were ironed out. Fran and Nick offered to come and stay with Jeannette for the weekend so Judy could relieve Joanne and Claire and save some money. Then the congregation graciously voted to pay for the trip as a way of thanking Judy and Charlene for volunteering their services as church secretaries. Everything was provided for them. It was obvious to Judy that the Lord really wanted her to go.

A few months later, Judy and Charlene were off to the conference. And every second of their experience was exciting. From the minute they boarded the plane, they were surrounded by women going to Renewing the Heart—and Judy had never been in the company of so many enthusiastic Christians.

When she and Charlene arrived at the Nashville arena the next day, Judy was even more struck by the energy there. She had always been around people and in churches that were relatively reserved, but here, at the conference, women were enthusiastically proclaiming their love for God, eager to profess their faith. That day, Judy felt the Holy Spirit's presence and love in her heart more powerfully than ever before. It seemed as though each of the speakers' messages was designed just for her. They all encouraged the women, reminding them to handle their feelings and relationships—both with people and with God—in a spirit of love.

Each speaker's topic seemed to go deeper than the one before, as well as pave the way for the next message. Patsy Clairmont talked about a woman's individual identity; then Kay Coles James discussed a woman's identity within her family; and finally Anne Graham Lotz reminded Judy of her identity within the world—that she was a child of God, and her true home was in heaven. Anne's message—that the cares of this world would pass—encouraged Judy to focus on God and look ahead to her heavenly future. Judy was reminded of her true priorities. She felt renewed and filled with hope. By the end of the day, Judy had realized that her mother's criticisms weren't important or true.

Seated in the arena, surrounded by thousands of women, she deeply felt the Lord's love. *I love you so much, Judy,* God seemed to say, *and your mother loves you, too. She doesn't mean the things she says. Just love her. Love her the way I love you—unconditionally.*

Judy looked up toward heaven. "Okay, Lord," she promised quietly. "I will."

It was a turning point in Judy's relationship with her mother. Reminded of God's incredible love for her, Judy was finally able to let go of her feelings and accept her mother's illness—zingers included.

Judy arrived home from the conference late that night, feeling refreshed and encouraged. The next morning as she walked to the kitchen to prepare breakfast, she found Jeannette sitting calmly in her favorite chair in the living room, staring at the pink-flowered upholstery.

"I love this chair! Isn't it nice?" her mother said absently, staring in wonder at the chair she'd sat in for years. "I'd like to get one just like it for my house."

Judy went over to Jeannette and placed her hand lightly on her shoulder. "Mother, this is your house," she said tenderly.

Jeannette jerked her head up to stare at her daughter. "It is?"

"Yes, it is."

"Oh," her mother said. She pushed up her glasses, but Judy could see that her eyes were glazed with confusion.

Judy's heart swelled with sadness. Sometimes her mother really *didn't* know what was going on or what she was saying. Judy sat on the couch, near Jeannette. "Well, how are you, Mother?" she asked kindly. "I haven't seen you for a couple days."

Her mother pulled at the knitted sweater that her stuffed bear was wearing. "Oh, I'm pretty good for an old lady. I do want to go to a dance, though," she said seriously. "Wouldn't that be fun?"

"We can't go to a dance," Judy said, suppressing a smile. "But we can go to your favorite restaurant. I want to spend some time with you."

Jeannette threw down her bear in frustration. "Judy, you're such a bore! You never want to do anything fun."

Judy took a deep breath. *Brush it off,* she told herself. *Laugh about it. Remember what you learned at the conference.* Then, turning to her mother, she said, chuckling, "It's my job to keep you in line. Come on, let's get some breakfast."

Jeannette blinked slowly a few times, then her own lips curled into an amused smile. "Okay, Judy."

Judy now could see that her mother wasn't intending to be mean—she was only confused.

There were times, however, when Jeannette showed signs of her former self. One night Judy took her mother out to a restaurant for dinner. As they entered the lobby, they saw an older gentleman waiting alone.

Pulling on Judy's arm with one hand and clutching her cane in the other, Jeannette hobbled over to him. "Excuse me," she said saucily, "but are you waiting for some nice young women to take you to dinner?"

The man chuckled, and Judy gasped in embarrassment. "Mother!" she said, steering the older woman away.

Peering innocently up at her daughter, Jeannette said, "I just wanted to make him laugh."

A giggle escaped Judy's lips, and she pulled her mother close to her side. "You did make him laugh," she said, "and you make me laugh, too. You're so much fun." Tears welled up in Judy's eyes. "I love you, Mother," she said softly.

"Oh, I love you, too, Judy," her mother replied. "You're the only daughter I've ever had."

Judy smiled, then winked at her mother as she said in turn, "And you're the only mother I've ever had."

And she wouldn't have wanted it any other way.

Judy Wiggin lives with her mother, Jeannette, in Sanford, Maine, where she continues to work part-time as church secretary and full-time as her mother's caregiver. Since attending the Renewing the Heart conference, Judy has shared her experience there with various women's groups and with her own congregation. Her renewed faith has given her the courage to reach out to her unsaved friends and evangelize— and it has also taught Judy to laugh at her mother's antics rather than

take them personally. Jeannette recently suffered a heart attack, making her physically even more frail than before, but Judy feels peaceful about her mother's future. She attests that God has turned her focus around, enabling her outlook to be one of hope and joy.

Heart to Heart

The hardest job I've ever had was digging ditches one summer for a golf course development company. A friend of mine told me about this great job at an exclusive golf course, and I accepted it without knowing what it was. The first day of work I showed up wearing a cute, white tennis outfit and was given a shovel and gruff instructions for digging holes for the irrigation system. It was the middle of summer in central Florida, and I was the only female on the dirty, sweaty crew. I dug holes all day, every day. With every shovelful of dirt I lifted, I fantasized about quitting. But I was determined to stick it out, and I'm glad I did, because I learned a lot about hard work, commitment, and perseverance that summer—and got a great tan in the process!

Judy is acquiring something far more valuable than a great tan as she perseveres in caring for her elderly mother, Jeannette. She's learning firsthand what Jesus taught in Matthew 25: Whatsoever you do for the least of them, you do it for Him. God wants us to place others before ourselves just as His Son did. Jesus came to serve, not to be served, and in the end He willingly gave up His life as a ransom for many. Judy shows us through her loving example that the one who will be first in God's kingdom is the one who puts herself last. Years from now when you get to heaven, if you run into a gentle woman with a quick smile, a Boston accent, and a crown full of jewels, ask her if her name is Judy.

Walking by Faith ~

Lisa

Standing on God's Promises

*Because of the LORD's great love we are not
consumed, for his compassions never fail. They are
new every morning; great is your faithfulness. . . .
The LORD is good to those whose hope is in him,
to the one who seeks him; it is good to wait quietly
for the salvation of the LORD.*
—LAMENTATIONS 3:22–23, 25–26

$\mathcal{K}$IMBERLY OSBORN GRIPPED THE PHONE ANXIOUSLY, HER knuckles white against the receiver. This was it—the moment she'd been anticipating all week. *Please let the test be positive*, she thought desperately as she waited for the nurse practitioner to come on the line. *Please let me be pregnant. All I want is to be a mom.* Pacing the floor, Kimberly let the phone cord twist around her petite frame. She glanced through the open bedroom door at her husband, Michael, who was sitting on the living room couch.

Married a little over a year, they had been going to a fertility clinic for four months. In college, Kimberly had been diagnosed with endometriosis and polycystic ovarian disease, and the doctor had told her that because of these conditions, her chances of bearing children were slim. Kimberly had been distraught because from the time she was a little girl, her major goal in life was to be a mother. So once she and Michael had decided they were ready to start a family, Kimberly didn't waste any time. She'd insisted that they go straight to an infertility specialist.

Michael's insurance with the navy covered the expensive fertility drugs and procedures, and his job in the military also provided the Osborns with financial security. Kimberly had another reason for wanting children right away—she was lonely. Michael had just been stationed in Philadelphia, and they'd moved to New Jersey, an hour from his shipyard, where they didn't know anyone. At first his career had sounded glamorous to Kimberly, with all the traveling and moving they'd be able to do. But soon the reality of being a military wife had set in. Michael's job frequently took him away from home, and as a result, Kimberly spent many days and nights alone. *A child*, she thought, *would fill my empty life.*

Kimberly untwisted herself from the phone cord and squeezed her green eyes shut. *Please let the insemination have worked*, she prayed silently.

Finally, after what seemed like hours, Iris, the nurse practitioner, came on the line to read the results of Kimberly's blood test, done two weeks after her artificial insemination. Iris's cheerful voice boomed through the receiver. "It's positive!"

Kimberly caught her breath, then asked hesitantly, "Really?"

"Yes, really," Iris assured her.

"Oh, that's great!" Kimberly said exuberantly. Her eyes glistened with tears of joy, and her delicate features curved into a glowing smile. *Finally I'm going to be a mom!* she thought happily. *Everything's going to be okay. I can stop taking those fertility drugs and going to the doctor three times a week because now I'm pregnant!* Kimberly hung up the phone and whirled around to tell Michael, who had entered the bedroom when he heard his wife's shrieks of joy.

"We're going to be parents!" she said, laughing and crying at the same time.

Michael let out a sigh of relief and wrapped his arms around his wife. "It's great to see you so happy," he said sincerely. "Still, I'm glad we're done with all this infertility stuff." Michael didn't want children as badly as Kimberly did—he was mainly going through the process to make his wife happy. He squeezed Kimberly. "Why don't we go out to dinner to celebrate?"

Michael and Kimberly spent that evening in a joyful frenzy. They went to a fancy seafood restaurant, and when they got back from dinner, they excitedly called their parents with the good news. Both sets of parents were glad, as this would be the first grandchild on each side. But Kimberly's mother, Ava, wasn't as overjoyed as Kimberly had expected.

"That's great, Kim," her mom said calmly over the line. "I'm happy for you."

Kimberly felt a twinge of hurt but quickly brushed it off. *Nobody is going to ruin my night,* she thought. "Well, I just wanted to tell you the good news!" she said blissfully. She hung up with her mother, then went to bed.

Kimberly's dreams that night were filled with happy, glowing images of her, Michael, and their new baby. And she was still in a giddy dreamland when she awoke early the next morning. Stretching luxuriously, Kimberly peered at the clock on the nightstand. It was just 5:30. *Hopefully I'll be able to go back to sleep*, she thought as she got up to go to the bathroom.

She padded down the hall to their tiny bathroom and switched on the bright, fluorescent light. Catching her reflection in the mirror, she smiled happily, thinking, *I'm a mom!* Life couldn't get any better than this.

As Kimberly relieved herself, however, she realized that something was terribly wrong. She began to tremble as she gazed in horror at the white toilet paper with which she had just wiped herself. On the paper was blood and a piece of tissue. She was having a miscarriage.

This can't be happening, she thought, stunned. The color drained from her face, and Kimberly bolted out of the bathroom. "No!" she screamed in panic. "Michael! Come here!" She stumbled down the hallway, crying, still holding the toilet paper.

Michael appeared immediately, his brown hair disheveled from sleep. "What's the matter?"

"The baby . . . the baby," Kimberly cried, pointing to the toilet paper. She hadn't thrown it away because even in her grieved state, Kimberly knew their doctor would want to see the tissue. "Will you . . . c-call the doctor?" she whispered, trembling.

Numbly, Kimberly followed Michael back into the bedroom, where he called the fertility clinic. The physician on call told them to keep the tissue and come immediately to the clinic.

Except for her constant sniffling, Kimberly was silent on the drive to the hospital. Outside, the late spring weather was dismal and cold—a reflection of how she felt inside. When they arrived at the hospital, the doctor examined the tissue and verified that she'd miscarried. Kimberly would have to immediately undergo a dilatation and evacuation (D&E).

The D&E was almost more emotionally painful than the miscarriage itself. Kimberly lay fully conscious on the operating table; they didn't give her any anesthetic. Michael stood beside her, holding her hand. The sucking sounds the machine made as the physician performed the procedure nauseated Kimberly. Suddenly, disturbing thoughts began to swirl through her mind: *What if it's too soon to be doing this? What if the doctor is wrong? What if I really didn't miscarry?* Digging her nails into Michael's hand, Kimberly closed her eyes, wishing she could shut out this nightmare and go back to the previous evening, when she'd first found out she was a mother and the world seemed full of wonderful possibilities. Now all her hopes had evaporated.

The doctor finished the procedure and sent Kimberly into the bathroom to clean up. In the rest room, she curled up into tiny ball on the cold floor, and resting her head on her arms, she wept.

It was just one week before Mother's Day.

"OH, HI, AVA," KIMBERLY HEARD MICHAEL SAY A COUPLE weeks later as he picked up the phone in the kitchen. Kimberly stiffened.

Michael was silent for a moment. "Well, actually she's not doing well," he said, then lowered his voice. "It's been two weeks since the miscarriage, and she's still crying and sleeping all the time. In fact, I think she's in bed right now, taking a nap."

Kimberly was in bed, but she wasn't asleep. She bit her lip to keep the tears from flowing. *If Mom's worried about me, why doesn't she talk to me herself?* she thought, frustrated. After the miscarriage, she and her mother had had a few strained, emotional conversations on the phone. Then her mother had stopped talking to her completely. It was too hard for her to hear Kimberly crying constantly, so she'd begun asking Michael how her daughter was doing. It wasn't that hard for Kimberly's mom to avoid talking with her, though—Kimberly was too depressed to answer the phone.

"Yeah, I know." Michael's quiet voice carried softly from the kitchen. He sighed audibly, then said, "But Kimberly really feels that she needs to do all this fertility stuff."

Kimberly cringed. Her mother hadn't agreed with her decision to use fertility drugs, which was why she hadn't been ecstatic over her daughter's pregnancy or very supportive after the miscarriage. Kimberly's mother and grandmother had both battled breast cancer, and Ava felt that Kimberly shouldn't be taking hormones because they would increase her already high risk of getting cancer in the future.

Hurt that her mother and husband were discussing her condition behind her back, Kimberly pulled the covers more tightly around herself. *Mom probably thinks I'm getting what I deserve,* she thought bleakly. *And Michael acts as if he doesn't even care.* Though Michael had been there physically—the ship he was assigned to was in the shipyard—emotionally, he hadn't been supportive at all. Like Kimberly's mom, Michael avoided talking with his wife about her pain, almost as if ignoring it would make her suffering go away. Kimberly felt that no one was there for her, and sometimes she felt she was drowning in pain and loneliness.

Only one thing had kept her from total despair—the hope that maybe next month she'd be pregnant again. The next day, just two weeks after she'd lost the baby, Kimberly was scheduled to go back to the fertility clinic for another insemination. She was determined to keep trying until she had a child.

Lying in bed, trying to focus on the novel she was reading and not the conversation her mom and Michael were having on the phone in the kitchen, Kimberly felt her eyes stinging with tears. For several minutes, she tried to make sense of the words swimming on the page in front of her, but all she could think about was getting pregnant. Frustrated, Kimberly put the book back on her nightstand. As she did so, something caught her eye. Sandwiched between two books on infertility was her old Bible, collecting dust. Kimberly picked it up and began thumbing through the pages.

She had grown up as a Christian but had fallen away from her faith when she began college in 1982. By the time she and Michael graduated and married, she had recommitted her life to Christ. In 1986 Michael received his duty assignment and they moved to New Jersey. They were having a difficult time finding a suitable church, however, and Kimberly hadn't read her Bible or prayed regularly in months.

She flipped to the psalms and began reading. "O LORD, you have searched me and you know me. You know when I sit and when I rise; you perceive my thoughts from afar." Kimberly's heart thudded. It was as if the words were speaking directly to her. She continued reading. "For you created my inmost being; you knit me together in my mother's womb. . . . All the days ordained for me were written in your book before one of them came to be" (Psalm 139:1–2, 13, 16).

This scripture was talking about babies! Pregnancy! Motherhood! Kimberly sat up in bed, feeling more hopeful than she had since the miscarriage. *Those promises were intended just for me,* she thought excitedly. She realized that God is in control of human life, and He could make her pregnant—all she needed to do was ask.

In the weeks that followed, Kimberly memorized the entire psalm and began quoting it as she prayed nonstop to God, asking Him to give her a baby. Meanwhile, she continued going to the fertility clinic three times a week for blood tests, inseminations, and checkups; charting her basal temperature; and taking powerful doses of fertility drugs. It seemed that with every breath she took, she petitioned God: *Lord, please let me get pregnant,* she'd pray as she breathed in; then, as she breathed out, *Please let me carry the next baby.*

The Lord didn't immediately bring Kimberly a baby, but He began to take care of her needs in another way—by sending her a close friend, Debbie.

*O*NE MORNING, A COUPLE OF MONTHS AFTER THE MISCARRIAGE, Kimberly was sitting quietly in the backseat of another military wife's car, on her way to be initiated into the Officers' Wives Club. She sighed softly, fidgeting on the seat. She still felt wracked by her volatile emotions. It was getting more and more difficult to keep going to the clinic, to keep feeling encouraged and hopeful, only to have that hope dashed when her latest blood test came back negative.

The car pulled up to a house not far from her apartment, and a striking, energetic woman bounced down the front steps and slid into the backseat next to Kimberly.

"Hi! I'm Debbie Eastin," the woman said, flashing a wide smile and holding out her hand.

Kimberly smiled back and said, "Hello. I'm Kimberly Osborn." She shook Debbie's hand and blinked, trying not to stare. Probably 10 years older than Kimberly, Debbie was wearing a bright pink outfit with matching bright pink shoes, and even color-coordinated lipstick. On anyone else, the outfit would have looked ridiculous, but somehow Debbie pulled it off.

It wasn't Debbie's clothing, however, that most captured Kimberly's attention. The entire right side of Debbie's fair-skinned jaw was black and blue.

Debbie caught Kimberly and the women in the front seat looking at her huge bruise. "Oh, my husband hit me!" she said, shaking her head.

Kimberly's mouth fell open, and she leaned toward Debbie with concern. "That's terrible!" Kimberly told her. "Are you okay?"

Debbie laughed good-naturedly. "No, no, no," she said, dismissing Kimberly's question. "Bill would never do anything like that. I just said that because I knew it was probably what everyone was thinking." She buckled her seat belt, then touched her jaw and winced. "Actually, I went to the dentist yesterday," she explained, "and he gave me a shot to deaden the pain. Too bad," she added, smiling ruefully, "because it bruised my face."

Debbie chatted all the way to and from the Officers' Wives Club meeting, keeping Kimberly and the other women entertained. She talked about her six-week-old daughter, Sarah Beth, who was home with her husband, Bill; her experiences as a military wife; and the migraines she'd been having lately. Debbie had thought that her headaches might be connected to problems with her teeth, which was why she'd had so much dental work done the day before.

What a fun, interesting woman, Kimberly mused. She exchanged phone numbers with Debbie, not sure what would come of it—after all, she hardly knew her.

A week later, however, Debbie called to ask Kimberly for a favor. "I have to go to the obstetrician tomorrow for a follow-up appointment," she said, "but I don't want to go alone. I've been having terrible headaches lately, and I don't know if I'll be able to make the half-hour drive back." She paused for breath, then asked, "Will you come with me to the doctor? If you're there, I won't have to worry about driving home if I have another headache."

"Sure," Kimberly said without hesitation. She didn't have many demands on her time aside from her part-time work at the library and frequent visits to the fertility clinic.

The next day Kimberly went with Debbie to her appointment, and on the way home, they stopped by the mall. The car ride and time spent shopping gave them the opportunity to bond. Soon, Kimberly was pouring her heart out to Debbie about her inability to get pregnant. Debbie began to confide in her as well, telling her she was lonely, too. Her husband, Bill, was a military pilot, and, like Michael, was frequently gone.

"How do you handle the loneliness?" Kimberly asked.

Debbie's brightly painted lips pressed into a thin, sad line. "Oh," she replied, "it's hard, but I've learned to deal with it—like keeping busy by going shopping with friends." She gave Kimberly a warm smile as she maneuvered Sarah Beth's stroller around the clothing displays and out the door.

That day sparked the start of an intimate friendship. Since the women couldn't lean on their husbands, they began to rely on one another. Debbie, who was a strong Christian, invited Kimberly to go with her to the Christian Women's Club. Soon they were attending meetings regularly together and either seeing one another or talking on the phone almost every day.

Kimberly relished the time she spent with Debbie and her daughter. She looked up to Debbie as a mother figure and Christian role model. Debbie was one of the most compassionate people Kimberly had ever known. She could always tell when Kimberly was depressed, and she consistently listened to her friend, then faithfully pointed the younger woman toward God.

"Kimmie, what's wrong?" Debbie asked pointedly one day, not two minutes after they'd begun talking on the phone. "I can tell you're upset about something."

I sure can't hide anything from Debbie, Kimberly thought, amazed. She swallowed the lump in her throat; her eyes were burning. "It's just so hard not being pregnant and going through all these tests," she told Debbie, her voice quavering, "and taking so many drugs and seeing babies everywhere . . ." Kimberly's voice trailed off as she tried to control her tears.

"Well, let's pray about it," Debbie said immediately. "Let's go to the Father and lay it all out for Him. We have a right to talk to God. We're His children, and He wants to help us."

Before Kimberly could even get her eyes closed, Debbie launched into a fervent prayer for her friend. When Debbie finished praying, Kimberly felt a wave of peace sweep over her. She'd never had anybody drop everything and pray for her the way Debbie did. It was incredible. And it was something Debbie was willing to do whenever Kimberly had a problem. But she didn't only pray with Kimberly—Debbie also consistently discussed God's Word with her. Many days, Kimberly would sit in Debbie's family room, rocking Sarah Beth while listening to her friend read from the Scriptures.

"Oh, let me read this to you!" Debbie would say excitedly. "I just love this passage." Usually the verses were already dated and underlined, but Debbie's enthusiasm about God never dampened. She always saw new truths and promises in His Word.

Kimberly's friendship with Debbie began in her a slow

process of spiritual growth. With Debbie as her mentor, Kimberly learned to pray out loud, read the Bible more consistently, and talk to God more confidently. She and Michael still hadn't found a church, but through Debbie's example, Kimberly's faith was strengthened.

Despite her renewed relationship with God, Kimberly was unable to put her infertility into perspective. As time went on and she didn't get pregnant, she became obsessed with having a child. The doctors at the clinic continued to give her hope that with this procedure or that surgery or that drug, she was sure to be pregnant in the next few months—and Kimberly clung desperately to that hope.

Her infertility affected her entire world. She was on so many fertility drugs that she had to tape a list of them to her calendar at home so she'd be able to remember which days she needed to take which pills. The quantity and variety of drugs also wreaked havoc on Kimberly's already fragile emotions and body, causing myriad side effects. She struggled with hot flashes, vision disturbances, and emotional outbursts. Bombarded by hormones, Kimberly felt she couldn't control her body or her feelings. If Michael looked at her the wrong way, she'd burst into tears or, depending on the day, lash out at him.

"You don't even care about having a baby!" she yelled at her husband one day after finding out that another insemination had failed.

Michael had just come home from work, and after setting down his briefcase, he folded his arms and said in frustration, "Well, I'm tired of doing this, Kimberly. I don't like having to plan our romantic nights together, I don't like it that you're always on so many drugs, and I don't like going to the doctor so much."

Michael's words cut her deeply, and Kimberly turned away from him, her shoulders shaking. "You just don't understand!" she sobbed.

Michael threw up his hands. "You're right," he said, exasperated. "I don't understand why you need to have a baby right now. Why can't you be happy with just me?"

"Michael," Kimberly said in a choked voice, her back still to him, "the only thing I've ever really wanted is to be a mother. Why can't you support me in that?"

"I am supporting you," Michael said quietly. "The only reason I'm doing this is because of you. I love you, and I want you to be happy." With a frustrated sigh, he turned and walked abruptly out of the room.

Sobbing, Kimberly sank onto the couch and held a pillow tightly across her middle. It was hard enough to deal with her infertility, but when Michael withdrew because of it, she felt even more hopeless. *Having children is the most important thing to me*, she thought sadly, *and Michael acts as if it doesn't even matter to him.* Kimberly buried her head in the pillow. *Lord, why are You doing this to me?* she asked numbly. *Why me?*

She wasn't sure she could take the pain much longer.

WEEKS PASSED, AND KIMBERLY CONTINUED TRYING TO GET pregnant. She underwent a laparoscopy for her endometriosis, secretly hoping that after the surgery, she'd finally be able to conceive, as the doctors had told her often happened. She also continued having artificial inseminations and taking fertility drugs. Finally, in August, four months after the miscarriage, she had a positive blood test.

Unlike their response to the first pregnancy, however, Kimberly and Michael didn't immediately tell their families. They wanted to wait until Kimberly got past the first 12 critical weeks. But Kimberly couldn't wait that long to tell Debbie.

"Debbie!" she eagerly called out, walking through her friend's front door one hot summer day. "Guess what?" She was beaming.

Debbie was sitting in the easy chair, giving Sarah Beth her bottle. As she studied Kimberly, a knowing smile crept across her face. "You're pregnant!"

Kimberly nodded happily. Her face glowed.

"Congratulations, Kimmie!" Debbie exclaimed. "Come

here and give me a hug!" She held Sarah Beth's bottle in one hand and threw her other arm around Kimberly's neck. "You deserve this. You'll be a wonderful mom."

They chatted excitedly about the news all afternoon. Despite her elation, however, Kimberly was still nervous. *What if I miscarry again?* she worried. *I don't know if I could handle that a second time.*

A few days later, Debbie's mother died suddenly. Kimberly, eager to support her devastated friend, helped Debbie get her things together and promised to take the Eastins to the airport the next day.

Early the following morning, Kimberly stood outside her apartment, holding a cake she'd baked for Debbie's family. Balancing the cake with one hand and her purse and keys in the other, she carefully made her way down the steep stairway. Halfway down, her sandals skidded on the worn concrete, and she lost her balance.

"Oh no!" Kimberly shrieked. The cake flew out of her hand and plopped on the sidewalk below, and Kimberly thudded painfully down the stairs after it, wincing as her bottom hit each of the remaining steps. When she finally reached the last one, she gingerly got up and brushed off the back of her shorts. Amazingly, except for an aching backside, she felt okay.

"Well, so much for the cake," she muttered. She checked her watch. *I'll have to clean up this mess when I get back,* she thought and hurried toward her car.

When she dropped the Eastins off at the airport, Kimberly was still feeling fine. The next day at the library, however, as she stood on a step stool, putting books away, her abdomen began to cramp. She nervously went to the rest room and discovered that she was spotting. Kimberly's heart pounded, and she felt lightheaded. *No—not again,* she thought, anguished. *What am I going to do?* After half an hour of worriedly running back and forth to the rest room to check her bleeding, Kimberly decided to go home. She wasn't going to sacrifice this baby to a part-time job at the library.

At her doctor's suggestion, Kimberly tried bed rest, but she continued to bleed for two days. When the bleeding finally stopped, she knew she'd lost the baby. This time Kimberly didn't have to go in for another D&E because the miscarriage had occurred so early in the pregnancy—but the emotional pain was just as intense.

The next week Kimberly quit her job at the library and glumly waited for Debbie to return from her mother's funeral. Again, Michael didn't know how to help her through her pain, and it seemed that even God had abandoned her. He was the One who had the power to make her pregnant, but He wasn't demonstrating it—and Kimberly felt as if He were mercilessly withholding some gift from her. Sitting alone in her dark bedroom, she struggled to pray. *It's my fault that I fell down the stairs,* she thought bitterly. *It's my fault I miscarried. God must be punishing me because of some past sin,* she concluded.

When Debbie returned a few days later, Kimberly finally got the emotional release she desperately needed. Debbie, though still grieving her mother's sudden death, was devastated to hear Kimberly's news.

"I know how much you wanted this," Debbie said, tears streaming down her face. "Kimmie, you'd be such a good mother. I've seen how you are with Sarie. I don't know why God isn't allowing this to happen."

Kimberly grabbed a tissue from the end table next to the couch and wiped her eyes. "Does . . . He . . . even . . . care?" she sobbed brokenly.

Debbie looked at her tenderly. "Yes, He cares very much," she said softly, squeezing Kimberly around the shoulders. Sitting back, Debbie crossed her legs and smoothed down her brightly patterned shorts. "You know, Kimmie," she said matter-of-factly, "life is like a parade. You're focused on your own float, but God sees the whole parade. Have faith in Him—He knows what He's doing. You've got to let God take control of this."

"I know," Kimberly whispered reluctantly. She knew Debbie was right, that she needed to release her obsession to the Lord, but Kimberly didn't know how to do that. Motherhood was something she'd always wanted. How could she give that up? And weren't babies good things to desire?

Kimberly continued going to the fertility clinic, yet slipped further into depression. She and Michael were doing all the right things to get pregnant, but they weren't successful—and Kimberly couldn't understand why. To make things even more difficult, Michael remained emotionally detached from their situation. Whenever Kimberly asked his advice, Michael would deflect the responsibility to her.

"Do you think I should try that new fertility drug?" Kimberly would question, hoping that Michael would give her direction or show some interest.

Michael would just shrug his shoulders. "I don't know," he'd say absently. "Do whatever you think is best."

Kimberly's heart would sink. *Why can't he be more involved?* she would wonder, frustrated.

As the weeks passed and Kimberly became more and more despairing, Michael suggested that she see a counselor. He didn't know how to help his wife through her grief, but maybe a therapist could. Kimberly went to several sessions, and though the therapist didn't have any answers to the questions Kimberly had about her grief or infertility, she did plant an idea in her mind.

One Saturday morning when Kimberly arrived for her session, the therapist pulled out a newspaper clipping and waved it excitedly in front of Kimberly's face. "Look at this!" she said, pointing to the article. The headline read: "Hard to Place Children—Could They Find a Home with You?" Pictured were several older children of various ethnic backgrounds.

Putting the article in Kimberly's hand, the therapist looked intently at her and asked, "Would you consider adoption? Look at these children!" she continued, pointing at the photographs. "They need homes. Why do you want to have your own baby so much when there are kids out there who need good, strong families?"

Kimberly frowned. The children in the photos looked 10 or 11 years old. *A child that age probably has a lot of emotional baggage,* she thought skeptically. *I don't think I could handle that right now.* She refolded the article and handed it to the therapist, saying slowly, "I don't know. I really want to have my own baby."

Shrugging, the therapist took the newspaper clipping and put it back in her purse. "Okay," she said. "But I think you should consider it."

"I will," Kimberly told her noncommittally. It was an interesting idea. She could see Michael and herself adopting an infant, not an older child; but she would rather have a baby of her own.

Kimberly left the session that day still focused on conceiving. But the therapist's words remained with her.

KIMBERLY RUBBED HER NECK TIREDLY AS SHE SURVEYED THE array of boxes stacked everywhere in their new apartment in San Diego. Several months after Kimberly's last session with the therapist, Michael's ship had been transferred to California. He had moved from New Jersey several weeks before Kimberly had, traveling with the ship, and wouldn't be arriving in San Diego for another month or two. So Kimberly bore the responsibility of getting their apartment put together.

First I've got to find the fan, she thought, waving a piece of paper in front of her face in an effort to create a breeze. Walking with determination to the stack of boxes, Kimberly started opening the ones marked "Miscellaneous." The fan had to be there somewhere.

San Diego was hot, especially in July, but Kimberly was still happy about the move. Moving meant change, and change was good. She could start over, go to a new fertility doctor, experience a different part of the country, even color her hair if she wanted. No one in San Diego knew her except the other military families moving with them from New Jersey. And that was the other wonderful thing about the transfer—Debbie was coming, too.

Debbie was spending most of the summer with her father up in Oregon, so she wasn't in San Diego yet. She'd be arriving the early part of August, just a couple of weeks from now—and Kimberly was having a hard time waiting. Life just didn't seem the same without their daily phone calls and visits.

Kimberly spent the next few weeks unpacking boxes, setting up the apartment, and finding her way around town. Finally, August 10th arrived, the day when Debbie was supposed to fly down from Oregon. But a week passed, and Kimberly didn't hear from her. Confused, Kimberly left several messages on her friend's answering machine, hoping that someone would call her back. She was getting worried.

Finally, after two weeks, Debbie called. "I'm sorry nobody's called you back, Kimmie," she said. She sounded tired.

"What happened?" Kimberly asked, her throat tight.

"Well, I passed out at the airport in San Francisco on the way here," she said soberly. "Someone took Sarie and me to the hospital. I was there for a week, and they couldn't figure out what was wrong with me. At first they thought I had an inner ear infection, but I was so dizzy, I couldn't even sit up, so they ruled that out." She sighed, then said wearily, "Now they think I might have Meniere's disease. They say it affects a person's sense of balance."

Kimberly's heart thudded. "Are you okay?" she asked anxiously.

"I don't know," Debbie said. "Bill took some time off from the ship and came here, so I'm not alone, but I have to go through more tests."

"Oh my goodness," Kimberly whispered. After promising to visit Debbie soon, Kimberly hung up the phone and sank into a kitchen chair. She had a bad feeling about this. Debbie's agonizing headaches were awful enough, but now she was having dizzy spells, too. *Lord, please watch over my friend,* Kimberly prayed, trying to ignore the sick feeling growing in the pit of her stomach.

Kimberly visited her friend the next day—and Debbie didn't

look well. Her skin was blanched, and she appeared weak and exhausted. A week later, they found out why.

Debbie had to go to the hospital for another CAT scan, and Kimberly offered to watch Sarah Beth while another friend drove Debbie to her appointment. When Debbie returned a few hours later, her face was chalk white and she was trembling. Dropping into a chair, she said in an unsteady voice, "Kimmie, you're not going to believe this, but they said I have a brain tumor." Debbie's hazel eyes were wide with fear.

"No," Kimberly whispered. Her muscles stiffened, and she clutched Sarah Beth tightly to her chest. *Brain cancer?* she thought numbly. *My best friend has brain cancer! Not Debbie! Why does it have to be her?*

Kimberly put Sarah Beth into her playpen, then, walking over to her friend, she bent down and wrapped her arms around her. Tears ran down her cheeks as she held Debbie silently.

A few minutes later, Bill came home—Debbie had called him from the hospital. Still trembling, Debbie looked at Kimberly. "I need to talk with Bill," she said hoarsely. "Could you take Sarie out for a little while?"

"Sure," Kimberly said, wiping away her tears. "We'll go for a walk."

Fortifying herself with a deep breath, she fastened Sarah Beth into her stroller and took her outside. The afternoon sunlight was blinding, which made it even harder for Kimberly to see through her tears. She walked past a few houses, then stopped and stood there, sobbing. *When you have cancer, you die—especially if it's in your brain,* she thought bleakly. *A brain tumor! What's the survival rate for someone with a brain tumor?*

Though her knees felt unsteady, Kimberly started pushing the stroller again. She walked past a few houses, stopped, and cried. Wanting to give Debbie and Bill as much time to themselves as possible, Kimberly continued to push, pause, and cry for about an hour. Finally, she turned around and took Sarah Beth back home.

Debbie was admitted to the hospital the following week,

and Bill asked Kimberly if she could take care of Sarah Beth while he and Debbie's father and sister stayed at the hospital. Michael's ship hadn't docked yet, and Kimberly didn't have any commitments in San Diego, so she immediately agreed to help out. It gave her the opportunity to return some of the blessings that Debbie had given her and to care for Sarah Beth, something she loved to do.

Debbie's brain tumor was successfully removed, and she stayed in the hospital for over a month, undergoing chemotherapy and receiving extensive physical therapy. Meanwhile, Kimberly cooked for Bill, cleaned the house, and took care of Sarah Beth. When Debbie finally came home, her shiny brown hair was gone, a side effect of the chemotherapy. Except for her face, which was swollen from the medication she was taking, she was extremely thin and weak.

At home, Debbie had to undergo additional physical therapy. The tumor had been at the back of her brain, on what the doctors called her "throw-up" nerve. For the rest of her life, she would have to fight off nausea and dizziness. Now, however, she had to relearn basic activities such as walking. Debbie slowly learned to crawl, then walk again, clinging to her walker or the bars that Bill had installed around the house. She was still so dizzy, however, that she often fell, bruising herself. It was difficult for Kimberly to see her friend so helpless and childlike.

Kimberly continued to help Debbie until Michael's ship finally docked in San Diego, a month after Debbie had left the hospital. Soon he and Kimberly found a strong Baptist church and began attending regularly. Kimberly also found another doctor to treat her infertility, and within weeks of Michael's return, they started the process all over again.

With Debbie no longer able to give her emotional and spiritual support, Kimberly relapsed into depression. And since Michael was frequently away, she felt even more alone.

Seeing Kimberly's fragile emotional state, Michael insisted that she start working—he wanted her out of her own little world. Debbie was physically well enough to be by herself during the day and had started counseling, hoping to sort out her feelings about cancer; and Bill had pulled some strings to get their two-year-old daughter into the military day-care center. Also, Debbie's father and in-laws came and spent some time with her. The Eastins didn't need Kimberly's help on a daily basis anymore.

Kimberly found a job downtown at an accounting firm, and she and Michael carpooled to work. But being out in the workforce did nothing to ease her depression, which worsened over the next few weeks. One Sunday at church, Kimberly lost control. She had entered the lobby with Michael, then waited as he grabbed a cup of coffee across the room. As she stood there, a greeter approached her.

"Hi. How are you doing?" the lady asked sweetly.

The question unleashed a storm of emotions, and without warning, Kimberly erupted into tears. Embarrassed and unable to control her weeping, she turned from the woman and bolted out the door. Michael, who'd watched the scene from across the room, cast an apologetic look at the greeter, then followed his wife to the parking lot, walking quickly to catch up with her.

"I've got to go home, Michael," Kimberly choked out. "I can't do this today."

Without a word, Michael unlocked the doors, got into the car, and drove them home.

Frustrated by her husband's silence, Kimberly began to fume. All of the pain she'd experienced as a result of Michael's reticence resurfaced. *Why won't he talk to me?* she thought, bristling. *Why does he always leave me to deal with everything alone?* She looked at his calm, quiet profile, then sighed angrily.

Michael braked at a stoplight and turned to his wife. "You really need to learn to cope with your problems better, Kimberly," he said calmly. "You're so dysfunctional. Why don't you tell me what's wrong?"

Angered at his detached tone, she said viciously, "You're my husband, Michael, not my therapist! I can't believe what a jerk you're being!"

"Come on," Michael said evenly. "You obviously need to talk about this." He pulled into their condominium parking lot, but instead of driving up to their condo, he passed it and kept winding his way through the complex.

Kimberly stubbornly folded her arms. "I'm not ready to talk until you're ready to really listen," she told him as tears cascaded down her cheeks.

Michael remained silent.

Suddenly, Kimberly decided she'd had enough. "Stop the car!" she said shrilly. "I want to go home—right now."

"No," Michael told her calmly. "I think you need to get this out."

Irritated that he wasn't acknowledging her words, Kimberly blew up. "I am not putting up with this anymore!" she shouted. With the car still moving, she unbuckled her seat belt and jumped out the door. She stumbled blindly on the asphalt, then regained her footing—and her reason. *I can't believe I just did that,* she thought, mortified. *That was really stupid. I've got to get myself under control.*

Michael jerked the car to a halt and backed up to where she stood, still shocked at what she had done. Leaning across the passenger seat, he said sharply through the open door, "Get back in the car."

Numbly, she climbed in again, and they drove home in silence. When they got inside their apartment, Michael turned to his wife. "Why don't you call that counselor Debbie has been seeing?" he asked gently. "She seems to have helped Debbie a lot."

Kimberly meekly agreed. After setting up an appointment with Debbie's counselor, Linda, for the next day, Kimberly hung up the phone, feeling immensely relieved. Finally, she'd be able to work through some of her volatile emotions.

She had hit bottom—things could only get better from here.

$\mathcal{K}$IMBERLY STARTED COUNSELING IN EARNEST, AND THIS TIME, the therapy brought her healing—in her own life and in her marriage to Michael. At Linda's request, Michael attended several sessions with Kimberly, and they finally began to talk again. Michael admitted that he was feeling insecure about being a father—he hadn't had a strong father figure growing up—and Kimberly was able to tell Michael how she felt about his passive role in the infertility treatment process. As he listened, he gradually became more receptive to her feelings.

At the same time, she and Michael became much more involved in their church. Kimberly sang in the choir, played on the baseball team, and began attending a Sunday school class. Taught by their preacher's wife, the class examined a woman's role in her family.

As the months passed, Kimberly's friend Debbie slowly regained her strength, and Kimberly talked with or saw her almost every day. A steadfast example of reliance upon God, Debbie always challenged Kimberly in her faith. Kimberly now read her Bible regularly, and it wasn't just to find more scriptures about having children—her Sunday school class and Debbie's friendship had pushed her to start examining what kind of wife and daughter she was. *Am I loving God as a daughter should?* she asked herself. *Am I loving Michael unconditionally?* It seemed as if every time Kimberly opened her Bible, God was talking to her, and she soaked it up.

Michael, too, was growing dramatically spiritually. He began taking his Bible to work and became more confident in sharing his faith. Kimberly was thrilled to see her husband seeking God. Throughout their marriage, she had counted on Michael to be the model Christian husband she'd longed for all her life, without realizing that it takes time to produce spiritual maturity. But as she herself matured spiritually and emotionally, she realized she'd placed unrealistic expectations on Michael. With Linda's help, Kimberly gradually learned to appreciate Michael for who he was—not who he could or should be.

As Kimberly worked through the issues in her marriage and in her own life, she began to feel more free. Amazingly, her infertility no longer had a death grip on her. Though getting pregnant was still important to her, she wasn't as driven as she had been before. But after devoting almost three years of her life to trying to conceive, she wasn't about to give up now.

God, however, had other plans for her.

One day Michael arrived home with interesting news. Putting his briefcase on the counter, he turned to his wife. "My boss told me about a huge adoption seminar that's coming to town," he said quietly, searching Kimberly's green eyes for her reaction. "He and his wife went to one, and they said it was really informative."

Kimberly raised her eyebrows in surprise. *I can't believe Michael's initiating this,* she thought happily. Before, she had always been the one who brought up the subject of children. "Well, let's go then," she said, giving him a thankful smile.

The all-day seminar was held the following Saturday. She and Michael heard the testimonies of birth parents, adoptive parents, and adopted children. They also listened to stories of people who had adopted drug-dependent babies, handicapped infants, and hard-to-place older children. The seminar even covered private adoptions—and this especially captured Kimberly's attention. She listened intently as the speaker described how people could adopt babies without the expense and wait of dealing with an agency.

"There are healthy infants from every racial group available for placement," the speaker explained. "You can find one through private adoption, and the fastest way to begin is by telling everyone you know and meet that you want to adopt." The woman held up a small white card. "Print up a business card with the word 'Adoption' on it and your name and phone number," she said. "Then pass it out wherever you go. Someone will get back to you sooner than you think. You *will* get a baby."

This idea of networking was new to Kimberly. When she and Michael left the seminar, she felt a glimmer of hope. *Maybe this is the way I can be a mother,* she thought. *Maybe Michael and I should try adoption.*

When Kimberly got home, she called her mother and described the day's events, mentioning what the speaker had said about networking to find a baby.

Ava, as usual, was calm and collected. "Well, that's nice," she said. "I'm glad you had a good time."

As Kimberly hung up with her mother, she thought, *That's the end of that subject, I guess.*

She forgot about her conversation with her mom until a few weeks later. Early one morning, she heard the phone ringing downstairs. Lying in bed, Kimberly squinted at the clock through sleepy eyes. "It's 5:00 in the morning!" she protested to Michael. "Don't answer that." Closing her eyes, she murmured, "It's either a wrong number or somebody's died, and if somebody has died, I don't want to know about it until I'm awake."

But the phone continued to ring, so at last Michael got up and went downstairs to answer it. After several minutes, he walked back into their bedroom, his face serious. "It's for you," he said.

Kimberly's eyes widened, and she sat up. "Who died?" she asked nervously, hoping that in her grumpy state, she hadn't been right about the reason for such an early call.

Michael didn't say anything, so Kimberly relaxed and shuffled downstairs. When she picked up the phone and heard the voice on the other end of the line, however, her brow wrinkled in confusion. It was her cousin Cindi calling from Illinois.

"Sorry to bother you so early, but I have a question for you," Cindi said brightly. "Your mother told me that you and Michael want a baby. Well, this morning an obstetrician friend of mine delivered a healthy white baby who's going to be put up for adoption."

"Oh . . ." Kimberly's voice trailed off, and her heart pounded. *Where is she going with this?* she wondered excitedly.

"My friend put you at the top of his waiting list of adoptive parents," Cindi went on. "The baby's yours if you want it, but we need an answer now."

Flabbergasted, Kimberly turned to call for Michael and

almost ran into him. He had followed her downstairs and was standing next to her, smiling his approval. "Of course we want the baby!" she said ecstatically into the receiver. She didn't even stop to ask whether the infant was a girl or a boy. Dizzy with joy, Kimberly fell back against Michael's chest. *This is a miracle!* she realized. *God just gave us this baby!*

Grinning from ear to ear, Kimberly continued to talk to her cousin, getting more details. The infant was a boy, and his mother was an unwed teenager. They'd have to get a lawyer right away who could take them through the process and inform them of the laws, especially because it would be an interstate adoption. And they'd have to fly to Illinois immediately.

Kimberly and Michael spent the weekend in a flurry of activity as they prepared to leave. *We don't have any baby things, or even a name picked out,* Kimberly thought in nervous excitement. Despite all the time they'd spent trying to get pregnant, they weren't prepared for a baby! Kimberly borrowed a car seat from Debbie and got a few necessities together, but she and Michael didn't tell anyone except her parents about the pending adoption. Illinois state law dictated that the birth mother had 48 hours to change her mind, and they wanted to be sure this would work out before they shared their good news.

Kimberly felt certain that it would work out. *This baby is mine,* she told herself gratefully. *This is the child that I've prayed for these last three years!* From the moment she'd said yes, Kimberly had felt an intimate connection to this infant she'd never seen or even known about before.

Two days after hearing the good news, she and Michael flew to Illinois, eagerly holding hands the whole way. They stayed with Kimberly's parents while they went through the adoption process. They had decided to have an open adoption if the baby's birth mother agreed to it. After trying to have a baby for so long, Kimberly could imagine how hard it would be to give up one's own child. She wanted to respect the feelings of the birth mother, especially since she was so young. The baby, however, hadn't seen his mom since she had handed him over in the hospital. He was temporarily staying with Nancy, a foster parent, until the Osborns could come get him—and that was where Kimberly first laid eyes on her son.

The morning after she and Michael arrived in Illinois, they went with her parents to Nancy's house. Standing at the front door, Kimberly's stomach flip-flopped as she rang the doorbell. She knew that the baby's attorney—the law required the adoptee to have one, too—had told Nancy not to give him to the Osborns if "they didn't look like nice people."

Fidgeting with the buttons on her best outfit, Kimberly wondered nervously, *What if she doesn't like us? What if I can't do this?* She shot a panicked look at Michael, and he reached over and squeezed her hand.

Nancy opened the door and welcomed the four of them into the house. "The baby's sleeping in the back bedroom," she said, pausing to look Kimberly and Michael over. "Come on. I'll show you where he is."

Kimberly's parents stayed in the living room while Kimberly and Michael followed Nancy down the hall. When Kimberly walked up to the crib and saw the tiny boy sleeping peacefully there, she caught her breath. He was swaddled in a baby blue blanket, and his four-day-old skin was pink and wrinkled. *He's beautiful!* she thought joyfully. "May I pick him up?" she asked Nancy. Quickly, she stopped herself. *Of course I can!* she realized. *He's my son.*

Kimberly picked up the baby, and for the next two hours, the infant didn't leave her arms. She cuddled and cooed and stroked his tiny face, awed that God was giving her this perfect little child. It didn't matter that he hadn't come from her body—there was an unbreakable bond between them.

After chatting awhile with the Osborns and Kimberly's parents, Nancy called the baby's attorney. "I think they're decent people," she said, smiling into the telephone. After she hung up, she turned to Kimberly and said warmly, "Looks as if everything's going to work out. You can consider yourself his mother."

After much heartache and waiting, Kimberly's dream of motherhood had finally come true. The name she and Michael picked out for their son, David Nathaniel, means "beloved, gift of God," and that was truly what the boy was—a gift from God.

OTHERHOOD WAS EVERYTHING KIMBERLY HAD HOPED IT would be. She absolutely loved being a mom to Nathan (as they soon came to call him), and it showed in the glow on her face. The time she spent cradling, comforting, and nurturing Nathan was fulfilling. And with the new addition, Kimberly finally felt they were truly a family.

She was also able to share her joy with Debbie. Though still dizzy and weak at times, Debbie continued to get stronger and healthier. She and Kimberly often spent their days together, taking care of their children. Just as Kimberly had once been Sarah Beth's first baby-sitter, Debbie was Nathan's first sitter as well, watching him from time to time when Kimberly went to get her hair done or out with Michael. Debbie loved Nathan as much as Kimberly loved Sarah Beth, and their time together was meaningful.

Still, Kimberly continued her fertility treatments. In the months after Nathan was born, Kimberly often lay on the table after an insemination, stretching out her arm to hold a bottle for Nathan, who was in his infant seat on the floor. Nathan, she felt, was an unrepeatable miracle. His adoption had come too easily; he had just fallen into their laps. There was no way she and Michael would be able to adopt another child so quickly. Kimberly wanted a brother or sister for Nathan—and she figured the best way to have one was by continuing the fertility drugs and inseminations. She knew that Michael's four years with the navy were fast running out, and they'd never be able to afford the expense once he left the service.

Nathan was a year old when Michael's time with the military ended—as did Kimberly's time with the fertility specialist. That wasn't the only change they were facing, though.

Small-town people at heart, she and Michael both wanted to move to a less-populated, slower-paced area. They were ready to put down roots. Again, Kimberly was excited about the move because it meant more change.

Michael found the perfect job as a drug and alcohol addiction therapist in a veterans hospital in Murfreesboro, Tennessee. Kimberly was happy for her husband, but Tennessee wasn't the first place she would have picked—in fact, on her list of possible states to move to, Tennessee had finished last.

But God knew what Kimberly needed. With His wonderful sense of humor and timing, two years after the Osborns moved to Tennessee, He brought Debbie and her husband, Bill, there. After leaving the navy, Bill got a job as a flight instructor in Memphis. Kimberly talked to her dearest friend on the phone several times a week and saw her once a month, despite the five-hour drive between their homes. Michael was in the Navy Reserves and went to drill in Memphis every month, so of course, Kimberly and three-year-old Nathan went with him to visit Debbie. Kimberly was grateful for that time with her friend. She felt it was God's way of giving each of them the support they needed and craved from one another.

Kimberly also found that having Michael around was a blessing. She hadn't realized that the long trips away had been just as difficult for Michael as they had been for her. He had loathed being away from home so often and was thankful to finally be out of the service. As they spent more time together, they grew closer.

After moving to Tennessee, they quickly found a wonderful church and dove right into church activities. Kimberly sang in the choir, and they both got involved in a Home Builders Bible study. Soon Kimberly began to meet other couples who were struggling with the infertility issues she and Michael had dealt with for so long. As she talked with these other couples, Kimberly felt God pushing her to facilitate a Bible study in their church that would help others through the dark valley of infertility. She needed to be encouraging them just as Debbie had encouraged her. She needed to give her testimony so that others could have hope.

God's clear call to her to begin a Bible study was nerve-wracking. *I don't have what it takes to be a leader,* she thought anxiously. *I'm not spiritually strong enough—I don't know enough about the Bible to encourage others in their walk with God.*

For almost a year, Kimberly halfheartedly prayed and thought about the possibility—and God continued to work on her resistant heart. Finally, one day she surrendered her concerns and asked God for help in doing the study. *Okay, Lord,* Kimberly told Him, *if You really want me to do this, let me know beyond a shadow of a doubt. I need Your help. Please put the materials in my hands. If You're the One doing this through me, You'll get all the glory, and that's the way I want it to be.*

HOLDING FIVE-YEAR-OLD NATHAN'S HAND AND SQUINTING in the bright sun, Kimberly walked to their mailbox one afternoon a few days later. As she eyed the box, she noticed that it was stuffed so full that the lid wasn't quite shut. *Why do we have so much mail?* she wondered.

She reached her hand into the mailbox and pulled out a large brown envelope. Immediately, Kimberly knew what it was. Chills went up her neck as she stared at the return address. It was from Focus on the Family.

Wondering whether she should home-school Nathan, Kimberly had written the ministry a letter a few weeks before, asking Dr. Dobson's advice on the situation. In passing, she had also mentioned her struggle with infertility.

Still standing in front of the mailbox, Kimberly eagerly ripped open the envelope. In addition to some home-schooling materials, there was also a tape, a newsletter, and a book that covered the topic of infertility. Enclosed was a note: "We thought these materials would help you. Here they are, with our best regards."

Well, Lord, she prayed, laughing inside, *it looks as though*

You've put the materials in my hands! Now she had resources to make the Bible study happen—and no longer had any doubt about what God wanted her to do.

The next day Kimberly called her pastor and arranged the details of the study. Shortly afterward, she and Michael began a 13-week program on infertility with three other couples in their church. They looked at different people in the Bible who had struggled with infertility and even discussed what it meant to be adopted into the family of God. As the couples shared with and prayed for one another, they bonded—and God began to work in their lives. Within two years of the study, three of the four couples had been blessed with children. One couple actually conceived after years of trying, and the others adopted children.

One of those babies ended up being the newest member of the Osborn family: Jonathan.

During the week of vacation Bible school at their church, a friend of Kimberly's, Melody, came up to her one day and asked casually, "Kimberly, did you know that Diane has been asking around, trying to find out if any couples are interested in adopting a baby?"

Kimberly looked at Melody in surprise. "No," she replied. "Whose baby is it?"

"Oh, I don't know," Melody said, shrugging her shoulders. "Diane told me the attorney she employed in her son's adoption process called her, asking if she and her husband wanted another baby."

A light went on in Kimberly's head. *That attorney is Jane Samuels,* she realized. *I have her phone number on my refrigerator!* She had gotten it from Diane over a year ago but hadn't done anything with it. At that time, Tennessee law dictated that the birth mother had a month to change her mind, and Kimberly wasn't sure she could handle it if the mother decided to take her child back after that amount of time.

Melody continued. "Diane and her husband prayed about it and decided not to adopt, but she promised to ask around. She thought you and Michael weren't planning on adopting again now that Nathan's getting older. But I thought I'd mention it just in case you were interested."

Despite her previous concerns, Kimberly definitely was interested, and so was Michael. They loved Nathan dearly and had a wonderful relationship with his birth parents—why couldn't it work again? The next day, she took Ms. Samuels's phone number off her refrigerator and called her. "We'd really like this baby if he hasn't already been promised to someone else," she said eagerly.

The attorney was blunt. "I'm sorry," she said, "but the baby has been promised to someone else, and I'm ready to send the couple's paperwork to the birth mother today."

Kimberly's heart sank, but she wasn't ready to give up. "You mean, the birth mother hasn't seen their biography yet?" she asked hopefully.

"No."

"Please . . . if you'll just wait one more day—I'll get ours to you by tomorrow," Kimberly pleaded.

Ms. Samuels reluctantly agreed, and Kimberly and Michael spent the evening writing up their biography. Kimberly gave it to the attorney the next day.

Meanwhile, Kimberly and Michael continued to pray that they would be able to adopt this baby, even naming him Jonathan Paul. Seven-year-old Nathan was just as determined to have a sibling. He had prayed for a baby brother every night for two years, and it tore at Kimberly's heart to see him, night after night, kneeling so hopefully before God. *What if God says no?* she often thought painfully. *What if we don't get another baby and Nathan doesn't understand why?*

She didn't want to dissuade her son from asking God for a sibling, however, so Kimberly simply sat by and listened, silently petitioning God as well. She knew that since her son was home-schooled, it was difficult for him not to have friends around; it was one of the reasons he wanted a brother so badly. Nathan never gave up, constantly hopeful that if he prayed long and hard enough, God would grant his request.

God did answer Nathan's prayer, but not in the way anyone had anticipated. In the following weeks, a divine mismatch occurred. The birth mother decided to give the baby to the first couple, but when the attorney called with the news, she contacted the wrong people. Ms. Samuels, thinking that she was talking with Kimberly and Michael, accidentally dialed the first couple's home and told them the birth mother had chosen another couple. Understandably, the original couple was devastated, but they grieved the situation and took comfort in knowing that this was God's will.

When the baby was born, he was eight weeks premature. Still thinking that she had talked to the Osborns, the attorney called the original adoptive parents and told them the baby had been born. At that point she realized her mistake. Explaining the mix-up, she assured them that they were supposed to be the parents. But by that time, the couple had already grieved the loss of the baby. And because he was born premature, they weren't ready for him, emotionally or logistically.

They decided not to take the boy—and the Osborns adopted Jonathan.

KIMBERLY SAT EAGERLY WITH HER FRIEND KRISTY IN THE Nashville arena just a week after Jonathan's birth. Long before she'd even known of his existence, she and Kristy had planned to go together to the first Renewing the Heart conference, only 45 minutes from their home in Murfreesboro.

Her hands clasped together, Kimberly listened intently as Lisa Harper, the emcee of the conference, explained her vision for Renewing the Heart and the obstacles she'd encountered when proposing the idea.

"Many people warned me that nobody would come to the conference," Lisa said as she gazed around the packed arena. "But I really felt God wanted this to happen. And now look— we're completely sold out!"

Lisa's words struck a chord in Kimberly's heart. For several weeks, she had felt God calling her to something big as well. During the break, she mentioned it to Kristy.

Sitting at one of the small tables on a balcony overlooking the arena, Kimberly smiled at her friend. "During my quiet times lately," she confided, "I've felt as if I were standing next to a deep chasm, with God telling me to step out into the nothingness and depend only on Him."

"Wow," Kristy commented, her blue eyes shining, "that's incredible. Do you know what He's telling you to do?"

Kimberly ran her hand through her wavy, brown hair. "Not right now, but when God tells me to step out, I'll know it's Him," she said. "It makes me nervous, though," she added. In fact, just thinking about it made her heart beat more rapidly. *What if I don't have enough faith to do something like that?* she wondered. *Could God really use somebody like me?*

Kimberly wouldn't find out for several months.

When Kristy and Kimberly left the Renewing the Heart conference, Lisa's words and her own calling were deeply etched in Kimberly's heart. Soon, however, she became absorbed in caring for Nathan and visiting her newborn son in the hospital. Jonathan was so small—two pounds, five ounces—that after his birth he stayed in the neonatal ward for a month and a half. Kimberly took Nathan to see him every day. It was about an hour's drive, but since she was home-schooling, she could work Nathan's schedule around visits to his brother. When Jonathan finally came home, the Osborns were ecstatic, though nervous about taking care of such a tiny baby. But Jonathan was healthy, and Kimberly was thankful for that.

Debbie never got to see Jonathan, however. Though she and Kimberly talked several times a week on the phone, they hadn't been able to see each other in some time. Then, shortly after Jonathan came home, Debbie's cancer recurred.

"Kimmie," Debbie said over the line one day, "I've been having those dizzy spells again."

Kimberly's stomach churned nervously. She swallowed, saying nothing.

"The other day I went to the dentist," Debbie continued, "and I had Sarie with me. I had a terrible dizzy spell and tried to walk home." Her voice caught in her throat. "It took me over an hour to go three blocks. I think the tumor's back."

"Oh, Debbie," Kimberly said quickly, "everything's going to be okay. It's probably nothing." Deep down, she knew that wasn't the case, but she wasn't ready to face the possibility of Debbie getting sick again.

The tumor was back, and it had recurred with a vengeance. A few weeks after their phone conversation, Debbie went into the hospital. This time the surgeons said that once the tumor was out, it would keep coming back, and more quickly each time.

Kimberly talked with her best friend again after the tumor had been removed. Kimberly wanted to visit Debbie in the hospital, but the Eastin family insisted that Kimberly didn't need to come—they had everything under control, and the doctors expected Debbie to pull through.

Three days later, Debbie passed away.

Her best friend's death devastated Kimberly. *I didn't even get to say good-bye,* she told herself mournfully. *What will I do without her?*

An hour after she found out that Debbie had died, Kimberly drove to Memphis. She stayed for five days, helping Debbie's family, going through her friend's personal effects, and making phone calls. It wasn't the same as saying good-bye, but it gave her the closure she needed. As Kimberly drove home, tears running down her face, she thanked God for the friend He'd given her in Debbie.

Debbie was gone, but her love and Christian witness would live in Kimberly's heart forever.

*O*NE MORNING ABOUT A MONTH LATER, KIMBERLY WAS IN HER kitchen getting ready to bake molasses cookies for Christmas—one of her favorite things to do. After tying a red and green Christmas apron around her waist, she measured out two cups of flour. *Now, where's the nutmeg?* she puzzled, looking in the cupboard. She found it and measured it out, then turned back to the recipe to determine what she needed next.

Suddenly, an inaudible voice cut through her cookie-making thoughts: *This is what I want you to do—have an infertility seminar for couples in your area.*

Kimberly stopped, stunned, as plans for a seminar continued to come to her.

Give it from a Christian perspective, but open it up to the public, the voice persisted. *Ask Ruby, Jonathan's birth mother, to give her testimony. Give yours, and have Michael contribute as well.*

The thoughts flew at her so quickly that Kimberly had to stop mixing the cookie dough and write them down. She was to have the seminar at their church at 10:00 in the morning on a Saturday. For several minutes, she wrote furiously. Then, her heart thudding, she stopped. What if these thoughts weren't from God and she was making everything up in her head? She needed to find out before this went any further. *Lord,* she prayed, *if this is really from You, tell me what day You want this on.*

Immediately, she got her answer: *Valentine's Day.*

Kimberly hadn't yet looked at the calendar for the following year. She took a deep breath. *Okay, God,* she prayed, *if You want it on Valentine's Day, it has to be on a Saturday.*

Walking over to the refrigerator, she stared at the calendar. February 14th was a Saturday. Kimberly leaned against the counter, trembling. *Lord,* she prayed, *You really want me to do this, don't You? Why?*

She wanted to be obedient but was scared to death. What if she couldn't pull it off? What if nobody came? Nervous, Kimberly called Michael, Kristy, and another friend, Donna, asking them to pray for her. Even though God had given her some confirmation, she still wanted more. What if she had somehow dreamed this up?

The next morning Kimberly got the assurance from God that she needed. When she opened up her daily devotional, the passage spoke of following God in faith and giving one's testimony to other people. The scripture for the day read: " 'For my thoughts are not your thoughts, neither are your ways my ways,' declares the LORD" (Isaiah 55:8).

Well, that's my confirmation, Kimberly realized thankfully. *I don't think I need anything more than that.*

She called her pastor to talk about the seminar, and things quickly fell into place from there. After praying about it, she decided to call the conference "Seminar of HOPE (Holding On, Praying Expectantly) for Infertile Couples." All the speaking spots were filled without Kimberly having to solicit anyone; people approached her about giving their testimonies. She sent fliers all over Murfreesboro, Nashville, and Rutherford County, to doctors' offices, newspapers, and radio stations, expecting a large group.

The turnout—13 registered couples—wasn't anywhere as big as she'd expected, but Kimberly definitely felt God's presence there. The speakers included a couple who spoke about in-vitro fertilization, bringing the little boy they'd conceived that way; an adoption agency representative who explained the process; Jonathan's birth mother, Ruby, spoke about her positive experience in giving her son up for adoption; and Nathan's birth parents, Trish and Matthew, who had an open, ongoing relationship with their son. Kimberly spoke about her struggle to become pregnant and how she'd put her infertility before her worship of God for so many years. Michael gave a man's perspective on infertility, and as he spoke, chills went up Kimberly's spine as many things fell into place for her.

"I was really nervous about having children," Michael explained. "My parents weren't healthy role models for me growing up, and I didn't want to be the kind of father my dad was. I also had a wild past and have done some things I'm not proud of. When I was a teenager, I dated two girls who ended up having abortions." He paused, swallowing his emotion. His voice shook as he continued. "If those babies had lived, I'd have two 20-year-old children today."

Sitting in the front pew, Kimberly's jaw dropped. She'd never dreamed that Michael had these issues. He had never told her about any of this.

"I struggled with a lot of grief and doubt when Kimberly and I couldn't get pregnant," Michael said. "I wondered if maybe God was punishing me for my past sins." He looked at the audience, smiled, and said, "But I know now that He just had different plans for Kimberly and me—to adopt. God knew that Nathan and Jonathan would need homes, and He brought our boys to us."

Kimberly smiled, too. Despite all of the pain and grief she'd gone through, God had met all her needs and given her the desires of her heart—two healthy, wonderful sons and a strong marriage. Now she was at this seminar to tell other couples about it, to encourage them with her testimony, and through it all, to give God the glory, honor, and praise.

Kimberly Osborn lives with her family in Murfreesboro, Tennessee. She stays busy home-schooling her oldest son, Nathan, and caring for Jonathan. In January 1999, she and Michael adopted their third child, Matthew Levi. The Osborns continue to keep in touch with Nathan's and Jonathan's birth parents, and Kimberly hopes to do the same with Levi's. Grateful for the way the Lord has worked in her life, Kimberly eagerly tells others of God's faithfulness and unending provision.

Heart to Heart

Kimberly's story struck a chord with me because I recently found out that my sister-in-law, Kandy, is pregnant. After rejoicing with my mom, who called me with the news, I got off the phone and cried. I'm 35 years old and single, and I don't know if I'll ever get married or have children. I've thoroughly enjoyed being single, but Mother's Day gets harder every year. So does Valentine's Day. I hope and pray that the desire of my heart for a family is in accordance with God's will for my life. But if it isn't, I still have to believe unquestioningly in His sovereignty and cling fervently to His promise that He will be a Father to the fatherless and a Husband to the husbandless.

Walking by Faith ~

Lisa

Pursued by God

My sheep listen to my voice; I know them,
and they follow me. I give them eternal life,
and they shall never perish; no one can
snatch them out of my hand.
—JOHN 10:27–28

*N*INETEEN-YEAR-OLD SALIMA KAHN STOOD BEFORE THE large, gold-framed bathroom mirror, eyeing herself critically. White lace and satin covered her slim body, from her slender neck to her wrists, displaying her newly manicured fingernails, then down to the tops of her white-satin pumps. *I look good*, she thought with satisfaction as she turned from side to side, admiring the stylish, tight-waisted wedding gown. *Mom really did a beautiful job.* Though Salima had refused to wear the traditional hot pink outfit required by her fiancé's Pakistani tradition, she would not disobey the strict modesty standards dictated by her Muslim culture, that women be fully covered.

I can't believe I'm getting married today! she thought happily. Biting her lip in nervous excitement, she leaned closer to the mirror so she could inspect her smooth complexion. *A stroke of mascara here, a dab of concealer there, and I'll be ready,* she thought. Well, almost. The long, heavy veil still had to be put in place. With shaky hands, Salima carefully picked up the thick, beaded headpiece from the bathroom counter and pinned it in her hair.

The effect was beautiful.

Ivory netting cascaded down her back and over her shoulders, almost to the floor, beautifully framing her loosely curled, shoulder-length, black hair. *I look like a real bride,* Salima realized, exhilarated. She smiled at the mirror, practicing her happy bride expression for all the well-wishers who would be at the reception. Glancing at the clock, she saw that only an hour remained until the ceremony. *Oh! What if I'm late? What if no one left a car for me to get to the wedding hall? What if—*

Suddenly, a voice broke into her thoughts: "Don't do it."

Salima turned, thinking her friend Jenny had come into the bathroom after completing an errand downstairs. But no one was there.

A little shaken, Salima faced the mirror again and began fussing with the folds of her veil.

Again she heard the voice; this time it came from within her: "Don't do it."

Either I'm losing my mind or it's just wedding-day jitters, Salima thought. Aloud, she said decisively, "This is my wedding day, and I'm going to have a great time. No one is forcing me to marry Muhammed. I chose him." Since Salima was half-Afghan on her father's side, and her parents—even her mother, who was American—were steeped in Muslim culture, Salima had known from a young age that her marriage would probably be arranged. It had been difficult to convince her parents that she should be able to choose her own husband. What would everyone think if she changed her mind now? No, she had no intention of backing out, strange voice or not.

Squaring her shoulders, Salima gathered up the folds of her dress and left the bathroom, determined to go through with the wedding.

ONE NIGHT, FOUR YEARS LATER, SALIMA FOUND HERSELF PACING the kitchen floor, her one-year-old daughter, Amina, pressed against her chest. Carrying her children—Amina and her unborn son—was a light load compared with the weight that descended every time she thought about, much less saw, Muhammed.

He should be home in an hour or two, she thought, gasping from the fear that seemed to suffocate her. *Then I'll tell him I just can't do this anymore. I can't stay married to him.*

She leaned back against the Formica counter and sighed. How could she have been so wrong about her husband?

When they had met in college, Muhammed seemed the perfect gentleman. One smile from the tall, dark, handsome senior and Salima swooned. Muhammed portrayed himself as a hard-working, modern-thinking Muslim; he'd won several leadership awards, was on the student council, and was a member of the International Students Organization. From the moment they met, he had charmed Salima, and they had become engaged after only five months of dating.

Not everyone had approved of the match. Salima winced as

she thought of Brian, an old college friend who had approached her a few weeks after she announced her engagement.

"I don't think you should marry Muhammed," Brian had told her, his voice filled with concern.

"Why not?" Salima had demanded, ready to spar verbally with anyone to defend her beloved sweetheart.

"There's a lot more to him than you realize, Salima. Just trust me on this," Brian had pleaded.

"Well, obviously you don't know him as well as I do!" she had snapped. Then, pulling herself to her full 4'11" height, she had marched off in a huff.

Now, only a few years later, she stood in her kitchen, broken and afraid, wishing she had listened to her friend. She smoothed Amina's dark hair, wet from her tears, and reflected on her marriage.

It had taken only six months for Salima to realize she had made a mistake. Under Muhammed's smooth smile and charisma lay a bitter, abusive, lying, overly possessive man who looked out only for himself. He was so jealous that not long after they married, he forced Salima to transfer from the public university she was attending to a parochial women's college. Muhammed didn't trust Salima's male professors—in fact, he didn't want his wife around any men, period.

Others never saw Muhammed's belligerent, controlling personality. In public, he proudly showed off his pretty, young wife and showered her with affection; in private, he verbally and physically abused her. In public, he gave Salima flowers; in private, he threw flower vases at her. During the years of their marriage, Muhammed had chased Salima with a knife, locked her in a bathroom, and thrown at her just about everything in the house that he could lift. He cursed, belittled, and threatened her daily. But the moment they stepped out the front door, his anger was replaced by charm.

Salima couldn't take it anymore.

Sitting on a kitchen chair, she rocked Amina back and forth, trying to calm both the toddler and herself. Tonight, as soon as

Muhammed returned from his nighttime job at a telemarketing firm, she would tell him it was over. She didn't care if her relatives or even her Muslim god, Allah, condemned her. She didn't care if she were ostracized by the Muslim community, which all her life she had tried but found impossible to please. She didn't care if she were left with nothing, so long as Muhammed was out of her life.

As far as Salima was concerned, living in a pit of fear and depression was not living at all, and if she didn't do something to stand up for herself, she would die inside.

*T*HE CLOCK IN THE HALLWAY HAD JUST STRUCK 11:00 WHEN the front door slammed. "Salima!" Muhammed's deep voice boomed angrily through the house. "Why are Amina's toys not put away? What have you been doing with yourself?" His footsteps pounded up the stairs to their bedroom.

Clad in her flannel pajamas, Salima sat on the edge of the king-size bed and waited for Muhammed to enter the room. She cradled Amina, holding a bottle of milk to her daughter's tiny lips. Again she felt the weight crushing her chest.

Salima, you have to do this, she told herself, *for your sake and the children's. Be brave.*

But courage was hard to hold on to when she faced Muhammed's dark, smoldering eyes and powerful 6'2" frame.

"Muhammed, I need to talk to you," she said, gulping.

Muhammed grunted. Turning his back on his wife, he walked to the closet to change out of his work clothes.

"Listen to me—there's something wrong here," Salima said in a soft, trembling voice. "Every time I see you, I feel as though I can't breathe. Muhammed, I want to be happy. I can't be married to you any longer."

Whirling around, Muhammed gave her a hard look, his black eyes boring through her. "You'll never leave me," he scoffed. "You're not smart enough or strong enough." He marched toward her until his face was inches from her own.

"You'd come back to me the minute you walked out the door." Salima winced as his hot breath hit her cheeks.

"No. I've made up my mind, Muhammed," she said quietly, tightening her hold on Amina. "I'm filing for divorce."

Furious, Muhammed grabbed the baby's bottle and ground the bottom end into Salima's eye. She yelped, overwhelmed with the sudden pain.

"Stop!" she begged, sobbing. She tried to quiet Amina, who was also wailing.

"I'll give you a divorce, woman!" Muhammed yelled. "I want the car, the TV, and my parents' wedding jewelry!" He stomped to their fire safe and, leaning over, lifted it off the floor and hurled it at Salima and Amina.

Oh, please don't hit us, Salima thought frantically. She couldn't move.

The safe tumbled through the air, fell onto the bed in front of them, and bounced back toward Muhammed. Cursing, he began to ransack the room, opening dresser drawers and flinging clothes out, grabbing shoe boxes and tossing them onto the floor, smashing vases and lamps into the wall.

In the chaos, Salima, holding her daughter tightly, slipped out of the room and called her brother, Ahmad, at work, and also a mutual friend, Ayub. She quickly explained the situation to each of them. "Please come help me," she whispered into the receiver.

A few hours later, she sat on the living room couch, looking gratefully at Ayub, who sat in the chair across from her. At Salima's request, Ahmad had taken Muhammed to the basement, trying to get him to calm down.

Ayub leaned his elbow on the table between them, resting his dark, curly-haired head in his hand. "I knew as soon as you called me what you and Muhammed were fighting about," he said, sighing. "I was sure you'd find out about this someday." He looked sympathetically at Salima.

Find out about what? she wondered. She grabbed a tissue and dabbed at her eyes, hiding her confusion.

"He couldn't have kept the other woman a secret forever," Ayub continued, unaware that he was giving Salima new information. "As a matter of fact, I ran into her and the little boy just the other day."

"What woman? What little boy?" Salima gasped, no longer able to restrain her curiosity.

Ayub's smooth, brown face turned pale. "Uh . . . you didn't know?" he asked weakly. "Then why were you two fighting?"

"Never mind that. Tell me about this woman."

Ayub sighed and ran his fingers through his hair. "Okay," he said resignedly. "Muhammed has been with her since before you married him. Right before your wedding, I found out she was pregnant, so I asked him, 'What are you going to do about this?' And Muhammed said, 'Well, I'm getting married to Salima. I'm not going to do anything about it.' " Ayub looked apologetic. "Salima, Muhammed has been seeing her throughout your marriage. His girlfriend and her son live only a few blocks away."

"Oh, I can't believe this!" Salima said angrily. "Well, that just goes to show I made the right decision when I told Muhammed I was leaving him." She got up from the couch and paced the carpet. "Maybe other Muslim wives would put up with his abuse and cheating, but I won't!"

Growing up, Salima had seen too many beaten-down older Muslim women with vacant expressions in their eyes. She had decided at an early age that she would rather die than let the light go out of hers.

A WEEK LATER, SALIMA SAT IN THE PASSENGER SEAT OF HER father's car, looking listlessly out at the bleak Illinois landscape. The sub-zero temperatures and browns and grays of early winter matched her gloomy mood. She and her father were driving to their relatives' house to watch the Sunday afternoon football game on television. When Salima's parents found out she was leaving Muhammed, they had been supportive—

not only because they were more modern in their thinking than their Muslim relatives, but also because they were having marital problems of their own. But Salima knew her extended family would disapprove when they found out. Divorce is taboo in Muslim culture, and her relatives would not want such a stigma attached to their name.

Salima turned to her father. "Thanks for coming all the way to Chicago to help me, Dad," she said, sighing. "I couldn't have made it through the week without you."

"You're my daughter. I'll always look out for you," her father said. Then, tightening his grip on the steering wheel, he added darkly, "Besides, I couldn't let Muhammed hurt you anymore."

Soon they pulled up to a large split-level house in an affluent neighborhood. As they walked up to the front door, her cousin Abdul opened it wide. "Ali, Salima, come in!" he cried. Ushering them in from the cold, Abdul led them into the family room, where the men were seated around the television. Salima nodded cordially to them, then went into the kitchen to greet the women.

"Salima, how are you?" her cousin Nasrine asked, eyeing her critically. Before Salima could answer, Nasrine turned her attention to other matters. "Why is your father here? You just visited your parents in Missouri a month ago."

"Uh . . . I've got some things going on, and I needed him here," Salima said, trying to give out as little information as possible. *Not that you care,* she thought bitterly. She and her cousin had never been close.

"Oh," Nasrine responded vaguely. "Well, I love your necklace. Where did you get it?" Her dark eyes scanned Salima's jewelry covetously.

A wave of approval followed as each of the four women leaned forward to examine Salima's neck. She mumbled a response, then seated herself in a corner, holding Amina and listening to the small talk that circulated around her. Most of the conversation centered on money and clothes.

These women are as superficial as ever, Salima thought in disgust. *You'd think they'd have more important things to worry about.*

A couple of years ago, Salima had decided to distance herself from her Muslim relatives because she was tired of competing with them and pretending to fit in. She had begun wearing American clothes, dropped her mosque duties, and nurtured her relationships with non-Muslim friends. She knew the Muslim community wouldn't approve of her actions, but she no longer cared.

After several minutes, Salima had had enough of the shallow conversation floating around her. "I'm going to go lie down with Amina," Salima told Nasrine. "I'll be in the living room."

Stretching out on the living room couch, Salima put her arms protectively around her small daughter. As she drifted in and out of sleep, she heard the sounds of the game on TV, punctuated by her male cousins' shouts and laughter during big plays. About an hour later, she heard band music coming from the TV. It was halftime. Figuring she'd better get up and socialize, Salima prepared to sit up and lift Amina off the couch.

Suddenly, she heard something that made her freeze: "I might as well tell you that Salima and Muhammed are getting a divorce." It was her father's voice.

Great timing, Dad, Salima thought irritably. She lay back down and listened as Ali explained her marital situation.

Abdul interrupted him angrily. "Muhammed is such a nice guy," he insisted. "He works hard for Salima. He loves her. How can she do this to him?" In his agitation, he switched from English to Persian.

The other men joined in, with the women occasionally voicing their opinions from the kitchen.

After a while, Salima sprang up from the couch. *I've had enough of this!* she thought indignantly. *I may not speak Persian, but I can understand everything they're saying, and it's not right.* Leaving Amina napping on the couch, Salima stomped into the family room. When she entered the room, the men immediately stopped talking.

Hands on her hips, Salima glared at them. "If you have something to say to me," she said hotly, "say it to my face—and do it in English."

Shocked, the men just stared, their mouths open. This was the first time their petite cousin had stood up for herself—especially to her male relatives. But she was too angry to care what they thought.

"You wonder how I can do this to Muhammed?" she asked, addressing Abdul. "Well, do you know what Muhammed has done to me? He hits me! I thought he was going to kill me when I told him I was filing for divorce. In fact, my father drove all the way from Missouri to protect me from Muhammed. That's why he's here."

Her relatives shrugged. "So?" her cousin Hussain said.

Salima bristled. "So, Muhammed hit my dad when he ordered him out of the house. And he called both of us names I won't repeat."

They were still unfazed. "Muhammed is a wonderful man. He has such a good character," Abdul protested.

Nasrine broke in from the kitchen. "You can't divorce Muhammed!" she said shrilly, leaning over the kitchen counter and looking at Salima with her piercing, dark eyes. "You'll shame our family. What will people say?"

"I don't care," Salima said decisively, gathering steam. "He got us $40,000 in debt and lied to me about our finances. I only found out because my divorce lawyer told me. I've had to work two and three jobs all these years because of him!" She looked at her dad for confirmation.

Ali nodded.

"And," Salima continued, confident that this would make her relatives understand, "he's been cheating on me."

They looked at her without expression. "Come on, Salima," Hussain said condescendingly. "You must've known about it. Besides, it's not that big a deal."

"I can't believe you're going to divorce him over that," Nasrine put in rudely.

Salima turned pale and grabbed the top of the large over-stuffed chair in front of her. "My goodness, you people, he has a son with another woman!" she blurted out, then turned to leave the room. She stopped and faced them again. "Oh, and by the way," she said, her voice shaking, "I'm pregnant."

"You can't be divorced and pregnant, too!" Abdul shouted at her. "You might as well get an abortion!"

The others voiced their agreement.

"My daughter, my unborn child, and I all deserve to have a chance at life, and a good life at that!" Salima said passionately.

Trembling with rage, she strode into the living room and began to gather up her things. Then, with Amina on her hip, she ran out of the house, sobbing. Her father followed, shouting angry words at his relatives as he left. After helping Salima into the car and fastening his granddaughter into her car seat, he got behind the wheel and sped away. As they turned the corner, Salima heard her cousins yelling insults at them from the front lawn. Holding her pregnant belly, she bent over and wept.

It was the last time she saw her Muslim relatives.

*T*HE NEXT SEVERAL MONTHS PASSED SLOWLY AS SALIMA TRIED to sort out her life as a single parent. Together with her attorney, she evaluated her situation and learned that she was destitute. She had no money, no transportation—Muhammed had taken their only car. The lack of sympathy and personal rejection Salima received at the hands of her Muslim family and friends severed any remaining ties she had to her Muslim heritage.

Though her family had deserted her in her time of crisis, Salima discovered she did have a few people in her life who would continue to support and encourage her. Laura and Annie, two close Christian friends she'd met at the parochial college, provided financial support and companionship. Often, Annie would show up on Salima's doorstep after work and say, "I'm taking you grocery shopping. You and Amina need food."

Since she didn't have a car anymore, that winter Annie and Laura chauffeured Salima everywhere she needed to go—to her prenatal checkups, to her attorney's office, and on other errands. They also gave her money and figured out ways to help her make a living.

A few weeks after Salima filed for divorce, Laura stopped by her house. "Annie and I were wondering if you'd do the bookkeeping for our real estate business," she said. "It's part-time, we'll pay you $200 a week, and you can do it from your computer at home. Could you do that for us?" Laura made it sound as though Salima would be doing them a favor.

Salima hugged her friend gratefully. "Of course!" she said happily. "And this way, I'll be able to keep Amina with me, too. Thanks for thinking of me." Soon, Salima had her own bookkeeping business. It was her only source of income, but it paid the bills and put food on the table.

The work also kept her in close contact with Laura and Annie, who often would stay for dinner or coffee when they came by to pick up checks or records or needed to discuss accounting concerns. Their compassion and attentive listening contrasted starkly with the condemning words Salima had received from her Muslim friends and relatives, and their companionship sustained her through what could have been a lonely time. Although Laura and Annie never mentioned their Christian faith, Salima deeply felt and appreciated their love and acceptance.

Meanwhile, the divorce proceedings continued. Salima got full custody of her daughter because Muhammed failed to show up in court. Soon after, Salima's mother, Julie, drove to Chicago to take her back to Missouri, where she could start over and prepare to have her baby. A few months later, Ahmad—named after Salima's brother—was born.

Ahmad had a voracious appetite. Unfortunately, as his mother soon found out, he was also allergic to formula. Salima's early days with Ahmad were spent buying medicine and going to doctors. This was difficult for her because she had to rely on her parents and her mother's American family for everything and so felt like a burden. Somehow, however, all their needs were provided for. The generosity of her parents and American relatives was astounding. It seemed that all she had to do was verbalize a need and someone would be offering to help a few days later.

In Missouri, Salima began the slow process of healing. Without an outside job, she busied herself with taking care of her children, and slowly her spirits were restored. With the exception of her mom and dad, no one knew she was a Muslim, so she was able to let go of that part of her identity without guilt. In doing so, she was also released from the expectation the Muslim culture had impressed on her since birth to be a "good Muslim girl." Salima no longer had to be the quiet, oppressed, abused wife who silently endured her lot in life. She was free to be the independent, vivacious, intelligent young woman she had once been.

During this time, her parents divorced after 29 years of marriage, and her father moved out of the house. Though difficult for Salima, her parents' failed marriage and her own broken relationship led her to seek new answers to the meaning of life. Her family's Muslim tradition certainly hadn't helped them preserve their most significant relationships; maybe other belief systems had better insight.

Salima lived with her mother in the central part of town, with 10 to 15 churches within walking distance. No matter which direction she went, Salima passed a church. One day, Salima borrowed her mother's car to take Ahmad to the doctor's office for more medicine. While braked at a stoplight, she read the marquee on a local church. It said, " 'Trust in the Lord with all your heart and lean not on your own understanding; in all your ways acknowledge him, and he will make your paths straight' (Proverbs 3:5–6)."

Well, that's really neat, she thought. She drove on, and the next church she came to had posted, " 'And we know that in all things God works for the good of those who love him, who have been called according to his purpose' (Romans 8:28)."

Salima marveled. The messages were comforting—so different from the condemnation and unbending wrath she'd experienced with Islam. In the following weeks and months, she secretly began to read the messages in front of these churches every time she left the house, and they helped to heal her. Interestingly, the churches all gravitated toward the same verses—Proverbs 3:5–6 and Romans 8:28. It seemed those scriptures confronted Salima every time she went for a drive.

Am I going crazy? she often thought. *Why am I always seeing these same verses?*

She didn't know it yet, but God was pursuing her.

$\mathcal{O}$NE MORNING A FEW WEEKS LATER, SALIMA STRETCHED luxuriously, then jumped out of bed. It was 7:00 A.M.—time for Ahmad's bottle. She walked to her son and daughter's room, just a few feet from her own, and lifted the restless baby from his crib. It was incredible to think that he was now almost a year old. Balancing Ahmad on her hip, she entered the kitchen and prepared her son's formula, then made her way into the family room, where she seated herself in a comfortable chair and flicked on the TV.

She cradled Ahmad in her arms, feeding him his bottle with one hand and clicking the TV remote control with the other. *There's not much to watch on Sunday mornings,* she thought after she'd clicked past a nature special on antelopes, a painting class, and aerobics for senior citizens.

She changed the channel again, then leaned slightly forward, intrigued.

"Folks, today I'm going to talk to you about a Christian marriage," said a man standing behind a podium. "This week we're addressing the husband's role in marriage—what a man should do for his family."

"Mama," three-year-old Amina said loudly as she toddled into the room.

"Shhh, honey. I want to hear this nice man," Salima told her and directed her attention back to the screen. *This should be interesting,* she thought.

". . . men, you need to love your wives. Treat them with respect. Put them in a place of honor. They should be most important in your life, after God," the preacher said passionately.

Salima stared at the TV, listening intently as she rocked Ahmad in her arms while Amina played quietly at her feet. *That man is right!* Salima agreed silently. *This is incredible. I've never heard anything like it before.*

The preacher talked for almost half an hour, explaining in detail what a husband's role should be in his family. The responsibilities outlined were not what Salima had experienced in her own home life with her father, and certainly not what Muhammed had displayed while they were married. But the pastor's explanation seemed right—it was what she had always wished for in a husband, yet never would have been able to put into words.

The program ended, and an announcer came on: "This program has been televised from Rushing Waters Community Church; Pastor Tony Edwards, speaking. Thank you for tuning in."

All that week, Salima found herself thinking about the program. She tuned in the next Sunday, and the next, until she'd watched the preacher six weeks in a row. *I want to visit this church,* she decided. Surprised at herself, she called the church and got directions. But it took her a few more weeks to gather up the courage to attend. She'd never been to a church before, but she was sure it would be very different from a mosque.

Finally, one Sunday morning, Salima decided to go. For several minutes, she stood uneasily in front of her closet before pulling out her one nice American outfit—a hunter green skirt and white blouse. She chewed her lip nervously as she dressed. *What if I'm not wearing the right thing? What if Mom gets upset about my going?* As she fidgeted with her hair and clothes, she realized, *I never would've been brave enough to do this when Dad was still living here.* Salima looked at the clock. It was 9:05, and the service was scheduled to start in 10 minutes. She was going to be late.

She walked briskly into the family room, bent down to kiss Amina and Ahmad, then turned to her mother, who was making coffee in the kitchen. "Thanks for watching the kids, Mom. I just want to see what this service is like," she said, lingering anxiously at the door. "I'll be back soon."

"Don't worry about them," her mother said, gesturing toward Amina and Ahmad. "They'll be fine." To Salima's surprise, her mom avoided the topic of church and instead focused on logistics. "Now, do you know how to get there? Are you sure you'll be okay?"

When Salima nodded, her mom waved her out the door.

In the car a few minutes later, Salima saw the huge wooden cross that stood atop the large brown-brick building before she noticed the church itself. She parked in a big lot filled with cars and walked in through the main, glass double doors.

"Hi! I'm so glad you came today," said a well-dressed man standing at the door. He smiled and shook her hand.

"Yes, it's good to see you," an older woman said enthusiastically and handed her a program.

Salima was taken aback. Nobody did that at the mosque, where the men and women entered through separate doors. *Do they know I'm not a Christian? Do I have "impostor" written all over me?* she thought worriedly as she smiled weakly at her greeters.

"You've arrived just in time for the sermon," the woman said, leading her into the sanctuary.

Since Salima was late, she was directed to slip into a pew at the back. She took her place and looked around. The inside of the church was huge and beautifully decorated with banners inscribed with different biblical names for God. A crowd of probably 3,000 people filled the auditorium, and this was just the first of two services.

Pastor Tony took the stand. "I'm going to tell you about a young man today," he announced, his deep voice reverberating through the sanctuary. Eloquently, he told the story of a son who had run away from his father and squandered his inheritance, which he had demanded early from his dad.

Hearing the sermon in person is even better than watching it on TV, Salima thought, not knowing that Pastor Tony's intriguing story was the parable of the prodigal son, one of Jesus' lessons in the Bible. She listened with rapt attention, especially when the pastor talked about how much the father in the parable loved the son, even though the boy behaved terribly. The hour passed quickly.

Pastor Tony got through about half the story and then said, "We'll examine the rest of it next week."

He prayed, and the congregation sang a chorus—but Salima was still focused on the parable. The service was over before she realized it. Not sure what to do next, she followed the crowd filing out of the church, got into her car, and left.

She was determined to come back the following Sunday. *I want to know how that story ends,* Salima thought.

"*M*OM, DO YOU HAVE A BIBLE ANYWHERE?" SALIMA ASKED A few weeks later, not certain what kind of response she would get. On the last day of Pastor Tony's series, she'd discovered that the parable of the prodigal son was from the Bible, and she wanted to read it.

Her mother looked up from the book she was reading, her eyebrows raised. "Actually, I have one that's years old," she said. "I used it in church long before your father and I were married." Salima's mom had nominally participated in the Christian church as a teenager but dropped her involvement while in college. Soon after her divorce from Ali, she had discontinued her Muslim practices, such as going to the mosque and praying to Allah. But when it became apparent that her daughter was serious about investigating the Christian church, she suddenly regained interest in Islam. Each Sunday, when Salima came home from church, her mom debated with her about what the minister had said about God.

"If God is so good, why are there starving children in Africa?" she would ask archly.

Salima would be stumped. "I don't know, Mom," she'd say. "I'll try to find out."

Her mom obviously wanted her to give up this new "obsession," but her questions just encouraged Salima to dig deeper into the Christian faith. Salima retrieved her mom's Bible from the basement and began to read it voraciously. The New Testament presented a problem for her, though. Although it was easy for Salima to accept God—she was excited to worship Him and didn't have any problem understanding that the Lord, and not Allah, was God—believing in and receiving Jesus as the Christ was harder. She had been taught since childhood that Jesus was *not* the Son of God. *Which is right?* she wondered.

Attending a Sunday school class at church helped clear up some of Salima's questions. She'd tried out several classes before ending up in one for young singles, led by two biblically knowledgeable young men named Kurt and Sam. They were willing to answer any obscure question she had and even lent her books to help her grow in her understanding. Whenever Kurt and Sam talked about God, their faces lit up, as if they were discussing their most beloved friend. *I want what they have,* Salima decided, and she made up her mind to learn everything she could about Jesus Christ, this Person who had so transformed her friends' lives.

After several months of reading, praying, and attending church and Sunday school classes, Salima went to a dramatic program put on by Rushing Waters called "The Judgment House." It was designed to nudge people toward making a decision about their salvation. The program was intense, set up for the audience to catch glimpses of both heaven and hell.

At first, Salima watched the play skeptically. *I'm a good person,* she rationalized. *There's plenty of time for me to learn about Jesus Christ.* She wasn't going to let this program push her into anything.

But when Salima entered "Hell," the devil character unnerved her. Clad all in black and hideous in stage makeup, he was frightening. "You're going to hell!" the devil sneered. He was talking to a teenager in the play, but standing within three feet of Salima, he looked directly at her. Actors all around him were screaming and crying in anguish. "You never made that final decision!" he said viciously. "You had plenty of time, but you procrastinated."

Shaking, Salima turned away and followed the crowd into the next scene—"Heaven." It was beautiful, filled with light and smiling faces. When the Christ character walked through the door, her heart jumped as he moved in her direction. Once again she was singled out from the rest of the audience. Taking her hand and clasping it tightly, "Christ" looked intently into her eyes as he said his lines.

Salima left the program that night feeling too emotional to make a decision but more aware of her soul than she had been before the program. Her studies and this program had finally convinced her that Jesus was the Son of God. But she was still too scared to make a decision. *I want to do this, but I'm walking away from everything I know for something I know so little about,* she thought. What would her family do? If they were upset about a divorce, they would have heart attacks if she became a Christian! One thing was certain: She would not tell them she was contemplating this because she didn't want them pressuring her to give it up. She felt as if she were about to take a huge step into uncharted territory, and it frightened her. Still, she knew she needed to make a decision.

The next Sunday during church, her pastor asked all those who wanted to accept Jesus Christ as their Savior to come forward. Salima sat frozen to her pew. She wanted to go up there, but she couldn't.

You know, God, I'm not really sure how to do this, how to give my life to You, Salima prayed. *So will You help me—help me to find You? Jesus, I want You to forgive me and to live in my heart now. I'm going to serve You forever.*

She sighed happily as she pictured Jesus holding her. She could see His loving, joy-filled face so clearly. Never before had she been able to visualize God; her Muslim tradition had forbidden it. But now, as she sat in the pew seeing herself embraced by the Lord, she felt her lifelong burden to be perfect vanish. Christianity's God was merciful, loving, and personal —not at all like Islam's distant, wrathful Allah—and that knowledge was freeing.

Tears came to Salima's eyes as she rose to her feet and— wondering why it had seemed so difficult a few minutes before—started down the aisle. From now on, she would live for the Lord God and His Son, Jesus. For the first time ever, she felt completely alive!

THE NEXT SEVERAL MONTHS PASSED QUICKLY. SALIMA WORKED at a day-care facility near her mother's house and ran a home business to make ends meet; she also continued to take care of her children and to read and study everything she could find about Jesus. It was a rich, satisfying time for her. God seemed to provide the right books and Bible verses, and as Salima learned more about Him and spent more time with Him through reading and prayer, she felt a closeness to Him that she had never imagined possible. Also aware of her kids' spiritual needs, she enrolled four-year-old Amina in a private Christian school for kindergarten, and she and the children became active in church, attending Sunday school classes and volunteering for church events.

This time of emotional and spiritual growth gave her the strength she needed to overcome her next obstacle: the reappearance of Muhammed.

A few months before her son's third and her daughter's fifth birthdays, Muhammed moved to Missouri, bringing his parents with him. He had been laid off from his job in Chicago and had decided, after three years of divorce, that he wanted to be a part of Salima's and their children's lives again.

Immediately, Salima felt her freedom had been stripped from her. She refused to go back to her ex-husband, because that would mean giving up her newfound Christian faith, and she knew that was not what God wanted her to do. To protect herself, her children, and her mother, Salima put up a privacy fence and security doors, changed phone numbers, and even got a restraining order.

But Muhammed was undaunted. He took her to court for custody and visitation. Now, instead of fighting each other at home, they were fighting in court. The Lord protected Salima and her children, for Muhammed received only supervised visitation, and Salima retained full legal custody.

Although Salima was confident that God would help her and give her the strength to deal with Muhammed, she was still intimidated by her ex-husband's forceful personality and powerful frame. With one word or look, he could terrorize her into compliance. Once, not long after he'd been in Missouri, he announced he was using his visitation to take Salima and the children to the local mosque the following Sunday. Salima felt sick about going but was too frightened to tell him no. Muhammed didn't yet know that she had converted to Christianity and was attending church with the kids. She wanted to keep it from him because she was afraid of what he might do if he found out. So when Muhammed told her that she and the kids would be going to the mosque with him, she reluctantly agreed. For days afterward, she fretted and prayed that God would help her figure out how to avoid going. *Lord, I'm not strong enough to be there!* she cried. *I don't want to hear the Arabic prayers, and I especially don't want Amina and Ahmad to be exposed to this.*

Sunday came, and Salima and the kids were healthy, her car was working, and the weather was nice—it seemed none of her prayers had been answered. She could find no way out of this. *Where are You, God?* she prayed. Salima had gotten rid of all her Muslim clothing and had only one scarf left, so she put on a long-sleeved shirt and a pair of pants to ensure that she was adequately covered. Then she reluctantly strapped her kids in the car and followed Muhammed, who was with his parents in the car ahead, to the mosque.

They pulled up to a small, nondescript brick building and parked in the gravel lot next to it. Muhammed and his parents got out of the car, all wearing the traditional, heavy Muslim clothing. Muhammed and his father walked around the building and entered through the men's door. Swallowing her anxiety, Salima picked up Ahmad and walked toward the mosque, with Muhammed's mother and Amina behind her. As she approached the women's entrance, she noticed a scribbled sign on a piece of paper tacked to the door, which was locked.

"This can't be the permanent door," she murmured. "There are probably several entrances, like there were at our old mosque."

She went to what she thought was the main women's entrance and peeked inside. Seeing no men there, she assumed it was okay for them to enter. "Okay," she said, taking a deep breath and reaching for her children's hands. "Let's go in."

The moment they passed through the doorway, chaos erupted. Salima, the children, and Muhammed's mother had stepped into the entrance of the men's door. The men, who were sitting on the floor inside, noticed Salima immediately, as her American clothes made her even more conspicuous. They jumped up and started yelling in Arabic.

"She's trying to come in the men's door!" the men shouted at Muhammed and his father, who were standing in front of Salima and the children.

Muhammed's mother dropped back, out of sight. Salima, however, remained where she was. "I'm sorry. I got the wrong door. I'm sorry," she tried to explain.

The men ignored her. "Is that your wife?" one man yelled at Muhammed. "Get her out!"

Muhammed argued with them for several minutes. Finally, his father calmed the men down and resolved the situation by pulling his son outside and motioning for Salima to follow with Amina and Ahmad.

Back in the parking lot, Muhammed was still adamant that they at least go to religious instruction classes, in another building nearby. He hastily got directions, and once again they piled into the cars, this time in search of the school.

For two hours, Salima followed Muhammed's car as they looked for the building without success. Finally, she waved him down.

"It's really hot, and the kids are tired, hungry, and crabby," Salima called through her car window. "Now Amina has to go to the bathroom. Let's find someplace clean so I can take her to the potty, okay?"

"Fine," Muhammed grunted.

They turned the corner and found a McDonald's, complete with a new playground. As soon as the kids left the bathroom, they raced to the slide, shrieking joyfully.

Salima looked over at Muhammed. "There's no way you're going to get these kids away from Playland and french fries," she told him. "Besides, we all need to get out of this heat. Let's just stay here."

"No. Let's go back to the mosque," Muhammed said stubbornly.

His father gazed at him wearily and said, "No. Let's leave it for today."

With a sigh of relief, Salima slid into a red plastic booth and watched her children play happily for the next two hours. As soon as her watch ticked to 1:00, she gathered up Amina and Ahmad and left. Muhammed's visitation was up for today, and neither she nor the children had to step another foot inside the mosque.

Thank You, Lord, she prayed gratefully. *How could I not have trusted You? You answered my prayers and took care of my children. You were always in control.*

TIME PASSED, AND AMINA AND AHMAD GREW IN THEIR understanding of God. Soon Ahmad, age four, was attending the Christian school with his sister. Not long after that, Muhammed realized his children were attending a Christian church.

Salima had started wearing a small gold cross in place of her former "Allah" necklace. When they saw it, both her father and Muhammed finally realized she was a Christian. They had taken one shocked look at the cross but never said anything. Shortly thereafter, Muhammed, who was incensed, took Salima to court, asking for unsupervised visitation and for the right to take Amina and Ahmad out of Christian school and church— he wanted them raised as Muslims. Again God protected Salima and her children, teaching her to trust Him and not worry. Muhammed was still allowed only supervised visitation, and the children were able to keep attending church and school.

Though Muhammed could not physically bring his children to the mosque, he still tried to teach them his Muslim faith. But Amina, already a precocious, intelligent six-year-old, knew better. She had prayed to accept Jesus on Mother's Day the year before. Salima often marveled at her daughter's words and actions.

One day, Amina proudly told her mother, "Mommy, today Daddy told me to sing him a song, so I sang, 'Jesus Loves Me.'"

"What did your dad say?" Salima asked curiously.

"He said, 'Don't you know any other songs? Sing a rock 'n' roll song for me.'" Amina giggled mischievously. "So I said, 'Okay,' and I sang 'Jesus Is the Rock and He Rolls My Blues Away.'" She clapped her small hands delightedly.

Salima shook her head as she smiled. God was knocking on her ex-husband's door, whether he liked it or not.

The Lord continued to teach Salima new things as well. Part of her learning came through listening to Dr. James Dobson on the *Focus on the Family* broadcast at work. When Salima heard of Renewing the Heart, the women's conference the ministry was promoting, she immediately ordered her ticket, even though she had no idea what it would be like. She had never attended anything like it as a Christian, and certainly never as a Muslim.

The day of the conference, Salima arrived at the large auditorium with her friend Suzanne. Renewing the Heart was a wonderful surprise for Salima. Never, until that day, had she really worshiped and praised God simply for the joy of doing it. She knew how to pray, read the Bible, and even sing, but this was a different experience. Closing her eyes, Salima could truly feel the presence of Almighty God as she joined thousands of other women in praise and worship.

The fellowship she experienced at the conference was also different from anything she had ever known. As a Muslim, Salima had never learned to accept and enjoy her womanhood, as women in that culture were taught to be silent, and the responsibilities and restrictions of Muslim life usually quickly squelched the love and joy in them. It had been difficult for Salima to release that old baggage, even as a Christian who had found new, eternal life. But here, in the Nashville auditorium, she saw all kinds of women—old, young, sick, healthy, rich, poor—and no matter what life had brought them, they were still praising the living God. That day, seeing other confident women of faith, Salima finally felt that she was valuable, not simply as a mother who was trying to raise two God-fearing children, but also as a woman and a daughter of God.

Back home, however, Muhammed was still dragging Salima into court, trying to get more time with the children and force them to attend his mosque. He continued to fight for unsupervised visitation, and one day the judge finally awarded it to him. Muhammed had argued that he, the foreigner, was a victim—every other divorced father he knew had two weeks of unsupervised visitation. The judge had listened and agreed, giving him what he wanted.

Distraught, Salima left the courtroom with her mother. *Lord, how will I protect my children now that Muhammed can spend time with them alone?* she cried out silently to God. *They're still so little.*

As she and her mother climbed into the car to drive home, Salima felt her world disintegrating around her. With difficulty, she tried to stifle her sobs.

"Salima," her mother said quietly, looking over at her, "if it will make you feel better, I want you to know I prayed and accepted Jesus Christ as my Savior, too."

Salima's eyes widened. She braked the car to a stop, then turned to her mother and said, "Mom, that makes me feel so much better. But what made you decide?"

"I've watched you, Salima," her mom said. "You and your friends are different—you're not the hypocrites I thought all Christians were. You've stopped cursing, you're trying to be cordial to Muhammed, and you've been incredibly calm throughout the court process." She stopped to wipe her eyes.

"Oh, Mom, you don't know how happy I am for you!" Salima cried exultantly. "Today I thought I was losing to Muhammed the love I've given my children, but God just brought me another gift of love—the knowledge that you're going to be in heaven with me and Jesus someday." Her tears of sadness had been replaced with tears of joy. She leaned over and hugged her mother.

God was faithfully taking care of her family.

*T*HE FOLLOWING EASTER, SALIMA STOOD OFFSTAGE IN HER white angel costume, nervously pacing and thinking about her dad, who was in the audience. It was a miracle that he had come to Rushing Waters's passion play production, which told the story of Jesus Christ's life from conception to crucifixion. She fidgeted with her wings and licked her dry lips. Her mother had been prompted to accept Christ by last year's production and had already attended the play this year. *If it got through to Mom, maybe Dad will get something from it, too,* Salima thought. For months, she'd prayed that Ali would come to the production and, at the very least, sit through the whole thing and not leave at intermission.

And now he was here.

Their relationship hadn't been on the best of terms lately. As a fairly new Christian, Salima had put her foot in her mouth

314 RENEWED HEARTS, CHANGED LIVES

when she'd tried to talk to him about Christ. She shuddered, her halo wobbling, as she remembered how abrasive she'd been.

"Dad, you're wrong!" she had said passionately. "You need to convert."

Now she hoped the play would get through to him in a way she never could.

At that moment, dozens of people were praying for her dad, the short, dark, curly-haired man who had never been in a church and looked very out of place sitting in the front row of the auditorium. Even the singers, who were sitting in the orchestra pit directly in front of her father, were sending up prayers to God on his behalf.

Salima anxiously smoothed back her hair, then poked her head around the corner to watch the end of the crucifixion scene. This scene was crucial. One of the characters, watching Jesus die on the cross, would finally make the decision to accept Him as the Christ, and then an emotional song—"I Choose Christ"—would follow. It was designed to influence the audience to choose God and prepare them for the salvation prayer the high priest character would lead at the end. Salima shuddered again. *What is Dad thinking about all this?* she wondered.

"Salima, you look nervous," Mary, one of the actresses, said as she approached her backstage. "You need to get down on your knees and pray."

Salima frowned and answered, "But I'm wearing white. My knees will be dirty when I walk out for my part in the heaven scene." How would it look for an angel to be soiled?

"God doesn't care if your knees are dirty," Mary reminded her. "You need to pray." She tilted her head and looked at her friend.

"You're right," Salima agreed. So, in her white angel costume, behind the red velvet curtain backstage, she fell to her knees. *Oh, God, I pray for my daddy,* she petitioned the Lord. *Please be working in his heart.* As she prayed, Salima felt a soft, peaceful breeze blow across her face. She could hear the high priest on the other side of the curtain leading the sinner's prayer, inviting the audience to accept Jesus Christ.

" . . . with all the power and glory and honor. Amen," the actor said.

Salima opened her eyes and brushed off her dirty knees. The end of the prayer was her cue to reenter for the final scene. She ran into the bright lights onstage, her angel wings jutting toward heaven, and took her place on the high part of the platform.

The audience stood up as "Christ" rode in on a white horse, and all the actors rejoiced, clapping and dancing. Gracefully twirling, her white robes flowing about her, Salima looked quickly at the audience. There in the front row was her father, standing and weeping. A wave of hope swept through her.

As soon as the curtain closed, Salima tore off her angel wings and ran toward her father in the lobby. "How'd you like it?" she asked eagerly, giving him a hug.

Ali wiped the tears from his face. "Can we go somewhere and talk?" he asked.

"Sure," Salima said, hopeful that the play had had its intended effect but unsure what her dad would say.

They went to a restaurant across the street from the church and settled into a booth. Her father leaned forward and looked down at his hands clasped in front of him. "Salima, I've got to tell you something," he said, his voice filled with emotion.

"What, Dad?" she asked, trying to calm herself.

Ali looked up at his daughter. "I did that prayer," he told her hoarsely. "You know, the one the guy at the end led. The one where you accept Christ."

Salima was speechless for a moment, half joyful and half skeptical. "You prayed that prayer at the end?" she finally asked.

"Yeah," he said. Tears ran down his brown cheeks.

Salima began to sob with thankfulness. It appeared to be true. The harsh lines in her dad's face were gone, replaced with a soft, peaceful expression that she'd never seen him wear before.

Father and daughter talked for several hours, making plans for him to attend church and Sunday school. Finally, they parted. Driving home, Salima was ecstatic, but a seed of doubt remained lodged in her thoughts. Her dad's swift decision just didn't make sense. It had taken her a long time to convert to Christianity. She hadn't been surprised when her mom had made the decision to follow Christ—she was American and had Christian roots. But her father? Salima thought for sure that her father would've reacted as Muhammed had when he'd attended an earlier show, thinking Amina was in the play. He had left, expressionless and seemingly unaffected. By contrast, her dad, who had been a devout and lifelong Muslim, was transformed within hours.

How was it possible?

Salima pulled up to a stoplight and turned on the radio. It was so late that she shared the street only with the car sitting in front of her. She glanced at the car's license plate, then rubbed her eyes and stared. It read, "GODSREL."

Salima blinked and then shook her head, silently berating herself for doubting. Yes, God certainly was real. Of course He could change her dad! Over the last several years, the Lord had repeatedly taught her that with Him, nothing is impossible— no heart is too hard, and no one is too lost.

And that included her family.

Salima Kahn and her two children, Amina and Ahmad, live in Missouri, where Salima works at Rushing Waters Community Church in the children's ministry department and teaches women's Sunday school classes. While her parents are both growing in their faith, Salima continues to pray for her brother, Ahmad, and her ex-husband, Muhammed, to accept Jesus Christ—believing now that God can change anybody.

Heart to Heart

I cried when I read Salima's story. And after I stopped crying, I picked up my Bible and turned to Matthew 18:12–14. I read about how a shepherd will leave his flock to go and find one sheep who is lost. And I read about how our Father in heaven is like that shepherd: He is not willing that any of the little ones be lost. Isn't it incredible to see that story played out in Salima's life? God pursued her through her friends and through billboards, and even through the television. He wasn't willing for her to be lost. Her story, along with the miracle of her parents' salvation, reminds me that no one is beyond the reach of God. He is the Good Shepherd who longs to find lost sheep. We must never lose hope for the Muhammeds in our lives.

Walking by Faith ~

Lisa

The Season of Singing Has Come

I'm on a plane as I write this concluding chapter, heading home after the final Renewing the Heart conference of 1998. We've had five conferences this year—in Greensboro, North Carolina; San Antonio; Nashville; Philadelphia; and we closed out the year in Tampa. And what a year it's been! Some of the memories are written on my heart. One of them is written on my hands. Let me explain.

As the first conference of 1998 approached, I decided we needed to do something fun to let the women know that this wasn't a stereotypical, stiff-and-formal women's conference. I also wanted to plan some lighthearted, humorous breaks in the schedule, as there would be much teaching and many tears as we dealt with some difficult issues. So I made plans to rappel in from the ceiling of the arena after lunch. I thought it would be a hilarious surprise for the women to see their hostess suspended 160 feet above them, and it would sure wake up those who'd gotten sleepy after eating!

I've been mountain climbing before and have rappelled off cliffs, so I didn't think it would be any more difficult to drop from the rafters of a huge indoor arena. I didn't realize that I'd have to crawl out on a narrow, rickety catwalk, which is essentially a suspension bridge made of chicken wire! After crawling and climbing where no sane person would go, I had to be lifted a few more feet onto a metal rail almost 200 feet above the floor of the arena—the *cement* floor of the arena.

As I sat trembling on the rail (have I mentioned that the "floor" of the catwalk is completely see-through?), I thought this was the dumbest idea I'd ever had. Then the crew member who was helping me told me that I was going to have to spin around on the rail so my legs would dangle over the side. I've raced mountain bikes, I've scuba-dived with sharks off Central America, I've snowboarded with teenaged boys, but I've never been so scared as I was at that moment.

However, once the praise and worship team started singing "I'll Fly Away, Oh Glory," I knew it was now or never, so I jumped. Women started pointing and laughing and cheering as I came zooming down a rope from way over their heads, and I grinned and waved briefly—then I gripped the rope so hard that I burned the skin off both hands! When I did the same stunt at the conference in Nashville, I looked up while coming down the rope from the ceiling and saw myself on one of the 20-foot video screens. It's a humbling and not very pleasant experience to see one's posterior crammed into a climbing harness and projected onto a movie screen bigger than life! One of my good friends told me after the conference that it wasn't my better side.

Another near-miss happened at the conference in Texas. I was backstage with Kay Arthur while Kay Coles James was speaking to the audience. We were talking passionately about spiritual issues when Tim MacDonald, who helps coordinate the logistics of the program, motioned to me. Tim is a dear friend, so I gave him one of those now-is-not-a-good-time looks and continued talking with Kay. Then both Kay and I felt led to pray. Kay Arthur spends hours every day reading the Bible, so when she prays, she has a lot to say! Suddenly, Tim grabbed my arm and pulled me out of the room. He gently tossed me onto the golf cart and said, "Hang on." We were about 100 yards from the stage, Kay James had already finished her speech, and I was supposed to be on stage. Tim sped to the edge of the arena and said, "Run!" I jumped out while the cart was still rolling and was racing toward the stage as Kay James was coming down the stairs. I walked briskly onto the platform and tried not to look like a bumbling idiot in front of 18,000 women. After I shared some announcements and a quick story, I dismissed everyone for the afternoon break and walked back to the golf cart to find Tim slumped over on the seat, laughing. He said that never in his life had he heard anyone make up announcements so well.

All of our mistakes, mishaps, and near-misses have reminded us that we are weak and He is strong. Recounting the stories (they get better with each telling!) at staff meetings provides levity and perspective. And rarely do we reminisce about our mistakes when we don't also remember His miracles.

One of my favorite miracles happened at the Greensboro conference. A radiant young woman came up to me at the end of the day and asked if I remembered her phone call from several months before. She said, "I asked if I could bring my friend who was an unbeliever to the conference." Then she turned and put her arm around the woman standing next to her and said, "This is my friend, and she's not an unbeliever anymore." Her friend had just committed her life to Christ during the altar call.

Another woman came up to me at a church in Nashville, and with tears streaming down her face, told me that her five-year-old daughter, Anna Kate, prays for me every night. She said that when she came to Renewing the Heart, she was depressed and struggling spiritually. She shared how God truly gave her a "new heart" and that the change in her life was so obvious when she returned home from the conference that Anna Kate noticed immediately. She said Anna Kate was so thankful to have a "new mommy" that she continues to pray for the conferences to have an impact on other women's lives, too. It is no less than a miracle to have a little girl praying that other mommies will find Jesus the way hers did.

After the conference in Tampa, one of the women who attended was driving away from the arena when she felt compelled to turn her car around. She drove back to the arena and went inside to pray with a counselor and commit her life to Jesus Christ. Then there was the mother in Philadelphia who walked down to the altar to pray for her adult daughter who wasn't a Christian. She tearfully told the altar counselor that she had no idea where her daughter was, but she just wanted to pray that her daughter would respond to the message of God's love. And then, out of the crowd of 20,000 women, her daughter walked right up to them and prayed the sinner's prayer with her mother.

God's grace is truly miraculous. We are awed at what He has accomplished with a little dream and a mustard seed of faith. He is sovereign; He certainly didn't need another Christian conference to accomplish His purposes. But He has graciously allowed us to be a vehicle to communicate His gospel. More than 100,000 women have attended a Renewing the Heart conference in the past 14 months. Women have come from all 50 states and from as far away as Japan. They range in age from 18 to 80, and they come in all different shapes, colors, and sizes. Mothers bring their daughters, husbands send their wives, and friends bring their friends who don't know Jesus. Women come looking for answers; they come looking for hope. And God does not disappoint—He gives hope; He is the answer.

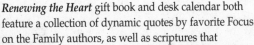

FOCUS ON THE FAMILY®

Welcome to the Family!

Whether you received this book as a gift, borrowed it from
a friend, or purchased it yourself, we're glad you read it! It's just
one of the many helpful, insightful, and encouraging
resources produced by Focus on the Family.

In fact, that's what Focus on the Family is all about—providing inspira-
tion, information, and biblically based advice to people in all stages of life.

It began in 1977 with the vision of one man, Dr. James Dobson, a licensed
psychologist and author of 16 best-selling books on marriage, parenting,
and family. Alarmed by the societal, political, and economic pressures
that were threatening the existence of the American family, Dr. Dobson
founded Focus on the Family with one employee—an assistant—
and a once-a-week radio broadcast, aired on only 36 stations.

Now an international organization, Focus on the Family is dedicated
to preserving Judeo-Christian values and strengthening the family
through more than 70 different ministries, including eight separate
daily radio broadcasts; television public service announcements;
11 publications; and a steady series of award-winning books and
films and videos for people of all ages and interests.

Recognizing the needs of, as well as the sacrifices and important
contribution made by, such diverse groups as educators, physicians,
attorneys, crisis pregnancy center staff, and single parents,
Focus on the Family offers specific outreaches to uphold and
minister to these individuals, too. And it's all done for one purpose,
and one purpose only: to encourage and strengthen individuals
and families through the life-changing message of Jesus Christ.

• • •

For more information about the ministry, or if we can be of help to your
family, simply write to Focus on the Family, Colorado Springs, CO 80995
or call 1-800-A-FAMILY (1-800-232-6459). Friends in Canada may write
Focus on the Family, P.O. Box 9800, Stn. Terminal, Vancouver, B.C. V6B 4G3
or call 1-800-661-9800. Visit our Web site—www.family.org—
to learn more about the ministry or to find out if there is a
Focus on the Family office in your country.

We'd love to hear from you!